Somebodyness

Harvard Dissertations in Religion

Editors

Bernadette J. Brooten

and

Francis Schüssler Fiorenza

Number 31

Somebodyness:
Martin Luther King, Jr., and the Theory of Dignity

Garth Baker-Fletcher

Somebodyness

Martin Luther King, Jr., and the Theory of Dignity

Garth Baker-Fletcher

Fortress Press, Minneapolis

Dedicated to my Parents:

Superia and Kenneth Fletcher

of Beloved Memory

Somebodyness: Martin Luther King, Jr., and the Theory of Dignity

Harvard Dissertations in Religion, Number 31

Book design and typesetting at the Harvard Theological Review

Managing Editor: Tamar Duke-Cohan

Editorial Assistants: Ellen B. Aitken and Laura Nasrallah

Library of Congress Cataloging-in-Publication Data

Baker-Fletcher, Garth, 1955–
    Somebodyness : Martin Luther King, Jr., and the theory of dignity
/ Garth Baker-Fletcher.
        p.   cm. — (Harvard dissertations in religion : no. 31)
    Includes bibliographical references.
    ISBN 0-8006-7087-6 :
    1. King, Martin Luther, Jr., 1929–1968—Contributions in Christian
doctrine of human dignity.   2. Dignity—Religious aspects—
Christianity—History of doctrines—20th century.   3. Human rights—
Religious aspects—Christianity—History of doctrines—20th
century.   4. Man (Christian theology)—History of doctrines—20th
century.   I. Title.   II. Series.
BT702.B35   1993
233'.5—dc20   93-19847
                                                                             CIP

The paper used in this publication meets the minimum requirements of American National Standard for Information Sciences—Permanence of Paper for Printed Library Materials, ANSI Z329.48–1984.   ∞ ™

Manufactured in the U.S.A.   AF 1–7087

97   96   95   94   93   1   2   3   4   5   6   7   8   9   10

Contents

Short Titles

Information appears here for frequently used works that are cited by short title. A few short titles do not appear in this list, but in each instance full bibliography is given on the page(s) preceding such references.

Ansbro, *King*
> John J. Ansbro, *Martin Luther King, Jr.: The Making of a Mind* (Maryknoll, NY: Orbis, 1982).

Bowne, *Personalism*
> Borden Parker Bowne, *Personalism* (Boston: Houghton, Mifflin, & Co., 1908).

Bowne, *Principles*
> Borden Parker Bowne, *The Principles of Ethics* (New York: Harper, 1892).

Branch, *Parting the Waters*
> Taylor Branch, *Parting the Waters: America in the King Years 1954–63* (New York: Simon & Schuster, 1988).

Brightman, *Moral Laws*
> Edgar S. Brightman, *Moral Laws* (New York: Abingdon, 1933).

Cone, "Black Theology—Black Church"
> James H. Cone, "Martin Luther King, Jr., Black Theology—Black Church," in Garrow, *King,* 1. 203–14.

Cone, "Theology"
> James H. Cone, "The Theology of Martin Luther King, Jr.," in Garrow, *Martin Luther King, Jr.,* 1. 215–33.

DeWolf, *Responsible Freedom*
> L. Harold DeWolf, *Responsible Freedom: Guidelines to Christian Action* (New York: Harper & Row, 1971).

DeWolf, *A Theology of the Living Church*
> L. Harold DeWolf, *A Theology of the Living Church* (New York: Harper & Row, 1960).

Downing, *Promised Land*
> Frederick L. Downing, *To See the Promised Land* (Macon, GA: Mercer University Press, 1986).

Gandhi, *Autobiography*
> Mohandas K. Gandhi, *An Autobiography* (Boston: Beacon, 1957).

Gandhi, *Non-Violent Resistance*
> Mohandas K. Gandhi, *Non-Violent Resistance (Satyagraha)* (ed. Bharatan Kumarappa; New York: Schocken, 1961).

Garrow, *Bearing the Cross*
> David J. Garrow, *Bearing the Cross: Martin Luther King, Jr., and the Southern Leadership Conference* (New York: Morrow, 1986).

Garrow, "Intellectual Development"
> David J. Garrow, "The Intellectual Development of Martin Luther King, Jr.: Influences and Commentaries," in idem., ed., *King.*, 2. 437–52.

Garrow, *King*
> David J. Garrow, ed., *Martin Luther King, Jr.: Civil Rights Leader, Theologian, Orator* (3 vols.; Brooklyn, NY: Carlson, 1989).

Hegel, *Philosophy of History*
> G. F. W. Hegel, *The Philosophy of History* (trans. J. Sibree; New York: Dover, 1956).

hooks, *Feminist Theory*
> bell hooks, *Feminist Theory: From Margin to Center* (Boston: South End, 1984).

hooks, *Talking Back*
> bell hooks, *Talking Back* (Boston: South End, 1989).

Kant, *Foundations*
> Immanuel Kant, *Foundations of the Metaphysics of Morals* (ed. Robert Paul Wolff; New York: Macmillan, 1969).

King, *Daddy King*
> Martin Luther King, Sr., with Clayton Riley, *Daddy King* (New York: Morrow, 1980).

King, "America's Chief Moral Dilemma"
> Martin Luther King, Jr., "America's Chief Moral Dilemma," address to the United Church of Church—General Synod, 6 July 1965; Martin Luther King, Jr. Center Archives, Atlanta, GA.

King, "Ethical Demands"
> Martin Luther King, Jr., "The Ethical Demands of Integration," in Washington, *Testament of Hope,* 117–25.

King, "Lost Sheep"
> Martin Luther King, Jr., "Lost Sheep," 18 September 1966; Martin Luther King, Jr. Center Archives, Atlanta, GA.

King, "Love"
> Martin Luther King, Jr., "Love, Law, and Disobedience," in Washington, *Testament of Hope*, 43–53.

King, "Modern Christians"
> Martin Luther King, Jr., "How Modern Christians Should Think of Man," folder 15. 14, box 112, Martin Luther King, Jr. Archives, Mugar Library, Boston University.

King, *Strength to Love*
> Martin Luther King, Jr., *Strength to Love* (2d ed.; Philadelphia: Fortress, 1981).

King, *Stride Toward Freedom*
> Martin Luther King, Jr., *Stride Toward Freedom: The Montgomery Story* (New York: Harper & Row, 1958).

King, "Three Dimensions"
> Martin Luther King, Jr., "Three Dimensions of a Complete Life," in idem, *The Measure of a Man* (Philadelphia: Fortress, 1988).

King, *Where Do We Go*
> Martin Luther King, Jr., *Where Do We Go from Here? Chaos or Community* (Boston: Beacon, 1967).

Morris, *Origins*
> Aldon D. Morris, *The Origins of the Civil Rights Movement* (New York: Free Press, 1984).

Muelder, "Philosophical and Theological Influences"
> Walter G. Muelder, "Philosophical and Theological Influences in the Thought and Action of Martin Luther King, Jr.," in Garrow, *King,* 3. 691–701.

Niebuhr, _Nature and Destiny_
> Reinhold Niebuhr, _The Nature and Destiny of Man,_ vol. 1: _Human Nature_ (New York: Scribners, 1941).

Oates, _Trumpet_
> Stephen B. Oates, _Let the Trumpet Sound_ (San Francisco: Harper & Row, 1982).

Paris, _Social Teaching_
> Peter Paris, _The Social Teaching of the Black Churches_ (Philadelphia: Fortress, 1985).

Smith and Zepp, _Search for the Beloved Community_
> Kenneth L. Smith and Ira G. Zepp, Jr., _Search for the Beloved Community: The Thinking of Martin Luther King, Jr._ (Valley Forge, PA: Judson, 1974).

Tillich, _Love, Power, and Justice_
> Paul Tillich, _Love, Power, and Justice_ (New York: Oxford University Press, 1960).

Washington, _Frustrated Fellowship_
> James Melvin Washington, _Frustrated Fellowship: The Black Baptist Quest for Social Power_ (Macon, GA: Mercer University Press, 1986).

Washington, _Testament of Hope_
> James M. Washington, _A Testament of Hope: The Essential Writings of Martin Luther King, Jr._ (San Francisco: Harper & Row, 1986)

Watley, _Roots of Resistance_
> William D. Watley, _Roots of Resistance: The Nonviolent Ethic of Martin Luther King, Jr._ (Valley Forge, PA: Judson, 1985).

West, _Prophesy Deliverance!_
> Cornel West, _Prophesy Deliverance!_ (Philadelphia: Westminster, 1982).

West, _Prophetic Fragments_
> Cornel West, _Prophetic Fragments_ (Grand Rapids, MI: Eerdmans, 1986).

PREFACE

The primary task of this work is to investigate Martin Luther King, Jr.'s ideals of dignity as a possible resource for a contemporary theory of dignity. King offered a complex idea of the person not as a "thing," but as a process, a becoming. For King, persons become dignified through a conscious process of reformation and transformation. King synthesized a creative doctrine of agape and nonviolent resistance into the dynamic process of the dignified person. Furthermore, this activity happens in the context of resistance to oppression. The center is the ethic of love, demonstrated in nonviolent resistance to oppression. King's view of dignity adds an important African-American viewpoint to current concepts of human dignity and self-respect.

The Problem

King reflected upon the enormous challenge that has plagued most African-Americans: How does one develop a self that preserves a sense of dignity and wholeness in the midst of a self-negating, racist society? While Cornel West offers a trenchant analysis that organizes the African-American community's historical reaction to racism into four "responses,"[1] his typology demonstrates the difficulty of placing King in an ideal typological framework which appreciates his contribution. A more direct way of understanding King's response to the negating effects of racism is to examine the sociological character of the segregated South.

Aldon Morris provides an excellent description of the southern system of segregation—the system to which King responded—as one of "tripartite domination" in which blacks were controlled "economically, politically, and personally."[2] He elaborates the economic oppression of Negroes, stating: (1) blacks were concentrated in the "lowest-paying and dirtiest jobs the cities had to offer"; (2) in the 1950s, seventy-five percent of the black males in a typical southern city were employed as unskilled labor, while only twenty-five percent of the white male population was comparably employed; (3) during the 1950s, over fifty percent of the black women were employed as domestics in contrast to only one percent of white women similarly employed; and (4) approximately twenty percent of the rest of the black female workforce was "lowly paid service workers" in contrast to less than ten percent of the white female workforce similarly employed.[3] This economic inequality meant

---

[1]West, *Prophesy Deliverance!* 69–91. West divides the African-American community's historical responses to racism into four ideal types: (1) the exceptionalist, (2) the assimilationist, (3) the marginalist, and (4) the humanist. West interprets King's doctrine of nonviolence as being part of a "weak exceptionalist" position. He criticizes King's nonviolent concept as based on a perception of the Negro as possessing a "peculiar capacity to love their enemies, endure patiently pain, hardship," and thereby "teach the white man to love" or "cure the white man of his sickness" (p. 72). West felt that King's position participated in the self-image of exceptionalism that was "defensive in character and romantic in content"(p. 75), and therefore inadequate to address fully the needs of all African-Americans. Such an assessment of King is inadequate in the following ways: it is too narrowly focused on King's views on nonviolence; it ignores the large corpus of King's thought that uplifts the dignity and equality of all people; and finally, it forces King into a framework that cannot comprehensively name King's actual contribution. West revises his view of King in *Prophetic Fragments*, claiming that King deserves a Gramscian honorific title of "organic intellectual" (p. 3). Such a title might be considered an uncritically praiseworthy view and a puzzling reversal from West's previous critical position. Both evaluations of King fail to analyze critically the vast amount of unpublished literature available in the King Archives of Mugar Library, Boston University, and the King Center of Atlanta, Georgia.

[2]Morris, *Origins*, 1.

[3]Ibid.

that whites held positions of authority over Negroes, and that Negro males and females served under the constant threat of unemployment and starvation if they did not conform to any whim, desire, or fancy of their white employers.

Negroes in the South were dominated politically because they were systematically excluded from the political and elective process.[4] Morris states that there were no black officials in city or state governments at this time.[5] Measures ranging from poll taxes and all-white primaries to intimidation and violence effectively disenfranchised blacks from partici-pating in the electoral process.[6] Morris identifies this disenfranchisment of blacks as resulting in social practices in which "blacks had few citi-zenship rights and were not members of the polity."[7]

Morris details the personal domination of blacks in the South by pointing to the manner in which segregation "determined behavior be-tween the races."[8] Negroes were expected to "address whites in a tone that conveyed respect" and to use formal titles rather than familiar names.[9] Conversely, although Morris chooses not to articulate it, whites expected to address Negroes in any familiar name that came to mind and to be answered respectfully by Negroes.[10] Morris carefully notes the strict and often lethal social prohibitions against any personal or intimate commu-nication between black men and white women.[11] Such personal domina-

[4]Ibid., 2.

[5]Ibid.

[6]Ibid. Morris is careful to footnote books and articles such as those of August Meier and Elliott Rudwick, *Among the Color Line* (Urbana: University of Illi-nois Press, 1976) 363; William H. Chafe, *Civilities and Civil Rights* (New York: Oxford, 1980) 32–37; and J. Mills Thornton III, "Challenge and Response in the Montgomery Bus Boycott of 1955–1956" in *Alabama Review: A Quarterly Jour-nal of Alabama History* 32–33 (1979–80) 171–72. These works demonstrate that "after the Supreme Court ruling abolishing the all-white primary in 1944, blacks began voting in the South in relatively small numbers" (Morris, *Origins*, 292).

[7]Morris, *Origins*, 2.

[8]Ibid.

[9]Ibid.

[10]Black males were summoned with "Boy!" and black females by any familiar name that came to mind, such as "Auntie!" This phenomenon was particularly distasteful to Negroes and was explicitly rejected by the civil rights and black power movements.

[11]Morris, *Origins*, 2–3.

tion "severely restricted the physical movement, behavioral choices, and experiences of the individual."[12]

King eloquently lists elements of this type of personal domination in his famous "Letter from Birmingham Jail":

> When you are humiliated day in and day out by nagging signs reading "white" and "colored"; when your first name becomes "nigger," your middle name becomes "boy" (however old you are) and your last name becomes "John," and your wife and mother are never given the respected title "Mrs."[13]

As a child in Atlanta, King began to experience the negating effects of racism and the concurrent need for a strong self when he was shunned by a white boy who had been his best friend. This incident led to his mother's advice: "You must never feel that you are less than anybody else. *You must always feel that you are somebody*" (my emphasis).[14]

King's view of the dignified person developed slowly. I shall look at the maturation process of King's view of the person by analyzing the "Autobiography of Martin Luther King, Jr." that King wrote while in seminary, as well as a paper he wrote at Boston University, "What Modern Christians Should Think of Man."[15] Such an investigation enables us to trace King's development of theological anthropology as a tension between a "mild neo-orthodox view" that went "back to certain experiences that I had in the South with a vicious race problem" and a contrasting "liberal leaning" that drew strength from "noticing gradual improvements of this same race problem."[16] Such a tension kept the young King divided between denying any "essential goodness in man" and affirming "some noble possibilities in human nature."[17] This tension was rooted in his early grappling with the essential dilemma of black personhood.

---

[12]Ibid., 3.

[13]Martin Luther King, Jr., *Why We Can't Wait* (New York: Doubleday, 1964) 81.

[14]Oates, *Trumpet*, 10.

[15]King, "Modern Christians."

[16]Ibid., 1.

[17]Ibid.

King's mature view of the human person, his strong adherence to a Christian realist doctrine that stressed *human freedom* as the keystone to understanding human dignity,[18] and his understanding of the power of "the Christian doctrine of love operating through the Gandhian method of nonviolence"[19] developed into a unique view of the person facing the dilemma of African-American personhood. For King, black persons who practiced the Christian ethic of love through nonviolent confrontation with the forces of segregation discovered that such an approach endowed the practitioner with a new sense of dignity.

> So the nonviolent approach does not immediately change the heart of the oppressor. It first does something to the hearts and souls of those committed to it. It gives them *new self respect*; it calls up *resources of strength and courage that they did not know they had.* [my emphasis][20]

Method

In order to understand King's view of the dignified self, I shall turn in the first chapter to an analysis of the formative social and historical elements that influenced King's ideas of dignity. I shall look at the notion of the creation of humans in the image of God that was prevalent in the black churches of that time, the view of personhood expressed in King's home, and the ideas of moral agency and human nature that King, as a young man, developed on his way toward a mature understanding of the person. This information can be obtained through King's early papers, found in the King Archives at Boston University and the Atlanta King Center, as well as through a careful reading of Martin Luther King, Sr.'s autobiography, *Daddy King*.

In the second chapter I shall describe King's early view of dignity between 1955–1960, the first few years of his public ministry. I shall trace the chronological evolution and the systematic clarification of his ideals of dignity. Specifically, I shall examine his sermons, speeches,

---

[18]See King, *Where Do We Go*, 97–98.
[19]Martin Luther King, Jr., *"Pilgrimage to Nonviolence"* in Washington, *Testament of Hope*, 38.
[20]Ibid., 39.

and writings, which have not been previously analyzed with the topic of dignity in mind.

In the third and fourth chapters I shall show the philosophical foundations of King's view of dignity. This is an important task, because if we are to understand King's view of dignity and self-respect as unique in some way, we need to relate his insights to the established philosophical understanding of self and dignity. Specifically, in the third chapter I uncover King's profound affinities to the philosophical school of Boston Personalism, and I look at the ways in which the thought of Borden Parker Bowne, Edgar S. Brightman, and L. Harold DeWolf helped to shape King's understanding of human dignity.

In the fourth chapter I examine those aspects of the thought of Immanuel Kant and G. F. W. Hegel, which, together with the nonviolence of Mohandas Gandhi, contributed to King's philosophical formulation of dignity. I examine Kant's famous Categorical Imperative as particularly influential to King's understanding of the inherent dignity of each person: "Now I say Man and, in general, every rational being exists as an end in himself and not merely as a means to be arbitrarily used by this or that will."[21] I describe the ways in which a Kantian moral view of persons as an "end" contributed to King's formulation of dignity. At the end of the fourth chapter I focus on King's view of nonviolent resistance, relating the influence of Gandhi's method of satyagraha to the civil rights struggle. The most important task in this chapter is to demonstrate how King's appropriation of the method of nonviolent resistance became the energizing philosophy and praxis for gaining a deeper sense of dignity.

In the fifth chapter I shall focus on the theological and ethical foundations of King's view of dignity by giving attention both to his theological anthropology, particularly his concept of *imago dei*, and to his understanding of agape as a formative element in gaining human dignity. I shall also investigate how his ambivalent view of the sinfulness and nobility of human nature colored his attempts to define nonviolent resistance in such a way that nonviolent struggle could become the catalyst for the formation of a new sense of self and a new dignity.

The second half of the fifth chapter emphasizes the centrality of King's agape ethic. King's view of love was influenced by the black church,

---

[21]Kant, *Foundations*, 52.

Anders Nygren, Paul Tillich, and Reinhold Neibuhr,[22] yet he synthesized
their views in such a way that agape was grounded in the concrete social
struggle of forming what King called a "new self-respect and sense of
dignity."[23] I turn again to a chronological and exegetical analysis of
King's speeches and sermons in order to understand the relationship
between agape, *imago dei*, and dignity. Furthermore, such textual exegesis will reveal that King's view of agape incorporates elements of a
justice that demanded social dignity for the person.

In the sixth chapter I shall look in depth at the development of King's
thought on dignity in the years from 1962 to 1968. I shall reveal how
certain themes such as the "Emancipation Proclamation," "opportunity,"
and "the dream" were developed in line with King's increasingly concrete understanding of the concept of dignity and self-respect. The method
of investigation will again be chronological textual exegesis.

In the seventh and concluding chapter I shall criticize King's view of
self, agape, and nonviolent resistance as this view relates to contemporary feminist/womanist discussions of self. Is King's view of the person
as a dynamic ongoing process limited by a presupposition of maleness
as the normative human person? Or, on the other hand, does the idea of
person as an open-ended dynamic process present future symbolic possibilities for a constructive inclusive vision of dignified persons? King's
views on women's roles, his view of marriage, and his relationship with
women in the civil rights movement help us to form a more complete
understanding of King's views regarding the human person. At this point
it will be possible to introduce King's notion of being "somebody" as a
potentially dynamic metaphor for stimulating liberating reflection on a
dignified and inclusive vision of humanity, particularly within the black
community. Finally, after describing and criticizing King's view of the
dignified person, I shall conclude with suggestions for a prolegomenon
for a contemporary theory of dignity that embraces a *constructive and
inclusive view of persons*, incorporating recent womanist works such as

---

[22]Anders Nygren, *Agape and Eros* (Chicago: University of Chicago Press,
1953); Reinhold Niebuhr, *Moral Man and Immoral Society* (New York: Scribners,
1932); Tillich, *Love, Power, and Justice*.
[23]Martin Luther King, Jr., "Nonviolence and Racial Justice" in Washington,
Testament of Hope, 6.

those of bell hooks and Jacquelyn Grant on the issue of male self
construction.[24]

Location in King Scholarship

At this juncture it is important to locate the precise niche that thi
work occupies in the burgeoning field of King scholarship. While sev
eral King scholars have looked at his mature theological and ethica
reflections, none have given such focused attention to King's view of th
person as a potential theoretical resource for conceptualizing humaı
dignity and selfhood.

Leading King scholars, such as Taylor Branch and David Garrow
have viewed King's life primarily through the lens of *historical biogra*
phy, giving scant attention to his theological and ethical thought. Whil
it is important and necessary that King's life be understood as contrib
uting to American history, his contribution to the field of theologica
anthropology and ethics also needs to be highlighted.

Taylor Branch's *Parting the Waters* and Stephen Oates's *Let the Trum*
pet Sound provide us with information about King's theological educaı
tion, some points about King's background in the black church, and
discussion of the affinities in thought between King and Reinhold Niebuhı
From these works we discover that King was an "evangelical liberal
whose primary influences were the "Boston Personalists" (L. Harol
DeWolf, George Davis, and Edgar Brightman) and the "Christian Reaľ
ist" (Reinhold Neibuhr). Branch and Oates offer a glimpse into the theo
logical education and "schooling" of King's mind, but their emphasis i
on the story of King's life, not on his theological and ethical develop
ment.

David Garrows's *Bearing the Cross* is perhaps the most exhaustivel
researched biography of King's life. While Garrow himself sees King
whole life as an embodiment of the self-sacrificial concept of "bearinį
the Cross," he does not demonstrate any interest in looking at King'
theological and ethical reflections. Instead we are treated to a thorougł
compilation of the *facts* of King's life, without attention to the develop
ment, changes, and blind spots of his theological thought.

---

[24]hooks, *Feminist Theory*, chap. 5, "Men: Comrades in the Struggle" 127–3.
and idem, *Talking Back*, chap. 18, "Feminist Focus on Men: A Comment" 67
81; Jacquelyn Grant, "Black Theology and the Black Woman" in *Black Theoı*
ogy: A Documentary History (Maryknoll, NY: Orbis, 1979) 418–33.

Other King scholars, such as William Watley, have written of King's theological contribution as primarily that of creating a *nonviolent ethic*,[25] or have approached King's theology with a view toward a comparative analysis of important *intellectual sources*, such as Reinhold Niebuhr, Paul Tillich, and Boston Personalism,[26] or have examined King's thought as *socio-political philosophy*.[27] Some have employed a *developmental-psychological framework of analysis*[28] for looking at King's personal self-development, or have even *systematized King's theology*.[29] The variety of approaches demonstrates the richness of available secondary litera-ture. These analytical frameworks, however, do not focus primarily on the unique manner in which King combined a theological anthropology and theological ethic of agape and nonviolence in order to address the problem of contemporary African-American dignity and personhood.

Objective

I hope to demonstrate that it is necessary to give special attention to the issue of dignity. When King's thought is viewed as a comprehensive theory of dignity, essential connections between theological ethics and theological anthropology are revealed. While various scholars have accu-rately described and systematized King's view of personality, God, agape, and even nonviolence, the connections between these categories of his thought and his dynamic view of dignity have not been adequately por-

[25]Numerous articles, dissertations, and essays have been written with the issue of nonviolence in mind. Of these, two books stand out: Smith and Zepp, *Search for the Beloved Community* and Watley, *Roots of Resistance*.

[26]One of the best examples of this approach is John Ansbro's *Martin Luther King, Jr: The Making of a Mind*, as well as Smith and Zepp, *Search for the Beloved Community*.

[27]Several dissertations follow this line of reasoning, see esp. Richard Busaca, "Social Movements and the Construction of Reality: A Study of the Civil Rights Movement and Its Role in the Transformation of American Politics" (Ph.D. diss., University of California, Berkeley, 1976).

[28]An excellent example is Downing, *Promised Land*; see also Frederick D. Harper, "*Maslow's Concept of Self-Actualization Compared with Personality Characteristics of Selected Black American Protesters: Martin Luther King, Jr., Malcolm X, and Frederick Douglass*" (Ph.D. diss., Duke University, 1973).

[29]See Thomas Mikelson, "The Negro's God in the Concept of God of Martin Luther King, Jr." (Th.D. diss., Harvard University, 1988); and Paul R. Garber, "King Was a Black Theologian," *JRT* 31 (1974–1975) 16–32.

trayed. The process and activity of dignity that King proposed synthe
sizes theological ethics and theological anthropology in the forge o
resistance to oppression.

Before entering the body of this work I want to clarify my usage o
the words "Negro," "black," and the masculine pronoun in quotations o
King's thought. King lived at a time when self-respecting African-Ameri
cans named themselves "Negro." He also lived to see that historica
period in which the revolutionary changes in the Negro's social situatior
enabled African-Americans to name themselves "black" with pride.
will use "Negro," "black," and "African-American" interchangeably ex
cept in quotations of King's speeches and sermons, where I will use the
words that were used at the time of the quotation. This will enable the
reader to appreciate the shifts in historical usage of each term, withou
valuing any name above the others.

King lived before our current sensitivity to the gender biases inheren
in the hegemonic use of masculine pronouns. For King "his" and "him"
referred to both male and female. King understood his ideas as being
comprehensive, although it is apparent to a reader in the late twentietl
century that King lacked a consciousness of feminism or a feminis
critique. I shall explicate the sexist assumptions within King's though
and actions in the last chapter. In quotations, I retain his usage of the
masculine pronoun, whereas in other passages pertaining to King's worl
concerning humanity, I employ inclusive language.

I also use the term "uplift" in a way that carries the particular valence
of the African-American community's historical understanding of tha
word. Edward Wheeler's *Uplifting the Race* presents an excellent work
ing definition of the way in which "uplift" has been understood in the
African-American community.

> Uplift entailed moral, social, economic and educational develop-
> ment. It included a sound family life and pride in ownership of
> property; it involved the adoption of moral standards and behav-
> ioral patterns that conformed to the norm in American civilization.
> The norm was correct not because it was American or white, but
> because any civilized society operated on such principles.[30]

[30]Edward L. Wheeler, *Uplifting the Race: The Black Minister in the New
South 1865–1902* (Lanham, MD: University Press of America) 28.

will use the word "uplift" as both a verb and a noun with the above connotations of meaning.

Finally, I use the terms "motif" and "motivic concepts" in a way that is colored by my musical education. In music a "motif" is a distinctive musical phrase or pattern that "recurs throughout a composition. . . as a unifying element."[31] To describe King's thought as "motivic" or as having "motivic concepts" is to indicate my interpretation of King's concepts of dignity as having a recurring, distinctive, and interweaving quality reminiscent of the development of motifs in a musical composition. While such usage of the term may seem peculiarly idiosyncratic, such particularity is appropriate to the fundamental importance of musical expression in the African-American community itself. Recent African-American theologians and musicologists have linked the aspirations of blacks for freedom from bondage and equal opportunity with traditional spirituals.[32] Jon Michael Spencer's *Protest & Praise* advances knowledge of the fundamental importance of African-American sacred music by revealing how the black preacher has been one of the primary vehicles of advancing spirituals into contemporary times "via the preaching event of black worship."[33] Spencer goes on to describe the black preacher's use of melodic intonation, rhythmic cadence, and antiphonic response as part of black sacred music history.[34] King's sermons are filled with examples of melodic intonation (the singing quality of King's baritone voice), rhythmic cadence (the repetition of a particular phrase—"I have a dream"), and the calling forth of antiphonal response of the people listening (heard in many of King's most memorable addresses). King's thought, when viewed in this light, is motivic.

Throughout my life the social contribution and religious power of the Rev. Dr. Martin Luther King, Jr. have held a singularly important place. I was born on 25 November 1955, five days before the official beginning of the Montgomery Bus Boycott. Dr. King's powerful baritone is part of the fabric of my earliest memories. His ideals, his vision of a better America, his proclamations of hope and love, and the television

[31]Willi Apel, *Harvard Dictionary of Music* (2d rev. ed.; Cambridge, MA: Belknap, 1969) 545.

[32]An excellent example of this type of work may be found in John Lovell, Jr., *Black Song: The Forge and the Flame* (New York: Paragon, 1972) 581–85.

[33]Jon Michael Spencer, *Protest & Praise: Sacred Music of Black Religion* (Minneapolis: Fortress, 1990) 225.

[34]Ibid., 227–35.

pictures of him leading demonstrations guided my parents' dinner conversations and their own dreams. As a result, it comes as no surprise to me that my work should focus on the thought of Martin Luther King, Jr.

My interest in the topic of human dignity stems from the same period of time. My most vivid recollections of the civil rights movement revolve around seeing adult black men carrying signs with the statement "I am a Man," written in large letters. I remember asking my parents why grown-up men had to protest in this way and remind white people that they were "men." My parents informed me of the terrible economic and social situation of racism that these men were fighting against and explained to me that the signs were worded in this way because the struggle for civil rights was a struggle "for dignity." So the term "dignity" was used frequently in the household in which I grew up.

The questions that I now bring to the subject of dignity combine three very important concerns: (1) how to understand human dignity as King did, (2) how King's view of dignity can be related to contemporary discussions of an inclusive view of persons, and (3) how such an academic exercise can be effectively related to the problems and concerns of young African-American males.

I acknowledge and honor many who have made the writing of this thesis possible. I thank the archivists at Boston University's Mugar Library whose professional courtesy and expertise enabled me to utilize the King Archives located in their facility. I thank Diane Ware at the Martin Luther King Center for Nonviolent Social Change in Atlanta, Georgia, for her enthusiastic help in my days of research in the King Archives located in the Center.

I also thank my advisor, Preston Williams, for his strong guidance and willingness to answer my many questions! Many thanks to Margaret Miles for being an exceptional and gifted inspiration and aid in the writing of the thesis. Thanks to Harvey Cox, Richard R. Niebuhr, Sharon Welch, and Gordon Kaufman for their encouragement, interest, and professional example. Thanks, as well, to the members of the Martin Luther King course in spring 1990 at Harvard Divinity School who helped me define the argument of the thesis.

I appreciate the time and interest shown for this work from my doctoral colleague Deborah Haynes, whose proofreading and discussion always helped me to sharpen arguments. Finally, I thank Karen Baker Fletcher, colleague and best friend, as well as wife, who despite the pressures of writing her own dissertation always took the time to read my work and to goad me toward excellence.

1

FORMATIVE INFLUENCES
AND DIGNITY

In order to describe Martin Luther King, Jr.'s contribution to our understanding of human dignity it is necessary to understand the historical and social setting to which he was responding. Beginning with the first campaign in Montgomery, Alabama, we find King describing the struggle for civil rights as a struggle for human dignity. In *Stride Toward Freedom* King described how the rallies or "mass meetings" served as places for breaking down class barriers because of the unity the people achieved in the fight for dignity.

Physicians, teachers, and lawyers sat or stood beside domestic workers and unskilled laborers. The Ph.D.'s and the no "D's" were bound together in a common venture. The so-called "big Negroes" who owned cars and had never ridden the buses came to know the maids and laborers who rode the buses every day. Men and women who had been separated from each other by false standards of class were

now singing and praying together in a *common struggle for freedom and human dignity.* [my emphasis][1]

Martin Luther King, Jr. was an American Negro, born and raised in
the South in the middle of the twentieth century, a time of de jure
segregation. The system of de jure segregation had arisen as a reassertion
of white dominance over a population of newly freed slaves. Except for
the terrorizing activities of such groups as the nascent Ku Klux Klan,
newly freed slaves made some progress from the end of the Civil War
until about 1875 with the passing of the first Civil Rights Bill in Congress. From 1875 onward, however, those rights were continually eroded
until the infamous *Plessy v. Ferguson* decision by the Supreme Court in
1896, the act that signalled the official beginning of de jure segregation.

Such facts focus our attention on the undeniable social reality of
racial oppression that formed and shaped young Martin Luther King,
Jr.'s personality. While it is not the intention of this thesis to present a
psychological or developmental picture of King, it is useful, nevertheless, to look at the social reality to which he was responding in order to
understand more fully why the concept of dignity was important to King.
In particular, I shall examine the influence of (1) "Daddy King" and
young Martin's family tradition of protest, (2) rural, southern black church
traditions, and (3) the wisdom of the "mothers" in King's family.

Daddy King

The enormously powerful character of Dr. King's father had a tremendous influence on King's understanding of dignity and self-respect. While
it is exceedingly difficult to penetrate the elder King's early childhood,
there are certain accounts that have survived.

Martin Luther King, Sr. rose from being the son of a sharecropper to
the pastorate of the influential Ebenezer Baptist Church of Atlanta. His
struggle to gain an education and social and ecclesiastical prominence is
legendary.[2]

The elder King completed his studies for a bachelor's degree in theology in 1930 from Morehouse College. He said of those years that they

---

[1]King, *Stride Toward Freedom*, 86.

[2]King, *Daddy King*. King, Sr. provides several moving accounts of his struggle
to become educated by starting in the fifth grade (p. 18) and talking his way into
Morehouse College (p. 75).

were the "toughest of my life,"[3] and that "though I'd never become an outstanding student in college, my stubborn determination got me through."[4] It is precisely that "stubborn determination" to better himself educationally that I consider to be part of the enormously powerful personal influence that Daddy King had on young Martin. The elder King recounted the tale of his educational "uplift" to his family numerous times, and it served as a constant source of both inspiration and irritation for young Martin Luther King, Jr.

King, Sr. was known for his boisterous and imposing ways, according to his son's own account.[5] While King, Jr. describes his father as an outstanding "personal example," providing a goad toward excellence, it is also apparent that his father was also a demanding and dominating figure in his son's life.[6] Young Martin learned to argue persuasively with his father, a skill that was honed and developed through his educational and ministerial career. King, Jr.'s ability to stand up to his father with a mixture of "filibuster, charm, and stubbornness"[7] could be interpreted as simply the normal growing pains of a young man and his father. Learning gently and forcefully to persuade such an imposing father may have also provided young King, Jr. with an important elementary exercise in nonviolence.

The elder King's influence must not be limited to his having been an inspirational personal exemplar. King, Sr. has been described as an "earthbound preacher, bursting with energy."[8] King, Sr. was one who knew how to mix a type of Christian "fundamentalism" with an overtly capitalist doctrine of economic success. This mixture of an "earthly" with a "heavenly" gospel was the constant menu of homiletic theology that young Martin Luther King, Jr. heard on a weekly basis from his father. For example, the Ebenezer Baptist Church secretary, Sarah Reed, quoted Daddy King in what she recalled as the elements of a typical sermon:

[3]Ibid., 87.

[4]Ibid., 88.

[5]King, (*Stride Toward Freedom*, 19–20) recounts how his father "stood up" to white people and how King, Sr.'s children stood in awe of their father's ability to do this without being physically harmed.

[6]See the commentary on King, Jr.'s battles with his father about his pastorate in Dexter Avenue Baptist Church and the bombing of his home in Montgomery, AL, in Branch, *Parting the Waters*, 111–12, 166–67.

[7]Branch, *Parting The Waters*, 112.

[8]Ibid., 41.

"Whether you have a million or not, you are just as important. Give respect and respect respect. Always give a full day's work for a full day's pay. Don't be sloppy on your job."[9] Mrs. Reed went on to relate to me that Daddy King would "talk about those things *everywhere*! From the pulpit, in private conversations, everywhere."[10]

Such an example is meaningful to the purpose of this volume, for it implies that such preaching had a positive and dignifying impact on the listeners. One particularly memorable phrase from the retinue of Daddy King's theology was his repeated injunction, "You can do it."[11] As Daddy King had risen up from illiteracy, poverty, and ignominy to education, prominence, and prosperity, so other Negroes could do the same. Such a message of "uplift" rang through young Martin's sermons as he called for Negroes (and America) to "rise up."

Taylor Branch portrays Daddy King with a mixture of admiration and contempt. Branch finds in the elder King a kind of crudeness and vulgarity that he describes in such statements as, "His sermons mixed straightforward Christian fundamentalism with boosterism."[12] Branch's account of the elder King's life, however, is complemented by King's own autobiography, *Daddy King*. In this work King, Sr. traced the powerful influence of his father's work ethic on his life. This determination to work hard was complicated by a dualistic "ethic" enforced by the white power structure of the time:

> Papa gave a hard, good day's work, never shirked, never cut any corners. But to the whites who owned the land around Stockbridge [GA], the cotton traders and the tradesmen, there was *one set of ethics for themselves and another bunch of rules that applied when they were dealing with any black person.* . . . "Cheatin' a nigger," they'd say, "ain't really doin' nothin' wrong. It's like playin' a game, 'cause most times they's too dumb to know the difference anyhow." [my emphasis][13]

---

[9]Sarah Reed, church secretary of the Ebenezer Baptist Church, Atlanta, GA, interview with author, 16 November 1989.

[10]Ibid.

[11]Branch, *Parting the Waters*, 43.

[12]Ibid., 41.

[13]King, *Daddy King*, 24.

Daddy King gave to this trenchant description of a double ethic an analysis similar to some of his son's statements: "To these whites, a Negro wasn't a human being, but just a thing."[14]

Although he did not have the systematic training of his son, Daddy King recognized that a dualistic and unjust ethic was unfair and morally repugnant. He devoted his life to fighting against this ethic and inculcated in his family a strong sense of the unfairness of segregation and racial discrimination. Furthermore, King, Sr.'s description of a double ethic demonstrates that he was aware of the connections between abusive economic treatment and the ideology of inferiority. The connection between King, Sr.'s understanding of a double ethic and his son's theory of dignity becomes apparent at this juncture, for King, Jr. attacked economic and civil abuses from their basis in a dehumanizing ideology of Negro inferiority. Knowing that King, Sr. struggled to right the negative implications of this double ethic adds support to the argument that King, Jr.'s concept of dignity originated in his family and church background.

Daddy King described his ministry as one of protest against "the system." Although he constantly worked against the forces that enforced segregation, Daddy King never lost hope that someday things would change. Yet such change would have to be over what he called the "political forces that controlled the entire region of the old Confederacy" who said unequivocally, "Never!" and meant it.[15]

Daddy King also described himself as a "chronic complainer" who "grumbled about all the conditions [he] saw segregation imposing on Negroes."[16] He described the degraded social position of Negroes in the following way: "the Negro continued to be an easy target of hatred, a 'thing' to be kept in his place, to be despised, brutalized, or killed."[17]

Daddy King repeatedly told his followers, "Never hate the white man!" The theme of "not hating" appears as a type of negative side to the emphasis on love found throughout King, Jr.'s ministry. Notice how Daddy King speaks of his "fight" for the Negro's dignity:

> We, in turn, were not fighting out of hatred for anybody. Our struggle was not so much against the systems people had created to keep us from living decent lives. Whites could only hate *us*. We

[14]Ibid., 24.
[15]Ibid., 96.
[16]Ibid.
[17]Ibid.

had no political machinery or systems to oppress them. We had no
signs to represent who we thought we were. Negroes did not divide
buses by race or build separate drinking fountains. The police did
not support our prejudices with the force of guns. We were *vulnerable*. Our victories and losses in the civil rights struggle had to
begin with that understanding. [my emphasis][18]

For Daddy King, the civil rights struggle was not merely a matter of
gaining citizenship rights, although that was a necessary part of it. It
was, as the previous quotations reveal, a struggle to overcome hatred
within one's self as well as the hatred that was practiced against every
Negro, a struggle against a *system of hatred* and not against individual
persons involved in the system, and a struggle toward greater freedom.
The theme of struggling against the system of injustice rather than fighting personal hatred, as we shall see, was echoed and developed in his
son's thought. Specifically, young Martin Luther King, Jr. seemed to
turn his father's doctrine of not hating inside out and to speak of the
necessity of the positive loving of the white oppressor. I shall develop
this in more detail in chapter five. It is also possible to argue that King,
Jr. simply extended his father's emphasis on working against systems
rather than individual persons and articulated his father's social critique
in the expository framework of such academic theologians as Reinhold
Niebuhr and Anders Nygren.

It is important to see that King, Jr. was first exposed to the idea of
struggling against systems rather than persons from his father and family, and *not* in the theological education he received at Crozer Theological Seminary and Boston University. Young King extended his father's
and grandfather's work for greater freedom, even calling his first book
Stride Toward Freedom. Freedom is a term that King, Jr. tied into his
description of the human person, as we shall see in chapter four.

The Reverend A. D. Williams

In an early chapter of his autobiography, Daddy King describes with
admiration how Martin Luther King, Jr.'s maternal grandfather, the Reverend A. D. Williams, had influenced his understanding of the necessity
of protesting for Negro rights. Rev. Williams had built Ebenezer Baptist
Church and was known throughout the Atlanta area as a leader. Branch
describes Williams as "the type who convened meetings, identified com-

[18]Ibid.

munity goals, and got elected to chair committees he himself proposed."[19] Williams had become the first president of the Atlanta chapter of the NAACP in 1909, just a few years after the 1906 Atlanta race riot. Williams was also a leader in the National Baptist Convention.

Williams believed and practiced political protest as the necessary way for Negroes to gain dignity. Further, Rev. Williams's influence over his son-in-law was enormous, because unlike King, Jr.'s father, Williams could (albeit in a very limited and controlled manner) influence the whites of Atlanta to make positive changes. This ability for the Williams-King family to make a positive difference in the dignity of Negroes was an important part of the environment within which young Martin Luther King, Jr. grew up.

Probably Williams's most important influence on Martin Luther King, Jr.'s thought is revealed by Daddy King in his autobiography, when he states that Rev. Williams believed that "progress never comes without challenge, without danger, and at times, great trial."[20] His understanding of "progress" was undoubtedly passed on through Daddy King to his grandson. Such a view is historically rooted in the protest tradition of Frederick Douglass, who stated the following in his 1849 speech, "No Progress Without Struggle":

> Let me give you a word of the philosophy of reforms. The whole history of the progress of human liberty shows that all concessions, yet made to her august claims, have been born of earnest struggle. The conflict has been exciting, agitating, all-absorbing, and for the time being putting all other tumults to silence. It must do this or it does nothing. If there is no struggle, there is no progress.[21]

Such a philosophy of protest engages all of a person's energies in active social, political, and economic public affairs. Such a view also implies a practical understanding of power relationships. Grandpa Williams, Daddy King, and young Martin realized that in order for Negroes to gain a greater sense of dignity, they would be forced to challenge the segregated system. Challenge, at times dangerous, could take the form of

---

[19]Branch, *Parting The Waters*, 32.

[20]King, *Daddy King*, 82.

[21]Frederick Douglass, "No Progress without Struggle," in Floyd B. Barbour ed., *The Black Power Revolt* (New York: Collier, 1968) 36–37.

mass protests and marches for certain rights, such as Daddy King's fight
to achieve equal pay for black and white teachers.

Rev. Williams's philosophical notion of challenge, which was based
on bringing about social change for the American Negro, identified the
minister's role as that of standing up for this change. Challenge came
through the minister's sense of "responsibility to the community."[22] The
minister, for Williams, was an "advocate for justice."[23] Daddy King
described Rev. Williams's view of the minister's role this way:

> It was through him that I came to understand the larger implica-
> tions involved in any church-man's responsibility to the community
> he served. Church was simply Sunday morning and a few evenings
> during the week. It was more than a full-time job. In the act of
> faith, every minister became an advocate for justice. In the South,
> this meant an active involvement in changing the social order all
> around us.[24]

Finally, Rev. Williams saw that the challenge initiated and led by
ministerial advocates for justice was part of the *mission* of Negro ministers. Daddy King reported that his father-in-law had "no sympathy for
those who saw no mission in their lives."[25] The "true man of God,"
according to Rev. Williams, was called to "lead the people of his church
not only in the spiritual sense, but also in the practical world in which
they found themselves struggling."[26]

Martin Luther King, Jr. challenged the very heart and soul of the
segregated system with the aid of his own coherent philosophy of challenge—namely, that of nonviolence. In chapter four, I shall discuss the
specifics of King's philosophy of nonviolence, but it is important to note
now that King's early understanding of dignity and of the role of the
minister, as well as his view that social progress came through dangerous challenge, had been shaped long before he entered seminary and was
exposed to Kant, Hegel, personalism, and the Niebuhrs. Without exag-
geration, I can concur with Dr. King's own assessment in *Stride Toward
Freedom* that his academic training gave him a "metaphysical founda-

[22]King, *Daddy King*, 82.
[23]Ibid.
[24]Ibid.
[25]Ibid.
[26]Ibid.

tion" for the concepts that he had already "received" from his ministerial family.[27] Martin Luther King, Jr. felt that his role in the nonviolent movement resisting racism was a part of the same "historical process" that had been initiated by his ancestors.[28] In Robert Penn Warren's interview with Dr. King, King stated that he saw himself in continuity with his father.[29] This interview reveals a great deal about King's understanding of the influence of his father and the historical struggle in which they were both engaged throughout their lives.

Warren begins the interview with the question, "Do you see your father's role and your own role as historical phases of the same process?" King's response is:

> Yes I do. I think my father and I have worked together a great deal in the last few years, trying to grapple with the same problem, and he was working in the area of civil rights before I was born and when I was just a kid, *and I grew up in the kind of atmosphere that had a real civil rights concern.* I do think it's the same problem that we're grappling with—it's the same historical process." [my emphasis][30]

Warren proceeds to ask about the differences between the elder King's "techniques, and opportunities and climates of opinion" and those of King, Jr., asking whether these differences were sharp or in "continuity."[31] King's response was that he saw "a continuity" with "certain and minor differences."[32] According to King, Jr. the primary difference between himself and his father lay in the philosophy of nonviolence:

> I think basically the roles are the same. Now, I grant you that at points my father did not come up under the non-violent philosophy. He was not really trained in the non-violent discipline, but even

---

[27]Martin Luther King, *Stride Toward Freedom*, 100.

[28]Martin Luther King, Jr., interview by Robert Penn Warren: "Who Speaks for the Negro?" 18 March 1964, Tape 1 and transcript, located in the Martin Luther King, Jr. Center Archives, Atlanta, GA, 1–2.

[29]Ibid., 1.

[30]Ibid.

[31]Ibid.

[32]Ibid.

without that the problem was about the same, and even though the
methods may not have been consciously non-violent they were cer-
tainly non-violent in the sense that he never, never advocated violence as a way to solve the problem.[33]

What stands out in this interview is King, Jr.'s sense of continuing
what his father had started, with the aid of the philosophy of nonviolence. Over and over again Dr. King points back to the virtually un-
changed problem of a racist system of segregation as the singular nemesis
for both father and son. Furthermore, he demonstrates that the ministerial role that he had grown up seeing—what in the interview he called
a "kind of atmosphere that had a real civil rights concern"—was the
same advocacy role his grandfather had encouraged his father to embrace as his own. Stressing the continuities, he downplayed the differences.

Rural Southern Black Baptist Tradition

Beyond what he experienced in his family, specific black church traditions influenced King's thought. Dr. King's spirituality was shaped in
a long and rich Christian tradition that can be characterized as *rural*,
sprung from the roots of farming and "country" people; *southern*, related
to the strong revivalist elements that typify both black and white
southerners; *black*, in the sense that there is an added element of Negro,
post-Reconstruction spirituality and culture; and finally *Baptist*, the particular denominational affiliation of the preachers in the King and Williams families and of such influential preachers in King's life as William
Holmes Borders and Vernon Johns.[34] All of these elements were part of
King's life before he went off to seminary and graduate education.

[33]Ibid., 2.

[34]For information regarding scholarly debate concerning rural southern black
religion, see Gerald L. Davis, *I Got the Word in Me, and I Can Sing It, You Know*
(Philadelphia: University of Pennsylvania Press, 1985) 1–13; C. L. Franklin
Give Me this Mountain (ed. Jeff Todd Titon; Urbana: University of Illinois Press,
1989) 1–46, particularly Franklin's description of the "Spiritual Preacher." See
also Cornel West's description of "kinetic orality": "the fluid and protean power
of the Word in speech and song along with the rich Africanisms such as antiphonality
(call-and-response), polyrhythms, syncopation, and repetition; the passionate physi-
cality, including the bodily participation in liturgical and everyday expressions;
and the combative spirituality which accents a supernatural and subversive joy,
an oppositional perseverance and patience" (West, *Prophetic Fragments*, 43).

In order to appreciate the rich influence of such a tradition, I shall limit my discussion of this tradition to what can be said about the *direct influences* on Martin Luther King, Jr., starting with his maternal great-grandfather who was a slave exhorter. The little that we know about him comes again from Daddy King who reported that Rev. A. D. Williams claimed that his own powerful style of preaching, his "gifts," were "inherited" from this slave exhorter. If indeed this slave exhorter was like his son, A. D. Williams, he must have been a "very impressive" figure who preached with a "thundering style."[35] Rev. Williams was said to have been raised in Greene County, Georgia, and called himself a "country preacher" even after living in Atlanta for many years.[36]

Daddy King also claimed rural roots from which he acquired a rough and ungrammatical language that caused him several embarrassing moments in his early days in the "big city" of Atlanta.[37] Daddy King painfully recounted these moments of feeling his rural background:

> They must have considered me a clown, a comical country bumpkin. Words like "totin'" didn't fit in an Atlanta vocabulary, not among Methodists, anyway, among those who'd escaped from the country life I was just emerging from. They didn't need any reminders, from preachers or anybody else, of what they'd left behind. I was that kind of reminder, with my dusty, uncreased clothes, my rough country style of speaking, my whole uneducated green farmboy personality.[38]

What is particularly moving about this account is Daddy King's empathetic response to these people's rejection of his "country" preaching personality. He was able to understand them, although the next phrase suggests his strong criticism of their viewpoint: "I was nothing to them, almost the way I'd been nothing to the white men back in the country, when I'd been just another one of somebody's niggers."[39]

[35]King, *Daddy King*, 84.
[36]Ibid.
[37]One such incident occurred when Daddy King was asked to preach at his girlfriend's father's church, which happened to be a "high-brow" Methodist church! (ibid., 57).
[38]Ibid.
[39]Ibid.

It is critical to remember the rural side of Dr. King's upbringing, for it is against the backdrop of rising above the illiteracy and roughness of the "country" that the King/Williams family struggled in the "big city" of Atlanta. Dr. King is often portrayed as having been born with a silver spoon, with all of the advantages of middle-class, bourgeois extravagances. Such a view, while indicating the young King's social advantages as the son of a prominent Atlanta preacher, does not adequately describe the dynamic of conflict *within* the King family. Daddy King often vividly described his awareness of being a "country" newcomer, with the feelings of being an outsider in comparison with the refined middle-class and educated manners of his wife, Alberta Williams, or the educated polish of his rival, Rev. Borders of Wheat Street Baptist. Still it is clear that "country" for Daddy King was a symbol for the vicious racism of whites and the powerless illiteracy of Negroes in the agricultural South.

As the pastor of Atlanta's Ebenezer Baptist Church, Daddy King did preserve one important aspect of the "country," namely the power of rural Baptist spirituality and worship. Daddy King described this form of worship by first remembering how he had "developed a strong voice and could sing nearly any song after hearing it just a few times."[40] He described how some rural churches did not allow any musical instruments except for the human voice, condemning all else as a form of the "devil's music."[41] This view, of course, can be shown to have much in common with the beliefs of many rural southerners—white and black.[42] Daddy King said simply, "The human voice was the rural church's organ and piano."[43]

Daddy King went on to speak of the prominence in rural Baptist spirituality of the "Country Circuit minister, or C. C. Rider."[44] These preachers "traveled by horseback, built a word-of-mouth reputation on an ability to cite the Scriptures—usually by memory, because not many of the country folks had ever learned to read."[45] These preachers could add

[40]Ibid.

[41]Ibid.

[42]For more on this topic see Hildred Roach, *Black American Music* (Boston Crescendo, 1973); and John B. Boles, *Black Southerners 1619–1869* (Lexington KY: University of Kentucky Press, 1984).

[43]King, *Daddy King*, 27.

[44]Ibid.

[45]Ibid.

o their impressiveness "if they could sing well," so Daddy King devel-
ped his skill to the utmost!

Along with emulating the C. C. Riders, Daddy King described how,
s a young man, he participated in the oral tradition of this type of
pirituality by studying the "old-time preachers" of the rural Baptist
hurches. While remembering that his own singing could bring congre-
ations to a "peak of emotional fervor," he honored the memory of those
ameless old-time preachers who had taught him how to be a minister.
Of them he wrote:

> And at these services I attended, so many of the old-time preachers,
> who could recite Scriptures for hours on end, provided me with a
> great sense of the gestures, the cadences, the deeply emotive qual-
> ity of their styles of ministry. And when I was alone, I would try
> to duplicate the things I heard them do, and having a good memory
> for songs and the parts of the Bible that were especially popular
> among country folks, the Psalms, for example, I was soon experi-
> encing a growing personal vision of spending a life in the ministry
> myself.[46]

The masterful rhythm, cadence, and "moan" in Dr. King's sermonic
elivery all went back to his father's and grandfather's rural black Bap-
ist spirituality. In fact, when I interviewed a few members of Ebenezer
Baptist Church, the one thing said about Dr. King and his father was
hat they both possessed a "common touch" and an ability to speak to
plain folks in plain language."[47]

All of the above leads me to infer that although Daddy King and
King, Jr. worked tremendously hard to overcome the illiteracy, crude-
ess, and some of the "backwardness" of the "country," they also appear
o have affirmed the powerful emotive style and vivid imagery of the
country" spirituality. Daddy King spoke of growing up "respecting and
oving it [rural Baptist worship]."[48] King, Jr. wrote of rejecting the fun-

---

[46]Ibid.

[47]This quality has been spoken of in more academic and expansive terms by
'ornel West in the chapter on Martin Luther King in *Prophetic Fragments* (p. 3),
here he names King as an "organic intellectual," and therefore "in touch" with
e language, needs, and everyday style of the people whom he served as pastor.

[48]King, *Daddy King*, 27.

damentalism and the otherworldliness of his father's heritage,[49] but h
never rejected the singing, style, cadence, and emotion that typified rura
black Baptist spirituality. Furthermore, while on the one hand King re
jected the fundamentalist theology and emotional excesses of the rura
black Baptists, on the other hand he affirmed the tone and vitality o
spirituality as a dignifying, necessary, and useful force to which he adde
the rational discipline of his synthetic philosophy of personalism an
nonviolence.

Motivating Daddy King to refine his "country" ways was the maste
ful eloquence of his rival, Rev. William Holmes Borders. It is reporte
that from an early age King, Jr. raised the jealous ire of Daddy King b
openly admiring and imitating the "commanding language and perfe
diction" of Borders.[50] While Borders and King, Sr. shared the commo
roots of a rural, black, southern, and Baptist spirituality, their primar
difference lay in the northern seminary education (including bachelor
and master's degrees) that Borders possessed.

King, Jr. was decidedly ambivalent about the "shout" tradition. Taylc
Branch describes how King convinced Abernathy to come and join hir
in Atlanta by recalling childhood experiences of his father "shouting" c
"walking the benches":

> "David, I told you that I remember watching my daddy walk the
> benches when I was a little boy."
> "I know," Abernathy said quietly. "Walking the benches" referred
> to ministers who leaped from the pulpit in mid-sermon to preach
> ecstatically as they danced up and down the pews, literally stepping
> over the swooning bodies in the congregation. Abernathy knew that
> King considered it the most vaudevillian, primitive aspect of his
> heritage. "He walked the benches," King repeated, in humiliation
> and wonder. "He did it to feed and educate his family. Now I've
> got to help him. Don't you see that?"[51]

---

[49]See Garrow, *Bearing the Cross*, 637 n. 23: "King later told an interviewe
'I revolted against the emotionalism of Negro religion, the shouting and stomp
ing. I didn't understand it and it embarrassed me.'" Further, Garrow (p. 3.
recounts that at Morehouse "the shackles of fundamentalism were removed
(King's own words as found in Lawrence D. Reddick, *Crusader Without Vic
lence: A Biography of Martin Luther King, Jr.* [New York: Harper & Brother
1959] 61–74).

[50]Branch, *Parting the Waters*, 54.

[51]Ibid., 267.

While I question Branch's usage of what might be considered deroga-
ory adjectives (e.g., "primitive," "vaudevillian," "swooning," etc.), it is
lear from even a cursory knowledge of King's preaching style that he
adically modified the tradition of shouting and walking the benches into
is own climactic perorations based on poetry and scripture. One need
nly remember his peroration on the phrase "I have a dream" in his
amous speech at the Lincoln Memorial to see how far King transformed
he dance of a minister's legs on the pew benches to memorable and
loquent dancing of poetic words. Having affirmed this transformation
nd modification, I nevertheless want to uplift the *tone of ecstasy* that
ermeates King's closing climactic perorations. This ecstatic tone was
erived from his personal knowledge of and facility with the rural south-
rn black Baptist tradition within which he spoke to the people. At the
nd of a traditional black sermon the preacher is called upon to "shout,"
hat is, to preach ecstatically "in the Holy Ghost," accompanied by "walk-
ng the benches," the activity of leaping and dancing. The people ex-
ected this, and as a young man King produced the imagery, fire, tone,
nd passion of the "shout" at the end of his sermons and speeches,
ithout the added element of dancing.

If King did feel, as Taylor Branch indicates, that such an act was
primitive" and "vaudevillian," at the very least we may affirm that he
onformed to the *ecstatic expectations* of his audience. King embraced
he tone, vitality, style, and cadence of rural southern black Baptist spiri-
uality. There is nothing in the corpus of speeches and sermons by King
hat publically denounces such a spirituality as "primitive" and "vaude-
illian."

To summarize, Martin Luther King, Jr.'s spiritual roots lay in the
ervent emotional, vital, fundamentalist, and otherworldly roots of rural
outhern black Baptist spirituality. Although he was apparently offended
nd embarrassed by emotional excesses and the stomping involved in the
shouting" tradition of this rural black spirituality, he appears to have
lso practiced and affirmed the undeniable power of the ecstatic, modi-
ring it in accord with his own emphasis on rational discipline. While
ing's father and grandfather appear to have preached and ministered to
benezer Baptist Church, utilizing the full range of emotionalism that
r. King rejected, he gained from them what Peter Paris has called a
prophetic principle of criticism."[52] This legacy is apparent when we

---

[52]Paris, *Social Teaching*, 10–11. Paris states: "The fundamental principle of
e black Christian tradition is most adequately depicted in the biblical doctrine

examine their emphasis on (1) the practical and transformative nature of religion, (2) the role of the pastor as advocate and leader in social change, and (3) the mission of the minister and church to challenge the system of segregation in order for progress in social justice to be attained. In order to complete the description of King's formative influences, I shall now turn to the wisdom and sayings of the "mothers"—the Williams and King women who raised him.

The Wisdom of the "Mothers"

Although little has been written about the women in the Williams and King clans, what information there is indicates their powerful and positive impact on the young King in particular.[53] In fact, their importance must be traced to earlier times, for Daddy King writes of the profound religious influence of his mother. Before looking more closely at Daddy King's mother I want to attend to the inherent problems of looking at these women's spirituality and wisdom.

The women in both the King and the Williams families have been greatly undervalued and virtually ignored by King scholars. What we know about their lives comes only in relationship to their husbands and sons, and that in bits and pieces. Their spirituality and sayings are referred to without any proper theological framework for adequately interpreting their beliefs. This is frustrating to the King scholar who desires to plumb the depths of their contribution to Dr. King's early view of human dignity. Fortunately, Daddy King mentions some important and fundamental themes of his mother's wisdom and theological beliefs.

Delia Lindsay King

Daddy King's mother, Delia Lindsay King, helped him from an early age to develop a love for God and for the church and thus provided strong encouragement for him to enter the pastoral ministry.[54] His father

---

of the parenthood of God and the kinship of all peoples. . . . The principle of *freedom and equality of all persons under God is not an abstract idea but a normative condition of the black churches*, wherein all who participate can experience its reality."

[53]One particular exception to the rule is Downing, *Promised Land*, which utilizes the Erikson-Fowler developmental model to reveal details of the influence of "the mothers" on Dr. King's faith journey.

[54]King, *Daddy King*, 26

on the other hand, resented the young man's interest in God and church, and when he was drunk would tease and pick on him. Daddy King recounted several features of his mother's belief in God: (1) God guides human beings with wisdom, (2) God "provides" despite hardships, and (3) God strengthens our will to "do what is necessary."[55]

Mother Delia believed and taught her son that God guides human beings with wisdom. Daddy King recounted that both his mother and father had violent tempers, but that his mother did not turn to liquor the way his father did "because of her abiding faith" that enabled her to "be at peace with herself."[56] For Mother Delia, God's wisdom not only guides the lives of human beings, but also provides for physical and emotional needs despite hardships:

> God's wisdom was the guide in Mama's life, and even in her times of great suffering, which came so many times in her life, she never lost sight of the Lord. No tears could blind her to His presence, and she could not close her eyes so tight in sorrow or in rage that she did not see God's hand reaching out to her.[57]

Such a God *enabled persons with a will to survive*. Daddy King completed this description of his mother's faith, "In the worst years, she *never surrendered to self-pity or doubt* (my emphasis)."[58] The quality of *never surrendering* to the forces that could have crushed her made her quite a strong and resilient person, according to Daddy King:

> Mama said that He gave her all the will to do what was needed. And so I came to admire both of them, the Lord and Mama, for being so *able* and so *strong*. [my emphasis][59]

These themes appear closely connected to Dr. King's view of dignity. Mother Delia's belief in the God who is "able" and who guides human will seems to be echoed (albeit with greater sophistication) in King's book of sermons, *Strength to Love*. In the sermon "Our God is Able,"

[55]Ibid., 27.
[56]Ibid., 25.
[57]Ibid.
[58]Ibid.
[59]Ibid.

I was fascinated to find King speaking of God as "able to give us interior resources to confront the trials and difficulties of life."[60] King goes on in the same sermon to articulate a belief in the *enabling power* of the God-human relationship:

> Admitting the weighty problems and staggering disappointments, Christianity affirms that God is able to give us the power to meet them. He is able to give us the inner equilibrium to stand tall amid the trials and burdens of life.[61]

This belief in God's enabling power is related to King's view of dignity in that having faith in such a God transforms human personhood. In the same sermon King goes on to state that God is "able to make a way out of no way, and transform dark yesterdays into bright tomorrows." For King this transforming power is *"our hope for becoming better men"* and "our mandate for seeking to make a better world (my emphasis)."[62]

Mother Delia's contribution to Dr. King's view of God and dignity is not explicitly acknowledged by King himself. I have discovered it upon examination, or to use womanist ethicist Katie Cannon's word, I have "disentangled" her strand from others so that it can stand out on its own. The task of lifting out her unacknowledged contribution was begun by her son, Martin Luther King, Sr. We may hope that her life and the lives of the other King and Williams mothers will be researched more completely by later womanist and black feminist scholars.

Jennie Williams

King's maternal grandmother, Jennie Williams, had a more direct influence on his early life. In King's "Autobiography of Religious Development," written in seminary, King recalled this grandmother as "saintly" and recounted that he believed himself to be "her favorite grandchild."[63] King went on to state that he remembered "very vividly how she spent many evenings telling us interesting stories."[64] We do not have to specu-

---

[60]King, *Strength to Love*, 111.

[61]Ibid.

[62]Ibid., 114.

[63]Martin Luther King, Jr., "An Autobiography of Religious Development," (ca. 1950), King Papers, Mugar Library, Boston University, 2.

[64]Ibid.

ate about the content of those stories, for Downing records that a general consensus of adults interviewed believed that "over the years she
Grandmother Williams] kept her husband alive in memory and story
and her grandchildren came to know him as something of a mythic
grandfather."[65] It was Grandmother, or "Mama" to young King, Jr., who
kept Rev. Williams "alive" for the household, since he died suddenly in
1931 when Martin was only one year old. Grandmother Williams was
instrumental in transmitting through storytelling much of Grandfather
Williams' theology, his views on social justice, and his concept of the
role of a minister to young Martin.

Downing calls these stories the "reminiscing of a grandmother who
needed to share the narrative of her prominent past."[66] While there is no
record of the specific information that Grandmother Williams passed on
directly to Martin, we do know that she was the "First Lady" of Ebenezer
Baptist Church. As the pastor's wife, she had a tremendously powerful
role, albeit one that in our current historical period would appear to be
too narrowly confined within stereotypes of sex roles. As the "First
Lady" who attended virtually every church service, it is probable that
she told Martin about the narratives and songs taken from Israel's Exodus tradition that formed part of Ebenezer's spirituality.[67] The congregation of Ebenezer, as is true of many African-American churches even
today, frequently sang about "crossing over Jordan" and making it into
"Canaan Land."[68] What caused such songs to take on a slightly different
meaning from their overtly "otherworldly" lyrics was that through Rev.
Williams's ministry, the "testimony to a hope that sought fulfillment in
the here and now" was given powerful expression.[69] So in a very real
way, the biblical narratives of Moses and the children of Israel became
a living and relevant symbol of the current struggle for freedom that
Negroes in Atlanta were experiencing. It is quite possible that sitting on
his grandmother's knees, young Martin, listening to the recounting of her
important memories, received his earliest training toward becoming a
symbolic "Moses" to his people.

One piece of strong supporting evidence of Jennie William's impact
on Martin Luther King, Jr. is found in his mother's recounting, "He

[65]Downing, *Promised Land*, 69.
[66]Ibid., 63.
[67]Ibid.
[68]Ibid.
[69]Ibid., 63–64.

remembered a lot of the Bible stories and when he was a man and he started preaching, he would remember those stories from the time he was a little boy."[70] Additional evidence of the impact of those stories on King's life is the preponderance of the theme of getting to the "Promised Land" and the identification of the Negro struggle for freedom and human dignity with the Exodus narrative in his sermons, speeches, and articles. Throughout King's career as a preacher and civil rights activist from 1955 to 1968 we find an Exodus motif that directly links him to his maternal grandfather through his maternal grandmother's stories. Take, for example, this section of his "Address at Hope Street Baptist Church" on 22 March 1956:

> Freedom doesn't come on a silver platter. Whenever there is any great move toward freedom, there will inevitably be some tension. Somebody will have to have the courage to sacrifice. You don't get to the Promised Land without going through the Wilderness. Though we may not get to the Promised Land, it's coming because God is for it.[71]

Twelve years later, a more mature, experienced, and visionary King proclaimed the night before his death:

> Well, I don't know what will happen now. We've got some difficult days ahead. But it doesn't matter with me now. Because I've been to the mountain-top. . . I want to do God's will. And He's allowed me to go up to the mountain. And I've looked over. And I've seen the Promised Land. I may not get there with you. But I want you to know tonight, that we, as a people, will get to the Promised Land. And I'm happy tonight. I'm not worried about anything. I'm not fearing any man. Mine eyes have seen the glory of the coming of the Lord.[72]

[70]Mrs. Alberta King, "Dr. Martin Luther King, Jr.: Birth to Twelve Years Old by his Mother," recorded 18 January 1973, tape recording, Martin Luther King, Jr. Center Archives, Atlanta, GA.

[71]Martin Luther King, Jr., "Excerpts from Address To a Meeting of the Montgomery Improvement Association on Thursday Evening, March 22, 1956 at Hope Street Baptist Church, Montgomery, Alabama," Martin Luther King, Jr. Center Archives, Atlanta, GA.

[72]Washington, *Testament of Hope*, 286.

Martin Luther King, Jr. could utilize the Exodus motif so powerfully because of those stories of Grandmother Williams. Her contribution to his early view of human dignity is invaluable.

Alberta Williams

Alberta Williams was Martin Luther King, Jr.'s mother, and she helped to shape and refine his moral character perhaps more than any other person in his life. Having been raised as the daughter of a prominent preacher, Alberta was accustomed to the demanding role placed upon a minister's family. Daddy King wrote about the absolute strictness and adherence to traditional Baptist moral views that Rev. A. D. Williams maintained, recalling somewhat humorously how he had to convince his future father-in-law that "moving-picture shows folks were running didn't have so much sin that good Baptist people couldn't enjoy!"[73] Daddy King went on to describe what this traditional Baptist morality and lifestyle entailed:

> Church folks then didn't drink or smoke or dance with each other. I had grown up that way in the country, just as Alberta had in the city. *Social life was built completely into the framework of the church.* But it wasn't as rigid as many people say. There were picnics and boatings and drives, plenty of good food among very warm, affectionate people. [my emphasis][74]

Courtship, under such a strict moral ethos, "was strictly chaperoned" by the "old saints of the church."[75] Thus even intimate expressions were made under the "closeness and sense of family that made for very strong bonds of emotional security," according to Daddy King.[76]

Upon examination of King's early life in which his mother and grandmother shared the responsibilities of maternal nurturing, Downing recorded that their household maintained this traditional and strict Baptist moral code. The King/Williams household was one that was "rather morally strict, a good bit provincial, and rather regimented."[77] Young Martin's life was strictly regimented:

[73]King, *Daddy King*, 71.
[74]Ibid.
[75]Ibid., 78.
[76]Ibid.
[77]Downing, *Promised Land*, 45.

> He usually went to bed early. When he started school, he left by
> eight and was home by three. Then there was time for playing in
> the afternoon. After that, homework had to be done.[78]

While I am not attempting a psychological analysis, I would argue that
such moral regimentation was important in the development of King's
thought. Throughout his mature life, King demonstrated an enormous
capacity for discipline and organization in both his thought and his personal lifestyle. The almost superhuman demands placed upon King (his
speaking engagements alone numbered over one hundred each year!)
required of him a personal adherence to a lifestyle of regimentation and
regularity. Beyond these personal factors, however, lies an even more
interesting connection. The philosophy of nonviolence that King developed required of its practitioners a life of *moral discipline*. Such a life,
King would later contend, helps the practitioner of nonviolence to gain
a greater "sense of dignity and self-respect." Thus the moral code of the
King/Williams household helped to prepare Dr. King for his adult responsibilities as civil-rights activist and minister and also informed the
intellectual environment for his interest in a philosophy of social change
that demanded a disciplined moral code.

"Mama," or "Mother dear," as King called his mother, also provided
him with a profound sense of being "somebody."[79] This sense of being
"somebody" was not merely because he was the son of a prominent
preacher, but was related to the ongoing dynamic within the black community, and particularly within the tradition of the black churches, that
affirms the *fundamental equality of all human beings under God*.[80] One's
equality was affirmed *despite* the threat to one's personhood presented
by the racism of the segregated "system" of the South. It is within this
tradition that I now turn to examine the famous racist "incident" in
King's early life, an incident that caused his mother to reaffirm his sense
of being "somebody."

[78]Ibid., 45–46.

[79]See ibid., 71, "the young King was special—he was somebody important."

[80]For more information about the unique ways that the doctrine of *equality of
all human beings under God* has been historically realized within the African-
American community, see Paris, *Social Teaching*; Washington, *Frustrated Fellowship*; and Henry H. Mitchell and Nicholas Cooper Lewter, *Soul Theology:
The Heart of American Black Culture* (San Francisco: Harper & Row, 1986).

It seems that Martin, Jr. had had a young white playmate from pre-school days until he was six, when the two were separated into different elementary schools, one white and the other colored. Soon afterwards the white boy's parents informed Martin that he "could no longer play with their son."[81] The following transpired:

> "But *why*?" he sputtered. "Because we are white and you are col-ored." Later around the dinner table he confided in his parents what had happened, and for the first time they told him about the "race problem." They recounted the history of slavery in America, told how it had ended with Abraham Lincoln and the Civil War, ex-plained how whites maintained their superiority by segregating Negroes and making them feel like slaves every day of their lives. But his mother counseled him, *"You must never feel that you are less than anybody else. You must always feel that you are some-body."* [my emphasis][82]

King recalled many years later that his mother "taught me that I should feel a *sense of somebodyness*."[83] I shall demonstrate in later chap-ters how Mother Alberta's notion of *somebodyness* became a central symbol in King's mature view of human dignity. For now I want to simply lift up the notion as a significant strand of tradition and as part of Mother Alberta's contribution to King's view of dignity.

Finally, Mother Alberta helped to instill in young King a sense of the *duty and power of Christian love*. After becoming aware of the "race problem," King evidently determined within himself that he would "hate every white person."[84] Following a number of similar incidents in which Martin was called by racist epithets, even slapped by a white woman and called "a little nigger," his determination to hate whites seemed to become more entrenched. His parents, and particularly his mother, in-sisted that it was his Christian duty to "love" whites even though they were doing hateful things to him.[85]

[81]Oates, *Trumpet*, 10.

[82]Ibid.

[83]Martin Luther King, Jr., transcript of a "Face to Face" interview on 29 October 1961, Martin Luther King, Jr. Center Archives, Atlanta, GA, 3.

[84]Stephen B. Oates, "The Intellectual Odyssey of Martin Luther King" in Garrow, *King*, 3. 704.

[85]Ibid.

Apparently the emphasis on a Christian duty to love whites came more from his mother than from his father who, in Martin's eyes, did not seem really to love whites himself. In fact, Martin remembered several incidents where his father was "straightening out the white folks" in the forceful style that typified his volatile character.[86] By contrast, his mother's gentle insistence upon the Christian duty of love flowed from what Downing referred to as a "deliberative and rational approach" to life that King appeared to emulate in his later scholarly efforts such as the "Letter from Birmingham City Jail."[87] There is a "fundamental tension" that King described between his encounter with the racism of whites (and his father's reaction to it), and the parental admonition (coming primarily from his mother) to love whites.[88] In his religious "Autobiography" King wrote on the question, "How could I love a race of people who hated me and who had been responsible for breaking me up with one of my best childhood friends?"[89] I believe that Downing is essentially correct in interpreting this question as pivotal in King's development of a synthesis of the philosophy of challenge with the Christian duty to love.[90] It was a problem with which King wrestled for many years and which created the need to resolve the two contending sides in the rational reflections on love that he later created. In chapter five I shall closely examine King's developed rational reflections on love and its centrality to his understanding of human dignity. At this point it is sufficient to indicate that the emphasis that King placed on the Christian *duty* of love was influenced greatly by the formation he received from his mother.

Many scholars have written about other persons influential in the intellectual and spiritual development of Martin Luther King, Jr.[91] I in-

---

[86]Stories about being insulted at a shoe store or his father's "standing up" to a white policeman calling him "boy" are recorded in Downing, *Promised Land*, 78, and Oates, *Trumpet*, 12.

[87]Downing, *Promised Land*, 67.

[88]Ibid., 85.

[89]King, "Autobiography," 12–13.

[90]Downing, *Promised Land*, 86.

[91]See David J. Garrow, "The Intellectual Development of Martin Luther King, Jr.: Influences and Commentaries," in idem, *King*, 2. 437–51. Garrow is particularly concerned with uplifting the important role of Morehouse professors George Kelsey, Lucius Tobin, and Samuel W. Williams. See also Stephen B. Oates, "Intellectual Odyssey of Martin Luther King, Jr.," in Garrow, *King*, 3. 302–4; Smith and Zepp, *Search for the Beloved Community*, is an excellent early work noted for its exceptionally detailed archival research; Ansbro, *King*, is a very

end this chapter's specific elaboration of the influence of Dr. King's "fathers" and "mothers" and his deep roots in the traditions of the rural southern black church to be a necessary addendum to these previous works on King's formative influences.

Summary

In this chapter I have examined some of the strands of the family tradition, the rural, black, southern Baptist spirituality, and the wisdom of the King and Williams women, all of which influenced Martin Luther King, Jr.'s view of dignity. While many essays and articles have turned our attention to the black community and "black church" as foundational to King's mature ideas,[92] attention has not been given to the details of King's *particular* black church and black community. In King we find that the influence of family and the influence of church are combined, perhaps even fused since service in the church dominated the lives of both the women and the men in his family. By carefully examining the various sayings, beliefs, and traditions to which his family adhered, I give substantive content to the claim that Martin Luther King, Jr. was a "product of the black church."[93]

What is the substantive content of the formative influences of King's family and church insofar as they are related to his understanding of dignity? First, I attributed to Daddy King several distinctive contributions: (1) Daddy King as *personal exemplar* both of the importance of bettering oneself in terms of education and of the value of stubborn determination to achieve one's goals despite the adverse claims of racism or of any person; (2) his *sermonic ethic* emphasizing the dignity of hard work; (3) his *sermonic theology* stressing human agency in the work of "racial uplift"; (4) his sharp critique of the "system" of segregation and the moral necessity of struggling against it and not against the individual persons representing it; and (5) his repeated stress that not hating the

---

thorough philosophical and theological text that attempts to ground King's thought in certain prominent figures of Boston Personalism such as the "evangelical liberal" thought of George Davis, L. Harold DeWolf, and Edgar Brightman, as well as the Social Gospel concepts of Walter Rauschenbusch; see also Walter G. Muelder, "Philosophical and Theological Influences," 691–701.

[92]See Cone, "Black Theology—Black Church" and idem, "Theology" for good examples of previous scholarly endeavors to outline the influence of the black church on King.

[93]Cone, "Black Theology—Black Church," 1. 204.

"white man" was fundamental to the dignity and Christian lifestyle of Negroes. Martin Luther King, Jr. turned this negative doctrine of "no hating" inside out by stressing the positive power of love as essential to dignity.

Through Daddy King's autobiography we gain access to King, Jr.'s maternal grandfather, the Rev. A. D. Williams. Daddy King refers to his father-in-law as his mentor and as the individual who taught him many things about the racial "struggle" for freedom. In concert with his father-in-law, Daddy King became known as a protester, organizing marches and demonstrations as Rev. Williams had done a generation before. Grandfather Williams's major contribution to the development of Martin Luther King, Sr. was his *concept of social change*, which stated that "progress never comes without challenge." Williams's view was both historical and pragmatic, understanding the intricacies of power relationships and the limited "place" of the Negro in effecting social change.

Other components of Rev. Williams's philosophy of social change included: (1) a *high view of the minister's responsibility* as leader, organizer, and motivating force for protest; (2) a view of the minister a *advocate for justice* who is *called* by the community's needs to stand up for justice, despite all the personal dangers such advocacy could initiate and (3) the *theme of mission* as connected with ministry for social change. It is important that Rev. Williams's philosophy of social change be duly appreciated, for through its application in Daddy King's ministry, Martin Luther King, Jr. was given a profoundly practical sense of the actual possibilities for social change in the segregated South. Furthermore, such a philosophy laid the mental groundwork for King, Jr.'s later adoption and appropriation of Hegel's view of history as conflictive struggle and Niebuhr's realist position on the power of social collectivities. King's appropriation of Hegel and Niebuhr, therefore, was not accidental, but part of his ongoing development of an adequate articulation of social change. King saw his work in continuity with his grandfather's and father's work in previous generations.

Dr. King's spirituality was deeply rooted in an African-American Christian tradition that was *rural*, *southern*, and *Baptist*. From the thundering style of preaching that was passed down from King's slave exhorter great-grandfather, to what some commentators have referred to as the "primitive, vaudevillian" elements of "walking the benches" and "stomping," King's nascent spirituality was formed within a vital and emotional Christian spirituality. By using Daddy King's memories I have recounted the rural background of "C. C. Riders," strong singing, shout ng, and the overflowing emotion that typified rural Baptist worship practices. Both Daddy King and his son criticized the illiterate and crude elements of being "country" (seen as a type of culture), while both retained certain key elements of "country" worship. For Daddy King these elements were the *earthy*, pragmatic style of preaching and delivery. His son maintained the fervently emotional *tone* and the *vital élan* of rural spirituality. While some commentators have emphasized King's discontinuity with and critique of traditional black forms of worship such as stomping and shouting, I have given evidence of King's necessary continuity with that tradition. For example, King maintained the climactic sense of the "shout" at the end of his sermons and speeches, but transformed the dancing and stomping element into memorable poetic peroration. From this, I have inferred that King held within himself a confidence in the vitalizing power of such spirituality, utilizing its unifying and elevating force as part of the process of gaining a greater sense of dignity.

By turning to the "mothers" and their moral wisdom, I have discovered several fascinating details worth reviewing. First, in Delia Lindsay King, Daddy King's mother, we find the possible source of several central theological and ethical beliefs that were carried though the family to Martin. These theological and moral sayings are (1) God guides human lives with sufficient wisdom; (2) God has the power to provide for our needs, despite hardships; and (3) such a God enables persons to have the will to survive, and even to affirm the motto of "never surrender." The influence of these thoughts is amply demonstrated in Martin Luther King, Jr.'s sermon "God is Able," although King did not explicitly acknowledge it.

Second, through the storytelling gifts of King's maternal grandmother, Jennie Williams, the narratives and ideals of Grandfather Williams were kept alive in the King household. Grandmother Williams is remembered by King himself as (1) being "saintly"; (2) being a memorable storyteller who passed on the beliefs of her deceased husband to their grandchildren; and (3) passing on to young Martin *important Bible stories and narratives*, of which the most significant is the *Exodus motif* of liberation and freedom. This Exodus motif was to have a profound impact on King's self-understanding and interpretation of his role in civil rights conflicts.

Finally, I examined the impact of King's mother, Alberta Williams. From his mother King received (1) a *strict moral code* that gave definite shape to his character and lifestyle from an early age and helped direct

his mind to embrace at a later point the *disciplined approach of nonviolence*; (2) an introduction to the notion of "*somebodyness*" as a distinc-
tively Negro way of interpreting the Christian doctrine of the *imago dei*
within the social context of the racist South; and (3) an emphasis on the
Christian's moral duty to love even enemies, which generated an enormous conflict within his mind about the practical application of the
Christian understanding of "love." This conflict motivated King to look
deeply into various ideals and doctrines of love throughout his college
seminary, and graduate school days, culminating in a synthesis of several authors' views into his own.[94] All three components of his mother's
moral and theological wisdom find significant development in King's
mature thought.

---

[94]I shall look specifically at King's view of love and its relationship to dignity
in chapter five. King synthesizes the thought of many theologians, chief among
whom are Anders Nygren, Reinhold Niebuhr, Paul Tillich, and the traditions of
his family and the black church that shaped his childhood.

2

KING'S EARLY CONCEPT
OF DIGNITY, 1955–1962

The concept of dignity is a recurrent theme in all of King's writings, speeches, and sermons. Repeated so often, dignity appears as one of the founding presuppositions of the civil rights struggle. In King's thought, dignity is a complex and multivalent term. It is necessary to inquire into how King used the word "dignity" and how his usage changed.

The first public instance of King's use of the term dignity was in the famous "Holt Street Baptist Address" that officially initiated the Montgomery bus boycott. The term appears twice in his closing statement:

> If you will protest courageously, and yet with dignity and Christian love, when the history books are written in future generations, the historians will have to pause and say, "There lived a great people— a black people—who injected new meaning and dignity into the veins of civilization." This is our challenge and our overwhelming responsibility.[1]

[1]King, *Stride Toward Freedom*, 63.

The preceding quotation yields three levels of meaning: (1) dignity for King is a necessary and inherent human condition or state, (2) dignity is an exalted or elevated state of humanity achieved through courageous protest, and (3) the protest for dignity will engender a higher sense of dignity for "civilization."

The first two meanings are inseparable, for one cannot protest courageously and with Christian love unless one believes that what one is struggling to achieve is a necessary state of humanity. The second presupposes the first, and yet the second also seems to go beyond the first in significance. The exalted or elevated state of humanity that comes about through protest calls for a greater or deeper humanity than the first.

At this point it is unclear exactly how this elevated and exalted humanity would become tangible. While not exactly explaining this transformation, the phrase "inject new meaning and dignity into the veins of civilization" provides an impressive rhetorical flourish that is one of the hallmarks of King's preaching style.

In the preceding phrase, is dignity a pregnant rhetorical symbol or an early sign of what King would develop within his understanding of dignity? It is necessary to remember the context of the statement—a church rally—in which King was attempting to "arouse the group to action by insisting that their self-respect was at stake and that if they accepted such injustices [as the verbal abuse of bus drivers and the arrest of Rosa Parks for not giving her seat to a white passenger] without protesting, they would betray their own sense of dignity and the eternal edicts of God Himself."[2] King went on to say that he would balance this challenge to the people's sense of self-respect with "a strong affirmation of the Christian doctrine of love."[3]

At this point we may ask what method King chose to convince the people that they were morally compelled to protest for their dignity. Is there a systematic methodology present, or is King, as some critics have claimed, merely a persuasive rhetor?[4]

---

[2]Ibid., 60.

[3]Ibid.

[4]The contention that King was a rhetor is implied in Malinda Snow's article "Martin Luther King's 'Letter from Birmingham Jail' as Pauline Epistle" in Garrow, *King*, 3. 861.

Method of Presentation

The "Holt Street Address" reveals King's early method for speaking of dignity. King's method had two fundamental moves in the social situation of oppression: first, appealing to the fundamental rights of American citizenship and second, appealing to the fundamental theological human right for dignity.

In the early paragraphs of the "Holt Street Address" King upheld the social situation of oppression as a contradiction to the basic rights of American citizens.

> We are here in a general sense, because first and foremost—we are American citizens—and we are determined to apply our citizenship—to the fullness of its means. But we are here in a specific sense—because of the bus situation in Montgomery. The situation is not at all new. The problem has existed over endless years.[5]

It is important to note that King did not elaborate upon what it means to be an "American citizen," for he presupposed that such a status implies freedom to exercise one's fundamental rights. Such a presupposition, however, is unspoken. One might ask whether the listeners also shared this view.

King moved on throughout the address to elaborate and support the fundamental contradiction he expressed in the opening paragraphs. First he spoke specifically of the arrest of Rosa Parks and of her upstanding character:

> Just the other day—just last Thursday to be exact—one of the finest citizens in Montgomery—not one of the finest Negro citizens—but one of the finest citizens in Montgomery—was taken from a bus and carried to jail and arrested—because she refused to give up—to give her seat to a white person.[6]

The contrast between Rosa Parks as an outstanding citizen of Montgomery versus the segregation ordinances of Montgomery that caused Rosa Parks's arrest was the next theme upon which King elaborated. The

[5]Quoted in Branch, *Parting the Waters*, 139.
[6]Ibid.

importance of this elaboration for us lies in the fact that King was not interested merely in making groundless assertions based on an emotional appeal, but in constructing a rational argument that would convince any reasonable listener of the moral claim of the Negroes in Montgomery to protest. In this first public speech, the power of the moral claim lay in its ability to reveal the disturbing contradictions between the ideal "American" rights of Rosa Parks (and Montgomery's Negroes) and the concrete segregation ordinances operative in the buses. In the climax of this section of the address, King returned to Parks's high moral character:

> And since it had to happen, I'm happy it happened to a person like Mrs. Parks, for nobody can doubt the boundless outreach of her integrity. Nobody can doubt the height of her character, nobody can doubt the depth of her Christian commitment. And just because she refused to get up, she was arrested.[7]

At this point King turned to appeal to the actual *degrading experience* of being racially humiliated, an experience that the Negroes present felt that they too experienced:

> There comes a time, my friends, when people get tired of being trampled over by the iron feet of oppression. There comes a time, my friends, when people get tired of being thrown across the abyss of humiliation, when they experience the bleakness of nagging despair. There comes a time when people get tired of being pushed out of the glittering sunlight of life's July, and left standing amidst the piercing chill of an Alpine November. We are here—we are here because we are tired.[8]

From this high point, so climactic in its impact, King had to allow the enthusiastic response to die down, and so he again reinforced the moral claim to protest.

> We had no alternative but to protest. For many years we have shown amazing patience. We have sometimes given our white broth-

[7]Ibid., 140.
[8]Ibid.

ers the feeling that we like the way we were being treated. But we are here tonight to be saved from that patience that makes us patient with anything less than freedom and justice.[9]

Once again King turned to the fundamental citizenship rights of the American to bolster the claim of the people to protest. Let us note, however, that the initial assertion in the following quotation is based on the claim of the people to be "Christian":

Now let us say that we are not here advocating violence. I want it to be known throughout Montgomery and throughout this nation that we are Christian people. The only weapon we have in our hands this evening is the weapon of protest. If we were incarcerated behind the iron curtains of a communistic nation—we couldn't do this. But the great glory of American democracy is the right to protest for right. . . . There will be no crosses burned in Montgomery. There will be no white persons pulled out of their homes and taken out on some distant road and murdered. There will be nobody among us who will stand up and defy the Constitution.[10]

Having established the right to protest on the basis of the contradiction between the basic rights of all Americans versus the social experience of oppression that Negroes underwent, particularly on the buses, King then moved to the fundamental theological basis bolstering the people's claims:

If we are wrong—the Supreme Court is wrong. If we are wrong—God Almighty is wrong. If we are wrong—Jesus of Nazareth was merely a utopian dreamer and never came down to earth! If we are wrong—justice is a lie.[11]

Then, with his attention on the topic of justice, King, the philosopher of religion, explained in theological language the interrelationship of love and justice in terms resonant with Paul Tillich's and Reinhold Niebuhr's understanding of the terms:

[9]King, *Stride Toward Freedom*, 62.
[10]Branch, *Parting the Waters*, 140.
[11]Ibid., 141.

We will be guided by the highest principles of law and order. . . .
Our method will be that of persuasion, not coercion. Our actions
must be guided by the deepest principles of our Christian faith.
Love must be our regulating ideal. Once again we must hear the
words of Jesus echoing across the centuries; "Love your enemies,
and pray for them that despitefully use you." . . . And I want to tell
you this evening it is not enough for us to talk about love. Love is
one of the pinnacle parts of the Christian faith. There is another
side called justice. And justice is really love in calculation. Justice
is love correcting that which would work against love. Standing
beside love is always justice.[12]

In his closing statement, King referred both to the protest as one conducted "with dignity and Christian love" and to the "great people—a
black people—who injected new meaning and dignity into the veins of
civilization."[13] It is important to note here that the term "a black people"
suggests that for King *dignity arises from a community*. Dignity is possessed by a people, not just by individuals. Later I shall demonstrate the
ways that this communitarian notion of dignity had ties both to the black
community and to personalism.

These statements reveal the underlying thrust of King's entire address,
namely, that the people were protesting for *greater dignity*. They believed this greater dignity to be both their Constitutional right as American citizens and a concept embedded in their fundamental Christian
beliefs. Furthermore, this dignity was something worth fighting for,
because it would ennoble them and grant them a fuller sense of self-
respect than would passive acceptance of the humiliation of segregated
practices.

The next step is to see how King developed and transformed the
loosely constructed contrasting method of presentation of the "Holt Street
Address" and of the various sermons, speeches, and rallies of the Montgomery bus boycott into a more formalized typology of history.

Montgomery Sermons

This section examines the way in which King's notion of dignity
began to take clearer shape and find richer content. It is particularly
interesting to note that King's view of dignity was strengthened by the

[12]Ibid.
[13]King, *Stride Toward Freedom*, 63.

concrete struggle and suffering endured by the boycotting Negroes of that city. In light of such suffering many of King's sermons emphasized the importance of perseverance, stressing that the power to endure until the end of the boycott was a strong measure of the new dignity that the people had gained for themselves.

One sermon that emphasized this aspect of dignity was "The Most Durable Power," first preached "just seven days before the United States Supreme Court ruled against Alabama's bus segregation laws."[14] Here the struggle to maintain nonviolent discipline again figures as an important aspect of this dignity:

> Always be sure that you struggle with Christian methods and Christian weapons. Never succumb to the temptation of becoming bitter. As you press on for justice, be sure to move with dignity and discipline, using only the weapon of love. Let no man pull you so low as to hate him.[15]

Dignity, as described above, is a quality that is *attained through the discipline of nonviolent struggle.* King viewed dignity as something worth struggling for by means of "Christian methods and Christian weapons"— a phrase that he later clarified to mean using "only the weapon of love."[16] He went on to describe this dignified struggle as a "struggle for justice":

> As you struggle for justice, let your oppressor know that you are not attempting to defeat or humiliate him, or even pay him back for injustices that he has heaped upon you. Let him know that you are merely seeking justice for him as well as yourself. Let him know that the festering sore of segregation debilitates the white man as well as the Negro. With this attitude you will be able to keep your struggle on high Christian standards.[17]

King saw this struggle as one that had to have the appropriate "attitude," which he labeled repeatedly as "high Christian standards." The application of these "high Christian standards" to the boycott enabled

---

[14]Washington, *Testament of Hope*, 10.
[15]Ibid.
[16]Ibid.
[17]Ibid.

the Negroes of Montgomery, under King's leadership, to attain a new, higher, and more ennobled view of themselves. Such a view is a development of the "calling" or "high destiny motif" of the Holt Street Address, indicated in the phrase "there lived a great people—a black people—who injected new meaning and a new sense of dignity into the veins of civilization." King encouraged the marching Negroes to go on marching, since through their marching they were gaining something far greater than a little more respect on the buses. They were gaining a deeper sense of dignity. He neither spelled out the sense of dignity that Negroes had attained in the past nor contrasted the old with the new. He simply indicated that through protest there would be a "new" and deeper sense of dignity.

It is important to note as well that the "high destiny motif" was intended to transform and deepen the dignity of civilization. The struggle was to enliven and deepen their oppressors' sense of dignity as well, not by seeking to humiliate or defeat the white citizens of Montgomery, but rather by convincing them of the justice of the Negro cause.

Expanding Reflections

The new sense of dignity attained through the boycott enabled King to reflect upon the struggle as one that broke self-imposed stereotypes:

> We have learned many things as a result of our struggle together. Our nonviolent protest has demonstrated to the Negro, North and South, that many stereotypes he has held about himself and other Negroes are not valid. Montgomery has broken the spell and is ushering in concrete manifestations of the thinking and action of the New Negro.[18]

King went on in this same address to make a list of things that added to the "New Negro." This list is important as a first reflection on the aspects of self-growth and self-respect that he would later label as part of the New Negro's sense of dignity:

[18]Martin Luther King, Jr., "Annual Address of Dr. Martin Luther King, Jr. for the First Annual Institute on Non-Violence and Social Change Under the Auspices of the Montgomery Improvement Association," 3 December 1956 at Holt Street Baptist Church, folder 1 of 7, box 127, no. 1.2, King Papers, Mugar Library, Boston University.

Some of the basic things we have learned are as follows: (1) We have discovered that we can stick together for a common cause; (2) Our leaders do not have to sell out; (3) Threats and violence do not necessarily intimidate those who are sufficiently aroused and non-violent; (4) Our church is becoming militant, stressing a social as well as a gospel of personal salvation; (5) *We have gained a new sense of dignity and destiny*; (6) We have discovered a new and powerful weapon—nonviolent resistance. [my emphasis][19]

In an article, "Our Struggle," published by the Montgomery Improvement Association, King took up the theme of *dignity as something that must be asserted*. The pamphlet carefully presented this thesis after following the general pattern established in the "Holt Street Address." First King presented the social problem to be overcome—segregation as the cause for a loss of self-respect in Negroes:

The segregation of Negroes, with its inevitable discrimination, has thrived on elements of inferiority present in the masses of both white and Negro people. Through forced separation from our African culture, through slavery, poverty, and deprivation, many black men lost self-respect.[20]

King moved on to present segregation as a fundamental contradiction to the highest moral claims of white Americans:

In their relations with Negroes, white people discovered that they had rejected the very center of their own ethical professions. They could not face the triumph of their lesser instincts and simultaneously have peace within. And so, to gain it, they rationalized—insisting that the unfortunate Negro, being less than human, deserved and even enjoyed second class status.[21]

Dr. King described the rationalization argument of white dominance in the paragraphs that followed. He took care to note how notions of su-

---

[19]Ibid.

[20]Martin Luther King, Jr., "Our Struggle," folder 1 of 7, box 127, no. 2, King Papers, Mugar Library, Boston University.

[21]Ibid., 1.

periority and being a "master race" enabled southern whites to remain comfortable with a system that degraded fellow human beings.

He then stated that after a while "many Negroes lost faith in themselves and came to believe that perhaps they really were what they had been told they were—something less than men."[22] The result was an "uneasy peace in which the Negro was forced patiently to accept injustice, insult, injury and exploitation."[23]

At this point in "Our Struggle," King described a turn in the self-image of Negroes that enabled a new sense of dignity:

> Gradually the Negro masses in the South began to reevaluate themselves—a process that was to change the nature of the Negro community and doom the social patterns of the South.[24]

It is necessary to pay attention to this *process of reevaluation*, since King seemed to see it as an important first step toward a new sense of dignity. King described the underlying motive for this process of reevaluation in this way: "We discovered that we had never really smothered our self-respect and that we could not be at one with ourselves without asserting it."[25]

Here again is the claim that *dignity is the assertion of self-respect*. King then drew out the implications of this assertion of self-respect:

> From this point on, the South's terrible peace was rapidly undermined by the Negro's new and courageous thinking and his ever-increasing readiness to organize and act. Conflict and violence were coming to the surface as the white South desperately clung to its old patterns. *The extreme tension in race relations in the South today is explained in part by the revolutionary change in the Negro's evaluation of himself and of his destiny and by his determination to struggle for justice. We Negroes have replaced self-pity with self-respect and self-depreciation with dignity.* [my emphasis][26]

[22]Ibid.
[23]Ibid.
[24]Ibid.
[25]Ibid.
[26]Ibid.

The preceding paragraph is most important in understanding how King's reflections on dignity expanded as he matured in his own leadership position in the civil rights movement. We see that now he has moved from a loosely inspired rhetorical masterpiece, setting contradictions beside each other in the "Holt Street Address," to a more reasoned and systematic exposition. It is possible to see the difference as simply a matter of rhetorical style, the one—"Holt Street Address"—a sermon, the other—"Our Struggle"—an article. Yet further studies of his sermons and speeches will bear out the position that King became increasingly systematic and capable of constructing a sustained argument on segregation as the social setting of oppression, the process of reevaluation that Negroes took on themselves, the discovery of a new sense of self-respect and dignity in the midst of nonviolent struggle, and the growing sense of a special destiny that involved the struggle for dignity on a global scale.

Another important aspect of "Our Struggle" is that King compiled a list of achievements gained by the protest. This particular list expands each of the points mentioned previously in his "First Annual Address for the Institute on Nonviolence and Social Change," except that the point regarding a "new sense of dignity and destiny" was replaced by the heading "We Believe in Ourselves."[27] In the paragraph that followed, King described this new sense of dignity without naming it:

> In Montgomery we walk in a new way. We hold our heads in a new way. Even the Negro reporters who have converged on Montgomery have a new attitude. One tired reporter, asked at a luncheon in Birmingham to say a few words about Montgomery, stood up, thought for a moment, and uttered one sentence: "Montgomery has made me proud to be a Negro."[28]

King bolstered the introductory remarks of "Our Struggle" with another reminder that the entire struggle at Montgomery arose from the struggle for dignity by one woman:

> When Mrs. Rosa Parks, the quiet seamstress whose arrest precipitated the non-violent protest in Montgomery, was asked why she

[27]Ibid., 2.
[28]Ibid.

had refused to move to the rear of a bus, she said: "It was a matter of dignity; I could not have faced myself and my people if I had moved."[29]

"Our Struggle" developed the idea of the moral primacy of nonviolence. It ended with a call for an "interracial society based on freedom for all."[30] King also expressed the thought that Negroes did not "wish to triumph over the white community," for such a triumph "would only result in transferring those now on the bottom to the top."[31] Rather, King upheld the method of nonviolence as the way by which to usher into existence the "interracial society based on freedom for all."

The Washington Prayer Pilgrimage, 1957

Dr. King reached a certain level of national prominence and notoriety when he was selected to be the closing speaker for the Prayer Pilgrimage For Freedom at the Lincoln Memorial in Washington, D.C., on 17 May 1957. Before a crowd of some thirty thousand people, King made an eloquent plea for the right to vote for Negro citizens as a "sacred right" hitherto tragically denied by the system of enforced segregation.[32] The importance of this plea for my argument is that it occurred near the beginning of this "Address" and demonstrates that King was developing his method of presentation. The presentation of the social situation of oppression—in this case, the denial of the right to vote—is followed here by the demand to "give us the ballot" as the *only morally correct solution* to the social injustice he had just previously described.[33] Unlike the "Holt Street Address," in this speech King did not spend a great deal of time speaking of the apparent moral, legal, and ideological contradictions between denying the right to vote to Negroes and white America's highest moral and democratic ideals. Instead, he pressed for the right to vote as part of the "sacred right" and as one of the "highest mandates

---

[29]Ibid.

[30]Ibid., 4.

[31]Ibid.

[32]Martin Luther King, Jr., "Address at the Prayer Pilgrimage For Freedom at the Lincoln Memorial, Washington, D.C., May 17, 1957, 12:00 Noon," folder 1 of 7, box 127, no. 2, King Papers, Mugar Library, Boston University, 1.

[33]Ibid.

of our democratic tradition."[34] His next statement directly tied the right to vote as a citizen to the dignity of being an autonomous person:

> So long as I do not firmly and irrevocably possess the right to vote I do not possess myself. I cannot make up my mind—it is made up for me. I cannot live as a Democratic citizen, observing the laws I helped to enact—I can only submit to others. So our most urgent request to the President of the United States and every member of the Congress is to give us the right to vote.[35]

This argument is followed by a peroration on the phrase, "give us the ballot," which showed how the granting of the right to vote would enable Negroes to gain dignity. Specifically, dignity in this instance means the *right to participate and be self-governing:*

> Give us the ballot and we will no longer have to worry the Federal Government about our basic rights. Give us the ballot and we will no longer plead with the Federal Government for passage of an anti-lynching law; we will by the power of our vote write the law on the statute books of the southern states, and bring an end to the dastardly acts of the hooded perpetrators of violence. Give us the ballot and we will transform the salient misdeeds of bloodthirsty mobs into the abiding good deeds of orderly citizens.[36]

King then moved on to describe the "urgent need for dedicated and courageous leadership"[37] in the presidency, the Congress,[38] in "white northern liberals,"[39] "moderates of the white south,"[40] and the "Negro community" itself.[41]

After encouraging the Negro leaders to "meet hate with love" and elaborating on the various types of "love," King linked the movement

[34]Ibid.
[35]Ibid.
[36]Ibid.
[37]Ibid.
[38]Ibid., 2.
[39]Ibid.
[40]Ibid., 2–3.
[41]Ibid., 3.

for Negro rights with the emerging international "great drama of freedom and independence."[42] King believed that the global ferment for freedom was "in line with the unfolding work of Providence," although he warned the listeners to "accept them [the global tides toward independence] in the right spirit."[43] Instead of turning the tables on whites by embracing a "philosophy of black supremacy,"[44] King insisted that the work of Providence is a work to free all people:

> God is not interested in merely freeing black men and brown men and yellow men; God is interested in freeing the whole human race. We must work with determination to create a society in which all men will live together as brothers and *respect the dignity and worth of human personality.*[45]

This "dignity and worth of personality" is for King the *moral telos of society.*[46] I shall discuss below how the theological anthropology of Boston Personalism is implied in the preceding statement. For the sake of the current discussion on King's developing view of dignity, it is important to note that here "dignity" is directly linked to the inherent worth of human personality.

King concluded the "Address" with the encouragement to continue the struggle for dignity "with dignity":

> The universe is on our side in the struggle. Stand up for justice. Sometimes it gets hard; it is always difficult to get out of Egypt, the Red Sea always stands before you with discouraging dimensions. Even after you have crossed the Red Sea, you have to move through a wilderness with prodigious hilltops of evil, and gigantic mountains of opposition. But I say to you this afternoon: Keep moving. Let nothing slow you up. Move on *with dignity, love, and respectability.*[47]

[42]Ibid., 3–4.
[43]Ibid., 3.
[44]Ibid.
[45]Ibid., 4.
[46]This phrase is my way of interpreting King to say "the highest moral end of society."
[47]King, "Address at the Prayer Pilgrimage," 5.

Again we are faced with the word "dignity" not only as something *in-herent* in the human being as a person, but as a quality of an *ennobled humanity*, and therefore tied to the other terms—"love" and "respectabil-ity." It might even be possible to infer from the final sentence that dignity is something that one struggles to keep as one fights to gain the fundamental right to vote as a dignified citizen. In this sense, I might clarify King's last sentence by saying, "Move on with dignity [for dignity], love, and respectability."

King's concluding paragraph articulated a "revised edition" of the final remarks of the "Holt Street Address":

> Keep moving amid every obstacle; keep moving amid every mount-ing of opposition. If you will do this *with dignity*—when the his-tory books are written in future years the historians will have to look back and say, there lived a great people, a people with "fleecy locks and black complexion" who *injected a new dimension of love into the veins of civilization, a people who stood up with dignity and honor and saved Western civilization in her darkest hour.* When that happens, "the morning stars will sing together, and the sons of God will shout for joy." [my emphasis][48]

In this version we find King calling for civilization's veins to be injected with a "new dimension of love" by a people who had "stood up with dignity and honor." This call contrasts with the phrase found in the "Holt Street Address" that states that "new meaning and dignity" will be injected into Western civilization. The distinction is not one to overlook. At the beginning of the struggle King could *hope* that new meaning and dignity would be attained by the bus boycott. Now, after the boycott had been successful and voter rights campaigns were gaining momentum, King could speak from the vantage point of experience, knowing that the "great people" of whom he spoke had indeed attained a deeper measure of self-respect and dignity, and in so doing, had injected a new under-standing of love into the currents of Western civilization. King was not merely a skilled rhetorician, but was also indicating a more experienced view of how dignity is attained.

Another important phrase embedded in the last two paragraphs of the Address" at the Prayer Pilgrimage provides further insights into King's

[48]Ibid.

maturing view of the process of attaining dignity. The phrase is a short
one: "Stand up." In the second to last paragraph it appears in the short
sentence, "Stand up for justice." In the last paragraph it occurs in the
phrase, "a people who stood up with dignity and honor."[49] The idea of
"standing up" to something or somebody has deep roots in the African-
American community. Stephen Oates writes of how Daddy King demonstrated "standing up," or as Daddy King also described it, "straightening
out the white folks."[50] Young Martin heard this expression frequently
enough for it to have influenced his memory of his childhood.

> Yes, Daddy was always "straightening out the white folks." He
> would not let white agents make collections at his house. He would
> not ride the city buses and suffer the humiliation of having to sit
> in a colored section. He would not let whites call him "boy." One
> day when M. L. was riding with his Daddy in the family car, a
> white patrolman pulled him over and snapped, "Boy, show me your
> license." Daddy shot back, "Do you see this child here?" He pointed
> at M. L. "That's a boy there. I'm a man. I'm Reverend King."[51]

In another 1957 speech, "Facing the Challenge of a New Age," King
fleshed out his notion of "standing up" as *courageous nonviolent resistance*:

> Finally, if we are to speed up the coming of the new age we must
> have the moral courage to stand up and protest against injustice
> wherever we find it. Wherever we find segregation we must have
> the fortitude to passively resist it.[52]

It is significant for my argument that King seemed consciously to
fuse "standing up" with the process of gaining greater dignity. That is,
King appears to have joined together Gandhian notions of nonviolence,[53]
various theological understandings of the term "love," and his own

[49]Ibid., 4, 5.
[50]Oates, *Trumpet*, 12.
[51]Ibid.
[52]Washington, *Testament of Hope*, 143.
[53]In chapter four below, see the discussion of King's appropriation of satyagraha
as Mohandas Gandhi articulated it.

African-American community's understanding of "standing up" into the all-encompassing process of striving to assert one's dignity. Although it seems ironic, King incorporated into the term "dignity" another term that suggests confrontation and even what white Southerners would have perceived as a threat of violence. The phrase "standing up" directs attention toward the *confrontational element* that necessarily existed for King and his followers during the civil rights movement. In a later chapter I shall speak about "standing up" in terms of King's view of agape; for now, it is enough to show how "standing up" is part of his overall view of dignity.

From a more critical standpoint, we may wish that King had been more precise in the various ways that he appeared to use the term "dignity." Was dignity for King something inherent and therefore part of the irreducible essence of the human being? Yes, but that is not all. Was dignity for King something that was to be asserted in a nonviolent confrontation with those who would deny one's dignity? Yes, but again dignity is not limited to this meaning. Was dignity for King something that needed to be realized more fully as one "stood up" for justice and against injustice? Yes, but once again, to fasten on to one interpretation is to miss others. For King dignity was a multivalent word. It could be used as (1) a *quality* of humanity, (2) a *way* of being human as one struggled to gain more citizenship rights, (3) a quality of *intentional determination for justice*, and (4) something *demonstrated* as one "stood up" to injustice.

The Typology of History and Dignity

In May 1957 King also published an article in the *Interracial Review* called "A View of the Dawn." In this article King took some early steps toward creating a historical typology of race relations that related directly to his maturing systematic idea of dignity.

The article began optimistically, embracing the current moment in history as standing "on the threshold of the most constructive period of our nation's history."[54] King then outlined what he interpreted as "the long sweep of race relations in America."[55] He discerned an "evolution-

---

[54]Martin Luther King, Jr., "A View of the Dawn," *Interracial Review: A Journal for Christian Democracy*, May 1957, folder 1 of 7, box 127, no. 2, King Papers, Mugar Library, Boston University, 82.

[55]Ibid.

ary growth over the years" in which three periods could be distinguished.[56] Each period, according to King, represented "growth over the preceding period,"[57] and Supreme Court decisions gave "legal and constitutional validity to the dominant thought pattern of that particular period."[58]

The first period, according to King's typology, extended from 1619 to 1863:

> This was the period of slavery. During this period the Negro was a *thing to be used, not a person* to be respected. He was merely a *depersonalized cog* in a vast plantation machine. [my emphasis][59]

It is important to note that King did not speak of this period in terms of atrocities, but in relation to the lack of dignity imparted to the slave. For King, the status of slave was the status of a "thing," not a dignified person. He did not speak of attempts within the slave community to maintain a measure of dignity, creativity, or rebellion. Instead, he created a typology, generalizing about the dehumanized, or as he put it, "depersonalized" context of race relations. He went on to link the Supreme Court's Dred Scott decision with this period:

> In 1857, toward the end of this period, there finally came a decision from the Supreme Court to give legal and constitutional validity to the whole system of slavery. This decision, known as the Dred Scott decision, stated in substance that *the Negro is not a citizen of this nation; he is merely property subject to the dictates of his owner.* [my emphasis][60]

In the preceding paragraph King referred once again to the connection between being a dignified person and being a "citizen." A citizen has rights, according to King, and therefore dignity and respect. A slave, on the other hand, was a "depersonalized cog," a "thing," and "merely property" in King's typology of the first period. He proceeded quickly to the next period.

[56]Ibid.
[57]Ibid., 82–83.
[58]Ibid., 83.
[59]Ibid.
[60]Ibid., 82.

King identified the second period of race relations as the time be-
ween 1863 and 1954. This was the "period of segregation."[61] It was
given "legal and constitutional validity" through the famous *Plessy v.
Ferguson* decision of the Supreme Court in 1896.[62] For King, this decision "established the doctrine of separate but equal as the law of the
and."[63] He went on to describe the second period as follows:

> Now it is true that this second stage of race relations was some-
> thing of an improvement over the first stage of race relations, be-
> cause it at least freed the Negro from the bondage of physical
> slavery. But it did not represent race relations at their best, because
> segregation is at bottom nothing but slavery covered up with cer-
> tain niceties of complexity. The fact is that in the area of race
> relations separate is always unequal, quantitatively and qualita-
> tively.[64]

King moved on to speak of the deterioration of the Negro's self-image
under the impact of the "separate but equal" doctrine: "Living under
these conditions many Negroes lost faith in themselves. Many came to
feel that perhaps they were less than human."[65]

In his next sentence, King turned away from this stunning and sober-
ing insight. Having identified the acceptance of an inferior human status
by Negroes, King insisted that there was an upward turn caused by the
Great Migration:

> But as this period gradually unfolded something happened to the
> Negro. . . . His rural plantation background was gradually being
> surplanted by migration to urban industrial communities. His eco-
> nomic life was gradually rising to decisive proportions. His cultural
> life was gradually rising through the steady decline of crippling
> illiteracy. All of these factors conjoined to cause the Negro to take
> a new look at himself.[66]

[61]Ibid., 83.
[62]Ibid.
[63]Ibid.
[64]Ibid.
[65]Ibid.
[66]Ibid.

This "new look" at the self, according to King, paved the way for a process of self-affirmation:

> The Negro masses began to re-evaluate themselves, and the Negro
> came to feel that he was *somebody*. His religion revealed to him
> that God loves all his children, and that *the basic thing about a*
> *man is not "his specificity but his fundamentum."* With this *new*
> *self-respect and new sense of dignity on the part of the Negro*, the
> second period of race relations in America was gradually passing
> away. [my emphasis][67]

This last paragraph is particularly important to my argument because it reveals that King turned to the word "somebody" as a particularly appropriate way of naming the new sense of self-respect and dignity attained by Negroes. In order to understand oneself as a somebody, in King's view, one had to (1) reevaluate oneself in light of social progress, in spite of all the negative oppressive factors, and (2) look into the theological bases of one's dignity—as one beloved by God and loved because of our fundamental human kinship under God. I shall explore this "fundamentum" of human beingness that Dr. King referred to in a later chapter on theological anthropology in the light of his usage of the term *imago dei*. What arrests my attention here is that as early as 1957 King was writing that Negroes, understanding themselves to have attained a new sense of self-respect and dignity, had achieved the status of being somebodies. To be *somebody* was a state of heightened self-awareness, self-appreciation, self-respect. It was a *reflected awareness* of one's fundamental state of being loved by God and therefore in kinship with all other human beings as a *human being*, and not as an inferior. Such an achieved awareness could, for King, also be named a "new sense of dignity." Below I shall explore the ways that the term "somebody" became an increasingly important way of naming dignity in King's later thought.

King believed the final, or third, period of race relations had begun on the date of the rendering of a decision in *Brown v. Board of Education* on 17 May 1954. To this third period, the present moment, King gave the positive appellation of "the period of complete and constructive integration."[68] In this period the Supreme Court gave "legal and consti

[67]Ibid.
[68]Ibid.

tutional validity to the dominant thought patterns of this period" by overturning the Plessy doctrine of "separate but equal": "The old Plessy Doctrine must go, that separate facilities are inherently unequal, and that to segregate a child on the basis of his race is to deny that child equal protection under the law."[69]

This decision provided a positive and promising outlook. King used glowing terms to describe the potential for positive social change that came directly from such a decision:

> And so as a result of this decision we find ourselves standing on the threshold of the third and most constructive period in the development of race relations in the history of the nation.[70]

King had no illusions, however, for he proceeded in this article to describe with caution the potentially positive future outlook. He spoke of standing "on the border of the promised land of integration" after having "broken loose from the Egypt of slavery" and having "moved through the wilderness of 'separate but equal.'"[71] Although King hoped for a positive future, one of "complete integration," he challenged the United States to "work passionately and unrelentingly for the complete realization of the ideals and principles of this period."[72]

After criticizing current attempts at "moderation" as a "tragic vice that all men of good will must condemn,"[73] King connected the Negro struggle for dignity to the worldwide uprisings against colonialism. He turned to words of the prime minister of the then "new nation of Ghana" to criticize America for not "treating our colored brothers in America as first-class human beings."[74] This was not the first time King had connected the American Negro struggle for dignity to the worldwide struggle against colonialism. What is significant is that here he quotes the direct comment of an African prime minister whom he had met face to face. King had met Kwame Nkruhmah during his 1956 trip to Africa. In a very real sense, it was the meeting of the leaders of two nations and

[69]Ibid.
[70]Ibid.
[71]Ibid.
[72]Ibid.
[73]Ibid., 84.
[74]Ibid.

indicates the growing international influence King had attained at a very early stage in his leadership.

The highest ideal of King's third period is described in the concluding paragraph of "A View of the Dawn":

> We will be able to bring into being a new nation where men will live together as brothers: a nation where all men will respect the dignity and worth of human personality; a nation in which men will not take necessities from the many to give luxuries to the few; a nation in which men will live by the principles of "the fatherhood of God and the brotherhood of man."[75]

The phrase about all people respecting "the dignity and worth of human personality" is one we have met before. Again, it resonates with one of the founding deontological principles of Boston Personalism as expressed by Edgar Brightman and Walter Muelder. For King, however, it moves off the pages of an academic text into the blood, sweat, and tears of the civil rights struggle. Furthermore, in King's hands it becomes a moral telos for American society. In this article King also set this moral telos within the theological context of the kingdom of God—the place in which the "principles of the fatherhood of God and the brotherhood of man" are incarnated. It would be remiss not to note that these two principles have often been cited as two fundamental theological tenets of the black Baptist church, and as the theological motto of the A.M.E. church.[76]

King's turning to the phrase "the fatherhood of God and the brotherhood of man" gives further insight into his understanding of dignity. He appears to be saying that dignity is rooted in a theological understanding of human kinship, with God as our common Creator and with each other as a human family. Such an understanding calls for a future, eschatological "day when we shall emerge from the bleak and desolate midnight of man's inhumanity to man to the bright and glittering daybreak of freedom and justice."[77] Such a day would be a time when all theologically

---

[75]Ibid., 85.

[76]For more information see Washington, *Frustrated Fellowship*, 27; and what Peter Paris (*Social Teaching*, 10) calls the "fundamental principle of the Black Christian tradition."

[77]King, "A View of the Dawn," 85.

based social ideals could become social reality, and thereby greater dignity would be realized.

In addition, this day could be interpreted as a time when the highest theological principles of the black churches would be integrated into the fabric of American society. This is an important insight into King's view of the importance of integration because it reveals the importance that he gave to the most prominent aspirations of the black church. To put it another way, King wanted to integrate even the theological ideals of blacks and whites in order to achieve a greater sense of dignity—the dignity of the kingdom of God—in America.

A Nontheological Reworking: Pride and Hope

At the Golden Anniversary of the National Urban League in 1960, King delivered the speech "The Rising Tide of Racial Consciousness." Here King turned to *social and psychological factors* to explain the Negroes' new sense of dignity.

The speech began with the question, "What are the factors that have led to this new sense of dignity and self-respect on the part of the Negro?"[78] King listed five factors that he believed supplied the social reasons undergirding such a change in self-regard.

The first factor King listed was "the population shift from rural to urban life."[79] He cited the Great Migration as an important factor toward broadening the world view of Negroes:

> For many years the vast majority of Negroes were isolated on the rural plantation. They had little contact with the world outside their geographical boundaries. But gradually circumstances made it possible and necessary for them to migrate to new and larger centers— the spread of the automobile, the great depression, and the social upheavals of the two world wars. These new contacts led to a broadened outlook. These new levels of communication brought new and different attitudes.[80]

[78]Martin Luther King, Jr., "The Rising Tide of Racial Consciousness," folder of 7, box 127, no. 3, King Papers, Mugar Library, Boston University; an abridged version is found in Washington, *Testament of Hope*, 145–51. Citations are to the manuscript.

[79]King, "The Rising Tide," 1.

[80]Ibid.

King then moved on to cite "rapid educational advance" as the second
contributing factor to a new sense of dignity.[81] He described this educational advance as a "steady decline of crippling illiteracy":

> At the Emancipation only 5 percent of the Negroes were literate;
> today more than 95 percent are literate. Constant streams of Negro
> students are finishing colleges and universities every year.[82]

King found in these educational advances a broadening of the Negro's
world view: "They [the educational advances] have given the Negro a
larger view of the world, but also a larger view of himself."[83]

The third factor King cited was "the gradual improvement of his [the
Negro's] economic status."[84] For King the Negro race had made "significant strides" in economic progress, which he qualified by the observation that "the Negro is still the victim of tragic economic exploitation."[85]
King compared the annual collective income of Negroes in North America
to the national income of Canada and cited other improvements:

> The annual collective income of the Negro is now approximately
> $18 million, which is more than the national income of Canada and
> all of the exports of the USA. This augmented purchasing power
> has been reflected in more adequate housing, improved medical
> care, and greater educational opportunities. As these changes have
> taken place they have driven the Negro to change his image of
> himself.[86]

In both the third and fourth factors King used the phrase, the new
sense of *pride*, while speaking of dignity.[87] Without reading too much
into the word "pride," it is nevertheless interesting to note that at this
stage, King saw pride as a necessary part of his understanding of dig-

---

[81]Ibid.
[82]Ibid., 1–2.
[83]Ibid., 2.
[84]Ibid.
[85]Ibid.
[86]Ibid., 3.
[87]Ibid., 2, 3.

nity. It will be important to see whether or not pride and dignity become synonymous in King's thought.

The fourth factor that had contributed to a new sense of pride was "the Supreme Court's decision outlawing segregation in the public schools."[88] King rejoiced in the decision of 17 May 1954, calling it "a joyous daybreak to end the long night of enforced segregation."[89] The decision, as far as King was concerned, "affirmed that 'separate but equal' facilities are inherently unequal and that to segregate a child on the basis of his race is to deny that child equal protection under the law."[90] The effect of this decision in King's view was that it "brought hope to millions of disinherited Negroes who had formerly dared only to dream of freedom."[91] Notice how King described the hope that this particular decision brought Negroes and how he connected hope with dignity:

> Like an exit sign that suddenly appeared to one who had walked through a long and desolate corridor, this decision came as a way out of the darkness of segregation. It served to transform the fatigue of despair into the buoyancy of hope. It further enhanced the Negro's sense of dignity.[92]

The connection of hope and dignity in King's thought should not be passed over lightly. These last statements show that hope was not a socially meaningless category, useful only in sermonic language. Rather, for King hope was based on meaningful social progress toward freedom and equality. Furthermore, King would probably have gone on to say that social progress toward freedom and equality enhances the dignity of all persons. Hope is based on concrete and actual social progress, not on the rhetoric of freedom and equality used by politicians. As such, hope, or at least the social aspects that increase hope—such as economic progress, educational advances, better housing—can be measured and described. Thus hope is another element of King's ever-maturing view of dignity.

[88]Ibid., 3.
[89]Ibid.
[90]Ibid.
[91]Ibid.
[92]Ibid., 4.

The fifth factor contributing to "the new sense of dignity" in Negroes was "the awareness that his [the Negro's] struggle for freedom is a part of a worldwide struggle."[93] This is a factor that King has noted before, but here he expanded his reflections:

> He [the Negro] has watched developments in Asia and Africa with rapt attention. On these vast prodigious continents dwell two-thirds of the world's people. For years they were exploited economically, dominated politically, segregated and humiliated by foreign powers. Thirty years ago there were only three independent countries in the whole of Africa—Liberia, Ethiopia, and South Africa. By 1962, there may be as many as thirty independent nations in Africa. These rapid changes have naturally influenced the thinking of the American Negro. *He knows that his struggle for human dignity is not an isolated event. It is a drama being played on the stage of the world with spectators and supporters from every continent.* [my emphasis][94]

King found in the international struggle for freedom and independence from colonialism a global community striving for dignity. This global community, including Asians and Africans as well as American Negroes, strengthened each other's struggles by being "spectators and supporters." Moreover, American Negroes gathered strength knowing that their struggle was not a unique and "isolated event" but rather a part of a grand "drama" that many people from many continents were acting out. Again, it is important to note that this idea of a global community of freedom was developed in King's later thought.

The rest of this particular speech resonated with familiar themes from previous speeches. What is particularly fascinating about this speech is that King barely mentioned two of his favorite themes—nonviolence and love—but referred to both in terms of dignity. For instance, in justifying why Negroes were inspired with "a new determination to struggle and sacrifice until first-class citizenship becomes a reality," King gave a brief historical sketch of all the nonviolent protests.[95] He ended with a telling statement: "The Negro would rather suffer in dignity than accept

---

[93]Ibid.
[94]Ibid., 4–5.
[95]Ibid., 5.

segregation in humiliation."[96] We are reminded once again that dignity for King increasingly involved "standing up" for one's citizenship rights against the system of segregation. To gain one's full or "first-class" citizenship in America involved struggling toward that goal. As before, King reminded his audience that America must be brought into a "full realization" of the "ideals and dreams of our democracy."[97] King's statements about the ideals and dreams of democracy indicate that he presupposed such ideals to be the epitome of freedom and equality and therefore of dignity. It is necessary to note again that being a dignified person involved *the free exercise of one's citizenship rights as an American.*

In the only vaguely theological mention in this address, King used language reminiscent of Martin Buber.[98] In this section, King attacked racial discrimination as something that is "morally wrong"[99] and contrary to the fundamental religious beliefs of Americans.

> The primary reason for our uprooting racial discrimination from our society is that it is morally wrong. It is a cancerous disease that prevents us from realizing the sublime principles of our Judaeo-Christian tradition. Racial discrimination substitutes an "I-it" relationship for the "I-thou" relationship. It relegates persons to the status of things. Whenever racial discrimination exists it is a tragic expression of men's spiritual degeneracy and moral bankruptcy. Therefore, it must be removed not merely because it is diplomatically expedient, but because it is morally compelling.[100]

King concluded this speech with his only direct reference to "nonviolent resistance" by justifying nonviolent confrontation as a "frontal assault on poverty, disease, and ignorance of a people too long deprived of the God-given rights of life, liberty, and the pursuit of happiness."[101] King did not avoid making a connection between American values and his understanding of godly values:

[96]Ibid., 6.
[97]Ibid., 8.
[98]King often quoted from Martin Buber's *I and Thou* (New York: Scribner, 1958) 8–9.
[99]King, "The Rising Tide," 7–8.
[100]Ibid., 8–9.
[101]Ibid., 19.

> We must work assiduously and with determined boldness to remove
> from the body politic this cancerous disease of discrimination which
> is preventing our democratic and Christian health from being real-
> ized. Then and only then will we be able to bring into full realiza-
> tion the dream of our American democracy.[102]

He followed this statement with a peroration on the American "dream,"
later expanded in his famous speech, "I Have a Dream." It is significant
that in "The Rising Tide" he once again mentioned dignity, the *moral
telos* for American society, as part of his understanding of the American
dream, "the dream of a country where every man will respect the dignity
and worth of all human personality, and men will dare to live together
as brothers."[103]

In "The Rising Tide of Racial Consciousness" there is an understanding of dignity that can encompass social, economic, and cultural factors
as well as theological ones. Such an understanding broadens our appreciation of King's contribution to the concept of dignity, because it reveals his view of dignity as one that includes factors both inside and
outside of the language of theology.

Summary

King's early view of dignity contained a rich mixture of factors. Initially King expressed a somewhat ambiguous sense of the term "dignity," using it both as a desired social telos and as a necessary and
essential human state of existence. Soon, however, he intentionally combined these two meanings into a single complex concept of dignity as
something inherent and essential to one's humanity when it is asserted in
the protest for greater rights of citizenship. Thus dignity is both an
inherent quality of humanity and a tangible sense of citizenship rights.
The two are closely interrelated, since one must protest with dignity as
one courageously asserts oneself for dignity.

Dignity had *moral value* for King. Over and over again King combined dignity with courage. It took courage to protest for dignity and to
stand nonviolently in the face of violent opposition. Such courage ennobled oneself. Yet courage does not stand by itself, for courage is
motivated by hope. Hope, for King, is not a vague theological or ethical

---

[102]Ibid., 19–20.
[103]Ibid., 20.

concept, but is based upon measurable social progress. Thus courage and hope, as moral values, take on new and particular meanings within King's concept of dignity.

At this early stage in King's thought the words "dignity" and "pride" could be interchanged to a certain extent. It will be necessary to ask, however, if King later distinguished the two.

Dignity, for King, was fluid; it could grow or be diminished. The power of a socio-political system could add or subtract from one's social dignity, but never take away that fundamental and inherent sense of one's personal dignity. If the socio-political system denied rights, as segregation did, then it had to be changed so as to grant rights that would allow for dignity to grow. King valued the growth of dignity in society, believing that it ennobles a nation and injects new meaning into civilization. This growth of dignity in society can be measured in tangible ways. In the civil rights movement one could measure dignity's progress by looking at (1) the Supreme Court's decision of May 1954 in *Brown v. Board of Education* as a significant beginning, (2) the victory of the Montgomery bus boycott of 1955–56, and (3) the protests all across the South that eventually led to the Voting Rights Act of 1964 and the Civil Rights Act of 1965.

Theologically, the growth of dignity would lead to a moral telos for American society wherein dignity and human personality are given the highest place. Over and over again King described the future attainment of this telos in terms of the kingdom of God coming here in America.

As Negroes protested with dignity for dignity, King understood them to be gaining a new sense of self-respect and dignity. This dignity came through the deeper self-awareness and sense of self-respect that nonviolent protest gave its practitioners. As Negroes courageously asserted their rights as American citizens, they attained a deeper sense of their kinship with other struggling peoples. This sense of kinship deepened their sense of humanity and their inner perception of dignity as something that can be fought for across racial and national lines.

As King's early views became more systematic, he began to present them in a more specifically historical fashion. Eventually this led to his creation of a historical typology that used the format of ideal types to present a view of the progress of racial dignity in North America. Yet King was also motivated to articulate, even in this early stage, a powerful symbolic notion, namely, that of being somebody. The notion of being somebody, despite and in the midst of a society that encouraged one to think of oneself as a "nobody," will later take on more signifi-

cance. For now, it is important simply to note the birth of the term a
a way of describing dignity.

To be somebody is to "stand up" to those forces that would deny
one's somebodyness. This act of "standing up" for one's dignity acquired
a new meaning for King, even though it had strong roots in the African
American community and in King's parents in particular. King expanded
the concept of "standing up" with his ideals of love and nonviolence
and in so doing, incorporated "standing up" into his unique understand
ing of dignity.

King's understanding of dignity involved concrete and measurable
economic and social factors, cultural factors, theological traditions, fun
damental American presuppositions and values, philosophical language
and ethical argument. To deal only with the theology and the ethics of
King's ideas on dignity would be to miss the concrete social, political
and cultural events that he valued as part of his understanding of th
term.

The rest of this work will demonstrate how King's view of dignity
was undergirded by his philosophical background, views of humanity
and theological and ethical understandings of love and nonviolence. In
the next several chapters I shall explore the underlying philosophical
theological, and ethical modes of reasoning that shaped King's view of
dignity.

3

PHILOSOPHICAL INFLUENCES: BOSTON PERSONALISM

n order to evaluate critically Martin Luther King, Jr.'s concept of dignity and the self, it is necessary to take a careful look at the philosophical influences on his thought and to uncover the philosophical strands that King integrated into his views of the self and dignity. In the next two chapters I shall examine several aspects of King's philosophical thought: (1) his apparent eclecticism, (2) the influence of the school of Boston Personalism,[1] (3) strands of the thought of Immanuel Kant in Personalism, (4) the dialectic of G. F. W. Hegel, and (5) King's philosophy of nonviolence.

King's Apparent Eclecticism

According to most evaluations, King was an eclectic philosopher, taking bits and pieces from a wide range of schools and positions across the

---

[1]Boston Personalism is a school of personalist theistic idealism that has been reared and nurtured in Boston University's School of Theology. Its leading exponents are Borden Parker Bowne, Edgar Sheffield Brightman, Georgia Harkness, Walter Muelder, and L. Harold DeWolf.

philosophical spectrum, quoting liberally from ancient giants such as
Augustine and Aquinas, as well as from Kant and even Nietzsche upon
occasion. Since King's rhetorical style required liberal use of quotations,
one may question whether it is fruitful to try to piece together a single
philosophical "system" out of the amassed quotations. Instead, we need
to look underneath the quotations toward an underlying personalism that
motivated his choice of texts. Warren Steinkraus has written three excellent essays on King's personalism.[2]

Steinkraus has also emphasized two important facts about King and
philosophy: first, King was a systematically trained philosopher who
began his studies of philosophy "as an undergraduate in Morehouse
College, continued when at Crozer Seminary by enrolling for courses in
the University of Pennsylvania, and took his doctor's degree in philosophical theology in 1955 at Boston University";[3] and second, King's
training enabled him to be thoroughly familiar with the history of philosophy "far better than in theology."[4] Steinkraus pointed out that in
Stride Toward Freedom alone, King cited "no less than eighteen philosophers" in order to support his description of the Montgomery bus
boycott.[5] This freedom to cite philosophers from the vast range of western philosophical history finds its coherent basis in King's adherence to
a personalist philosophy. In order to appreciate more fully why King felt
such freedom in citing these various philosophers in order to support his
own personalism, I turn to King's claim to be a "personalist idealist."
The following quotation from *Stride Toward Freedom* elaborates upon
King's understanding of personalism, as it was taught to him:

> I studied philosophy at Boston University under Edgar S. Brightman
> and L. Harold DeWolf. Both men greatly stimulated my thinking.
> It was mainly under these teachers that I studied personalistic phi-
> losophy—the theory that the clue to the meaning of ultimate reality
> is found in personality. *This personal idealism remains today my
> basic philosophical position.* Personalism's insistence that only per-
> sonality—finite and infinite—is ultimately real strengthened me in

[2] Warren E. Steinkraus, "Martin Luther King's Personalism and Non-Violence,"
"Martin Luther King's Contributions to Personalism," and "The Dangerous Idea
of Martin Luther King, Jr.," all in Garrow's *King*, 3. 891–931.

[3] Steinkraus, "Martin Luther King's Personalism and Non-Violence," 891.

[4] Ibid.

[5] Ibid., 891 n. 3.

> two convictions: It gave me *metaphysical grounding for the idea of a personal God, and it gave me a metaphysical basis for the dignity and worth of all human personality.* [my emphasis][6]

I disagree with David J. Garrow's claim that this section of *Stride Toward Freedom* is unreliable because it may have been ghostwritten.[7] I contend that it is a reliable source for information about King's philosophical background even if it was ghostwritten by Bayard Rustin or Stanley Levison; based on my archival research, it is an accurate recounting of the facts of King's philosophical training and academic background. Moreover, King did not refute its claims, and it was published in many forms. Personalism for King was "the theory that the clue to the meaning of ultimate reality is found in personality." Furthermore, as Steinkraus has also pointed out, personalism provided King with an adequate *metaphysic* to be wedded to his "religious convictions" (see chapter one above), and his "theory of social change," which I shall discuss later in this chapter.[8] I now turn to the school of Boston Personalism that directly influenced King's philosophical adherence to its claims, beginning with Borden Parker Bowne and going on to Edgar S. Brightman and L. Harold DeWolf.

Bowne and Kant

Borden Parker Bowne is widely considered the founding force of Boston Personalism. He took on Kant's epistemology as essentially adequate with one important exception, namely, what he called the "theistic standpoint."[9] The "theistic standpoint" affirmed that all personal thoughts and experiences are "embraced in the thought or plan of the infinite Mind and Will on which they all depend."[10] Thus thought was elevated to an absolute transcendental perspective for Bowne:

> From a theistic standpoint the universe itself is no proper static existence, but only the divine thought finding realization through

[6]King, *Stride Toward Freedom*, 100.
[7]See Garrow's argument in "Intellectual Development," 2. 437 and 2. 439 n.

[8]Steinkraus, "Martin Luther King's Personalism and Non-Violence," 893.
[9]Bowne, *Personalism*, 108–9.
[10]Ibid., 109.

the divine will, and that thought for us must find expression in the order of our experience.[11]

Bowne was concerned that Kant's doctrine of knowledge could lead to an "agnosticism" of uncertainty, whereas he called for a personali system that would honor the "living world of experience" by pointing personal "intelligence" and the Infinite Mind as its source.[12] For Bowr human beings know anything at all as "living persons":

> We are not abstract intellects nor abstract wills, but we are living persons, knowing and feeling and having various interests, and in the light of knowledge and under the impulse of our interests trying to find our way, having an order of experience also and seeking to understand it and to guide ourselves so as to extend or enrich that experience, and thus to build ourselves into larger and fuller and more abundant personal life.[13]

Personality, for Bowne, was the only sure ground upon which we ca rationally know anything. "Personality is the real and only principle philosophy which will enable us to take any rational step whatever."

Bowne desired to go beyond what he saw as Kantian rationalism incorporating a "spiritual principle":

> The world of experience exists for us only through a rational spiritual principle by which we reproduce it for our thought, and it has its existence apart from us only through a rational spiritual principle on which it depends, and the rational nature of which it expresses.[15]

Bowne combined the terms "rational" and "spiritual" in the previous paragraph. He went beyond Kant's rationality to a personalist view the human person and a personal God who *is* "thought" in the absolu

[11]Ibid.
[12]Ibid., 110.
[13]Ibid., 263.
[14]Ibid.
[15]Ibid., 110.

ense of the word. Thus the "spiritual principle" is the thinking of human persons in combination with the "thought" that is God.

This concern for a *rational* and *spiritual* basis for knowing the world
and God is omnipresent in King's thought. King repeatedly demonstrated
confidence in God as "toughminded and tenderhearted."[16] King reassured
his congregation in the sermon "A Tough Mind and a Tender Heart" that
they had a reasonable assurance in trusting in a God who combines the
"toughmindedness" of demanding justice with the "tenderheartedness" of
being responsive to human longings and pain.

In his doctoral dissertation King relied on Bowne's description of God
as an Infinite or "Absolute" Personality:

> The idea of personality is so consistent with the notion of the Ab-
> solute that we must say with Bowne "that the complete and perfect
> personality can be found only in the Infinite and Absolute Being,
> as only in him can we find that complete and perfect selfhood and
> self-expression which is necessary to the fullness of personality."[17]

Bowne affirmed the distinctiveness of each individual personality
within the sphere of humanity.[18] He wrote of a "living self" that was
invisible."

> We ourselves are invisible. The physical organism is only an in-
> strument for expressing and manifesting the inner life, but the liv-
> ing self is never seen.[19]

> This invisible living self can only be manifested through our deeds.
> For each person his own self is known in immediate experiences
> and all others are known through their effects. They are not re-
> vealed in form or shape, but in deeds, and they are known only in
> and through deeds.[20]

[16]King, *Strength to Love*, 15–16.

[17]Martin Luther King, Jr., "A Comparison of the Conceptions of God in the
thinking of Paul Tillich and Henry Nelson Weiman" (Ph. D. diss., Boston Uni-
ersity, 1955) 270.

[18]Bowne, *Personalism*, 268.

[19]Ibid.

[20]Ibid., 268–69.

I wonder if many years later in the famous "Drum Major" sermon, a highly reflective Martin Luther King, Jr. did not express a similar respect for the power of one's deeds in revealing the invisible self. King offered the following as his own epitaph:

> Tell them not to mention that I have a Nobel Peace Prize, that isn't important. Tell them not to mention that I have three or four hundred other awards, that's not important. Tell him not to mention where I went to school. . . . I'd like somebody to mention on that day, that Martin Luther King, Jr. tried to give his life serving others. . . tried to love somebody. . . . I want you to say that I tried to love and serve humanity. . . . I won't have the fine and luxurious things of life to leave behind. But I just want to leave a committed life behind.[21]

King appears to have affirmed Bowne's assertion that "out of the invisible comes the meaning that transforms the curious sets of motions into terms of personality and gives them human significance."[22]

Out of this epistemological basis, Bowne elaborated a concern for ethics, clearly seen in his *Principles of Ethics*. In agreement with Schleiermacher's view, he presented fundamental moral ideas as a procession of "the good, duty, and virtue."[23] All three were represented in an ethical system that expressed the "moral consciousness of the race."[24] The ethical system that Bowne created from these fundamental moral ideas affirmed the following five points: (1) the moral task consists of the rational expression of good will;[25] (2) the moral life chiefly consists of service to the common good;[26] (3) the greatest need in ethics is "the impartial and unselfish will to do right" as a counter balance to wars, corruption, and the abstraction of most ethical systems; (4) the greatest need within ethical practice is "the serious and thoughtful application of

---

[21]Washington, *Testament of Hope*, 267.

[22]Bowne, *Personalism*, 270.

[23]Bowne, *Principles*, 20. These ideas were based on Bowne's particular reading of Friedrich Schleiermacher, "Second Speech," in *On Religion: Speeches to its Cultured Despisers* (London: Collins, 1987) 76–77.

[24]Bowne, *Principles*, 20.

[25]Ibid., 304.

[26]Ibid., 305.

he intellect to the problems of life and conduct";[27] and (5) moral righ-
eousness must continually be reaffirmed by always "adjusting itself to
new conditions."[28] It is especially noteworthy that these five bases of
Bowne's ethical system affirm human rationality and intentionality as the
personal foundation for a proper ethical system.

Bowne revealed his underlying personalist epistemology by stressing
these qualities strongly. In his *Principles of Ethics* Bowne did not posit
the existence of a "moral law" theologically or metaphysically, but insisted upon those ethical duties within human beings which we are socially obligated to perform and should will to do. Bowne used the terms
"moral sphere" or "moral field." Both terms appealed to Bowne's historical understanding of "principles of social morality"[29] based on a "feeling
of obligation, the idea of a right and a wrong with corresponding duties
is universal."[30] According to Bowne, this "feeling of obligation" developed progressively from "tribal" origins. This historical progression is
not a Hegelian dialectic or a Hegelian understanding of the progression
of history. Rather, Bowne described the development of a "common
rational nature, yet there is a vast diversity in intellectual beliefs."[31]

Bowne was confident that "as this diversity and contradiction do not
shake our faith in the oneness and community and infallibility of reason,
so the similar fact in ethics need not shake our faith in the unity and
infallibility of the moral nature."[32] This unity and infallibility of the
moral nature, for Bowne, was shared by "savage" and "Christian" and
was thus a cause of a "good degree of moral uniformity" among humanity in general.[33] Bowne warned his late-nineteenth-century seminary student readers to maintain a chaste judgment about the difference between
"savage morality" and "civilized morality":

> Indeed, making due allowance for ignorance and embryonic devel-
> opment, we may well doubt whether savage morality is not quite

[27]Ibid., 307.
[28]Ibid.
[29]Ibid., 156.
[30]Ibid.
[31]Ibid., 157–58.
[32]Ibid., 158.
[33]Ibid., 157.

equal to civilized morality. If the former show more animalism, the latter show more diabolism. In our dealings with the lower races, we have little to boast of on any score; and in any civilized community one can find, under hatches, infamy and bestiality enough to satisfy all demands in that line.[34]

Bowne's allusion to the existence of "lower races" nevertheless reinforces, in my mind, the strength of his personalist ethic because it reveals that while he conformed to contemporary racist notions of a "higher race" (Anglo-Saxon and European) and "lower races" (African and tribal), at the same time he affirmed a universal and uniform human moral nature. Bowne valorized a common human moral condition with the phrase "common rational nature." Later personalists overcame the late-nineteenth-century racial provincialism in which Bowne was embedded. In order to see the development of personalist metaphysics and ethics along both Kantian and Hegelian lines, I now turn to the thought of Edgar Sheffield Brightman.

Edgar Sheffield Brightman

Brightman was one of the most influential personalists in the generation of Bowne's students. Walter Muelder wrote the following of Brightman and A. C. Knudson:

Students of Bowne in the generation of A. C. Knudson and E. S. Brightman affirmed that the self is the locus of value, perspective, and meaning. *Personality is the ultimate empirical reality, God being the person of persons. Person is conscious activity. To be is to act and to act is to will.* Conscious activity is most clearly evident in acts of valuation and selection. *Ethics is an important personalistic discipline.* [my emphasis][35]

Brightman's influence on King was direct and immediate, for he was King's doctoral advisor until his death in 1953. Through Brightman King gained a deeper appreciation of Kant and Hegel, both of whom were very important sources of inspiration for Brightman, particularly in his *Moral Laws*.

---

[34]Ibid.

[35]Muelder, "Philosophical and Theological Influences," 692.

Brightman's most influential book, *Moral Laws*, articulated an under-standing of personalism that had the distinctly Kantian format of pre-senting moral ideals as principles, laws, or universal categories. Brightman created eleven "laws" that articulated his understanding of the "moral law." Before turning to these laws, I want to define what Brightman meant by "moral law" and to demonstrate that Brightman built upon the rational basis for morality that Bowne had established earlier.

Reason, for Brightman, was "a special function of experience; a func-tion which surveys, orders, unifies, and systematizes."[36] This "function" of reason can be seen in the development of art and music, which for Brightman were "structures of reason no less than mathematics and logic."[37] Reason was also responsible for the development of "physics, chemistry, and all the sciences."[38] Thus, in Brightman's view, to "deny the right of reason is to deny the *very structure of the mind* and the achievements of the highest culture."[39] He proceeded to demonstrate "the essential elements of rational thought in ethics, by means of which moral laws are derived from moral experience"[40] by delineating four steps: observation, generalization, criticism, and interpretation.

Observation involved the "observation of experiences of value, obli-gation, and law as voluntarily chosen or controlled, and of other expe-riences related to them."[41] Generalization, the next step, entailed the "formulation of such general likenesses or tendencies as they appear" with the recognition that with generalizations come "contradictions."[42] Criticism then arose "with a view toward eliminating these contradic-tions."[43] Criticism was a negative state, however, which implied the "mere absence of contradiction" and not the "action, forward meaning of life, and richness of meaning" that an appropriate ethic must present. The final step, that of interpretation, consisted of two "phases," interpretation and systematization.

---

[36]Brightman, *Moral Laws*, 84.
[37]Ibid.
[38]Ibid., 85.
[39]Ibid.
[40]Ibid.
[41]Ibid.
[42]Ibid.
[43]Ibid.

Interpretation, for Brightman, involved a "recourse to hypothesis—a 'guess' as to the probable rational connection of our experiences."[44] The hypothesis may then be tested "by a twofold systematization; the practical system of living and the theoretical system of our most general and best established hypotheses, which we call laws."[45] Brightman was supremely confident in ethics as a "science" and as a "rational account of moral experience" that is a "system."[46] This "system" sees the relations of the parts to the whole, a "connected whole" in which the "coherent relations of a proposition to other propositions, to experiences, and to the system of which it forms a part" are clearly demonstrable.[47] For Brightman, "all truth partakes of system and of wholeness," a proposition that is overtly Hegelian (as I shall elaborate in the next chapter).

Moral law, for Brightman, was "a universal principle to which the will ought to conform in its choices."[48] It must conform to the standard of universality and to the "obligation of the will in choosing" to be a moral law and in this way can be distinguished from both "codes" and "convention."[49] Codes, for Brightman, were "sets of principles in accordance with which society expects or demands that the individual shall choose" that may or may not be in accordance with the moral law.[50] Convention was an even less clear concept for Brightman. He claimed that it could be "sometimes an aid and sometimes a detriment to morality" because it does not create an obligation of the will, but only a "situation and a problem" of conformity.[51] Brightman appealed to varied philosophers who, while quite different in approach, shared a fundamental "conviction that there is a moral law."[52] His list included Spinoza, Ralph Cudworth, Kant, and Jeremy Bentham. It is interesting that Brightman appealed directly to Kant's concept of the moral will. "Kant called the moral will 'practical reason' (with the accent on the 'reason')

[44] Ibid.
[45] Ibid., 85–86.
[46] Ibid., 86.
[47] Ibid., 86–87.
[48] Ibid., 45.
[49] Ibid.
[50] Ibid.
[51] Ibid.
[52] Ibid., 47.

and held that moral law must be universal and necessary—a priori as he called it."[53]

Brightman articulated a highly complex and propositional understanding of moral laws that included eleven laws. Brightman listed them in the following manner:

I. The Formal Laws
  1. The Logical Law (consistent will)
  2. The Law of Autonomy (self-imposed ideals are obligatory
II. The Axiological Laws
  3. The Axiological Law (consistent values)
  4. The Law of Consequences (consider and approve foreseeable consequences)
  5. The Law of Best Possible
  6. The Law of Specification (develop values relevant to the situation)
  7. The Law of the Most Inclusive End
  8. The Law of Ideal Control (control empirical values by ideal values)
III. The Personalistic Laws
  9. The Law of Individualism
  10. The Law of Altruism
  11. The Law of the Ideal of Personality (judge and guide all acts by an ideal of personality)[54]

Brightman explained the subdivisions of formal, axiological, and personalistic with the idea of an unfolding development. Brightman saw this system of moral laws as developing "from abstract formalism to concrete value and still more concrete personality."[55] Formal laws "have to do with the will alone, and state the principles to which a reasonable will must conform irrespective of the ends (values) which it is trying to realize."[56] Axiological laws "show the principles which the values a good will is seeking ought to embody."[57] Finally, personalistic laws "show

[53]Ibid.
[54]Ibid., 89–90.
[55]Ibid., 90.
[56]Ibid.
[57]Ibid.

what ought to follow in conduct from the fact that value is always an experience of persons."[58]

While it is beyond this present volume to give a full description and critical assessment of these laws, a few aspects of them have direct bearing on the subject of dignity and King's underlying philosophical understanding of personalism. First, together with John Ansbro,[59] I affirm that King's study of moral law with Brightman was reinforced by his personal experiences of the "evil of segregation" that "systematically does violence to the human personally."[60] Second, King's own family and church traditions presented him with a mental framework for enthusiastically receiving and translating Brightman's laws into the concrete situation of racism. Third, Brightman's first two logical laws—the logical law and the law of autonomy—reveal an overt indebtedness to Kant's second formulation of the "categorical imperative." This is particularly true of the law of autonomy which states that "all persons ought to recognize themselves as obligated to choose in accordance with the ideals which they acknowledge, self-imposed ideals are imperative."[61] In the next chapter, a section on Kant shall examine this relationship more closely. Ansbro demonstrates how the logical law, the law of autonomy, the law of best possible, the law of consequences, the law of the most inclusive end, and the law of ideal control are suggested in King's self-evaluation of various nonviolent movements from Montgomery to Albany, Selma, and Birmingham.[62]

In addition to being deeply indebted to Kant's formulations on morality and the dignity of the human person, Brightman was also an "admirer and critic" of Hegel and, according to Walter Muelder, started King along that same path.[63] Brightman incorporated a dialectical methodology that stressed a phrase heard repeatedly in King's writings, "the truth is the whole."[64] Muelder interpreted this expression as signifying

[58]Ibid.

[59]Ansbro, *King*, 76–86.

[60]Ibid., 76.

[61]Brightman, *Moral Laws*, 106.

[62]See Ansbro, *King*, 79–83. Ansbro is quite specific in finding certain aspects of King's thought that refer to these moral laws.

[63]Muelder, "Philosophical and Theological Influences," 693.

[64]King first heard of this expression in his History of Philosophy course in 1950 (teacher unknown); see Hegel notes, folder 14, King Archives, Mugar Library, Boston University.

the "philosophical method of rational synthesis or synopsis which follows a dialectical process of comprehensive analysis."[65] Such a method
of analysis stressed "rational coherence" as well, or, in other words,
"thought must not only be internally or propositionally consistent, but
coherent with experience taken as personal and social wholes."[66] Muelder
emphasized that while early personalists were "essentially Kantian in
their epistemology," those who studied under Brightman "stressed wholes
and the dynamic dialectic of criticized experience."[67]

In Muelder's view this focus on criticizing social systems rather than
persons was sharpened by Brightman's underlying Hegelian attention to
the "whole" of a system.[68] I would add that such an emphasis on systems rather than persons received intellectual articulation through King's
personalist training, but the seeds of such thought had been planted by
the protest tradition of his family.

It is fascinating to note the combination of Kantian and Hegelian
notions in one of Brightman's late essays, "Philosophical Ideas and
Enduring Peace." In this essay Brightman reiterated his understanding of
personalist principles: (1) "personality is the seat of value"; (2) "personality idealizes"; (3) "personality is free" (based on the Kantian notion
that "to be a person is to choose, and to choose or to select is to
exercise freedom");[69] (4) "personality is social"; (5) *"personality is growth
through dialectical tensions"* whereby Brightman defined human personality as an "arena of oppositions, which have well been called tensions";[70]
and finally (6) "religious personality is rational love."[71]

[65]Muelder, "Philosophical and Theological Influences," 693.
[66]Ibid.
[67]Ibid.
[68]Ibid.
[69]Edgar S. Brightman, "Philosophical Ideas and Enduring World Peace" in
Approaches to World Peace (eds. Lyman Bryson, Louis Finkelstein, and Robert
M. MacIver; New York: Harper & Row, 1944) 546. See also Kant's *Foundations*,
74–75 in which "freedom must be presupposed as the property of the will of
rational beings."
[70]Brightman, "Philosophical Ideas," 550. Brightman went on to stress that
such growth requires the "convincing of all men of their *universal social nature,
of men's need of each other, of the interdependence of nations and cultures.*"
[71]Brightman defines "rational love" as follows: "In the interrelations between
love and reason we have the loftiest form of dialectical tension experienced by
the human mind" (ibid., 553).

Walter Muelder has written of Brightman's expression "rational love" that "reason here means adequate and complete coherence of all experiences, and love means cooperative commitment of persons of good will to mutual respect and the creation of shared values."[72] These six points that Brightman passed on to King through his personalist philosophy provided a powerful reinforcement to the views that King received from his church and family, belief in the dignity of all persons and of progress gained only through conflict and sacrifice. That is to say, in stressing the fundamental freedom and value of the human person and the struggle for growth that evolves in a dialectical process, Brightman particularly reinforced the claims from the African-American matrix of family and church already well established in King's mind.

L. Harold DeWolf

Martin Luther King, Jr. considered L. Harold DeWolf to be both a "mentor" and a "friend" who stayed close to him throughout his career.[73] Stephen Oates has stated that DeWolf was very impressed with King, calling him a "scholar's scholar" and ranking him as "one of the best five or six graduate students he had taught in thirty-one years at Boston University School of Theology."[74] Even before Brightman died suddenly in 1953 and DeWolf took over the duties of advising King's dissertation, King had taken DeWolf's "Personalism" course in 1952.

My examination of the syllabus, bibliography, and King's own notes on this course has led me to agree with Paul Deats's assessment of personalism as having a "certain eclectic character" because of its wide-ranging diverse heritage.[75] This heritage was elaborated in the course's primary text, Albert G. Knudson's *Philosophy of Personalism* (1927) Knudson relied on a reading of Plato that valorized "the superiority of thought over sense and the objectivity of ideals."[76] Knudson's text selected various "contributions to personalism" from a wide range of historically significant figures: Augustine's writings on "the role of

---

[72]Walter G. Muelder, "Edgar S. Brightman: Person and Moral Philosopher," in Paul Deats and Carol Robb, eds., *The Boston Personalist Tradition* (Macon GA: Mercer, 1986) 120.

[73]Muelder, "Philosophical and Theological Influences," 699.

[74]Stephen Oates, "The Intellectual Odyssey of Martin Luther King," 719.

[75]Paul Deats, "Introduction to Personalism," in *The Boston Personalist Tradition*, 4.

[76]Ibid., 3.

self-knowledge in metaphysics and of the significance of the will,"[77] Aquinas and Descartes for introducing the "primacy of self-certainty,"[78] and the line of philosophers from Berkeley to Kant, Hegel, Lotze, and Bowne.

DeWolf informed his class that they were "expected to master" Knudson's *Philosophy of Personalism* and that they would be tested on it for the midterm examination.[79] Thus, if we say that King is an "eclectic philosopher," it is important to root this eclecticism in the underlying eclecticism of Boston Personalism and not in King alone. King learned to draw from a wide range of historical sources and significant authors from within the particular philosophical framework of personalism, as he learned it from DeWolf.

DeWolf's own contribution to Boston Personalism was to add three "communitarian laws" to Brightman's previous eleven, along with a "metaphysical law." These new "laws" were initially formulated in DeWolf's *Responsible Freedom* and were meant to be an addition to Brightman's earlier formulation. DeWolf remarked that these laws would "take into full account the fact that individuals are not only affected by and are in turn obligated to other individuals, but are also in reciprocal relations with the communities of which they are members and also frequently with other communities."[80] These "communitarian laws" began with a *principle of cooperation* that stated that "every person ought, when possible, to cooperate with others in the production and enjoyment of shared values."[81] The second communitarian principle is the *principle of social devotion*: "Every person ought to devote himself to serving the best interests of the group and to subordinate personal gain to social gain."[82] DeWolf said of this law that it stressed his belief that a person could not "achieve a maximum of values" for the self unless that self subordinated itself to the interdependent communal context in which it lived:

> A person concerned only with the cultivation of values for himself
> or herself cannot achieve a maximum of values even for self. We

[77]Ibid.

[78]Ibid., 4.

[79]L. Harold DeWolf "Personalism" syllabus in folder 15. 23, box 113, King Archives, Mugar Library, Boston University.

[80]DeWolf, *Responsible Freedom*, 223.

[81]Ibid., 166.

[82]Ibid., 168.

are by nature socially interdependent and need to subordinate our self-interest to the interests of various communities to which we belong.[83]

I shall explore the claims of this paragraph with greater attention to its theological implications in the next chapter. For now I want to draw attention to the claims of social interdependence and the subordination of self-interest in favor of the interests of various communities as an important influence on Martin Luther King, Jr. Without a doubt, one of King's favorite topics was the *interdependence of all humanity*. In sermons King often referred to the famous quotation from John Donne concerning the interdependence of humanity:

No man is an island, entire of itselfe; every man is a piece of the Continent, a part of the maine; if a clod bee washed away by the Sea, Europe is the lesse, as well as if a Promontorie were, as well if a Manor of thy friends or of thine owne were; any man's death diminishes me, because I am involved in Mankinde; And therefore never send to know for whom the bell tolls; it tolls for thee.[84]

King often repeated another sentence expressing the belief he shared with DeWolf that all humanity is interdependent: "All men are caught in an inescapable network of mutuality, tied in a single garment of destiny."[85] King saw this interdependence as being part of the "*structure of the universe*." At other times he referred to this interdependence as "the inter-related structure of reality."[86] By this, I understand King to mean that the *moral* and *spiritual* universe, as well as the geographical, are to be thought of as one interrelated and interdependent structure consisting of many various parts. King was impressed with what for his time was the new sense of "geographical togetherness" that humanity held be

---

[83]DeWolf, "Ethical Implications," 224.

[84]Quoted in its entirety by King in "Facing the Challenge of a New Age" (1956) in Washington, *Testament of Hope*, 138, as well as in "Remaining Awake Through a Great Revolution," (1968 National Cathedral sermon) in Washington, *Testament of Hope*, 269–70.

[85]Martin Luther King, Jr., "The Man who was a Fool," in idem, *Strength to Love*, 70.

[86]Ibid.

cause of the "jet age" and "technological and scientific genius."[87] While King was deeply appreciative of this sense of closeness created by humans, he challenged America to develop a "moral and spiritual genius" to work in cooperation with its technological and scientific genius for the sake of interdependence:

> Through our scientific genius we have made of the world a neighborhood; now through our moral and spiritual genius we must make of it a brotherhood.[88]

King articulated his sense of interdependence in specifically *moral* language, particularly with the deontological term "ought."

> Whatever affects one directly affects all indirectly. I can never be what I ought to be until you are what you ought to be, and you can never be what you ought to be until I am what I ought to be.[89]

In this quotation King rearticulated DeWolf's principle of social devotion, but in his own particular manner. The difference between the two can be seen most clearly if we look to King's immediate usage of a concrete social illustration, taken most often from the crisis between Negroes and whites in America, to demonstrate the usefulness of the claim in a social situation of oppression.

> All humanity is involved in a single process, and all men are brothers. To the degree that I harm my brother, no matter what he is doing to me, to that extent I am harming myself. For example, white men often refuse federal aid to education in order to avoid giving the Negro his rights; but because all men are brothers they cannot deny Negro children without harming their own. They end, all efforts to the contrary, by hurting themselves. Why is this? Because men are brothers. If you harm me, you harm yourself.[90]

[87]Ibid., 138.
[88]Ibid.
[89]Ibid., 70.
[90]King, *Stride Toward Freedom*, 106.

While I would criticize King's male-exclusive language as drawing a
human moral universe that is too small (in other words, exclusively and
explicitly "male"),[91] I note that King was able to tie this personalistic
ethical principle into his immediate social battle for the rights and dignity of Negroes. King desired America to move beyond its technological
and scientific genius to the moral and spiritual genius of an "ethical
commitment" to "brotherhood."[92] The term "brotherhood," in this context can be understood to mean that *state of loving recognition of human
interdependence created by the ethical commitment to full citizenship
rights and human dignity for all persons*. "Brotherhood" for King was
the communal "ought," the moral telos that DeWolf and personalism
helped him to articulate. Moreover, King's ideal of "brotherhood" adhered closely to DeWolf's third and final law, the principle of the ideal
of community.

> Every person ought to form all of his ideals and values in loyalty
> to his ideal of what the whole community ought to become; and
> when possible to participate responsibly in groups to help them
> similarly form and choose all their ideals and values.[93]

King contributed his vision of the ideal community, which he called
variously "brotherhood," "integration," or "the beloved community," as
an ideal of the interdependent context of American communities. He was
also engaged, through massive nonviolent demonstrations as well as
through his speeches and sermons, in the *responsible formation* of the
ideal American community. Martin Luther King Jr.'s speech "I Have a
Dream" has been appropriated in recent times as a particularly evocative
symbol of the ideal American community.[94] Therefore, without diminishing King's unique way of wedding his particular social struggle to the

[91]My perspective, of course, is informed by my own historical location in the
late 1980s and early 1990s, whereas King wrote and spoke to a prefeminist era
audience that, on the whole, was not concerned about such things.

[92]King, "Remaining Awake," found in Washington, *Testament of Hope*, 26.

[93]DeWolf, *Responsible Freedom*, 171.

[94]I must qualify this statement by drawing attention to the fact that some
recent American appropriation of the King "Dream" has been to silence and
dismiss his radical social critique and to utilize King's charisma as a power to
bolster confidence in a status quo social policy. For a fine analysis of recent

philosophical framework of personalism, DeWolf stated that his own work and that of King were remarkably close:

> At nearly all points his system of positive theological belief was identical to mine and occasionally I find his language following closely the special terms of my own lectures and writings. [95]

King was deeply influenced by the content, eclectic style, and ethical norms of DeWolf's personalism. As he attempted to address the problems of racism that he confronted, he repeatedly turned to the ideals and ethical norms embodied in the laws of DeWolf and Brightman. King's articulation of these personalistic principles, however, was wedded to something else that enabled him to engage effectively in social action, namely, a *philosophy of nonviolence*. Muelder, Steinkraus, and DeWolf agree that it was King's ability to synthesize personalism with nonviolence that made his philosophy unique. Before proceeding to a further discussion of King's understanding of nonviolence, I want to investigate two underlying philosophical influences found both in personalism and in King's thought, namely, the work of Immanuel Kant and G. F. W. Hegel. My discussion of both figures will not take the form of a summary of their own work, but will describe the manner in which they were taught to King by the personalists and will describe King's own understanding of Kant and Hegel, starting with his notes from graduate school.

---

conservative" political manipulations of King's "Dream" in this manner, see Jesse L. Jackson's sermon, "Protecting the Legacy: The Challenge of Dr. Martin Luther King, Jr.," in idem, *Straight from My Heart* (Philadelphia: Fortress, 1987).

[95]L. Harold DeWolf, "Martin Luther King, Jr., as Theologian," in Garrow, *King*, 1. 266.

4

PHILOSOPHICAL
INFLUENCES: KANT,
HEGEL, AND NONVIOLENCE

Four primary themes in Kant's philosophical system exerted an important influence over the thought of the Boston Personalists who taught King: Kant's doctrine of knowledge, the idea of the moral nature of the person, the existence of a moral law, and the primacy of autonomy. Although all four themes have some bearing on King's own formulation of dignity and personhood, I shall focus on Kant's discussion of the moral nature of the person and its claims about human dignity. I shall also examine Hegel's philosophical influence and King's synthesis of Gandhian nonviolence as elements that constitute King's philosophical background.

Kant's Moral Nature of the Person

In his *Foundations of the Metaphysics of Morals* Kant developed a view of the person that became foundational to King's thought. Kant elaborated an understanding of human persons as "rational beings" and as morally "objective ends."[1] King often quoted Kant's declaration of persons as ends, for in this declaration King saw a demand for respect of persons, regardless of race or social status.

Kant began the second section of the *Foundations of the Metaphysics of Morals* with the claim that all "moral concepts have their seat and origin entirely a priori in reason."[2] The "will," or "practical reason," is the human capacity to "act according to laws, i.e., according to principles."[3] Kant is interested in advancing morality beyond "common moral judgement" or "popular philosophy" to a "metaphysics"[4] that pertains only to these principles and is not constrained by empirical data. The will is that "faculty of choosing only that which reason, independently of inclination, recognizes as practically necessary, i.e., the good."[5] The will is constrained by objective principles of reason, or a *command of reason*" that Kant calls an "imperative."[6] These imperatives are expressed by an "ought," which articulates its relationship to the will as one of "constraint":[7]

> Imperatives say that it would be good to do or to refrain from doing something, but they say it to a will which does not always do something simply because it is presented as a good thing to do.[8]

Kant's concept of the categorical imperative was significant in King's notion of dignity. Kant presented the categorical imperative as "an action as of itself objectively necessary, without regard to any other end."[9] The categorical imperative pertains to actions taken to be objectively necessary, rather than fulfilling a subjective end.

One of Kant's formulations of the categorical imperative addressed the topic of human dignity directly by utilizing the language of "ends and means." It arose after Kant had carefully distinguished between what

[1]Kant, *Foundations*, 52, 53.
[2]Ibid., 32.
[3]Ibid., 34.
[4]Ibid., 33.
[5]Ibid., 34.
[6]Ibid.
[7]Ibid.
[8]Ibid.
[9]Ibid., 36.

ne called "subjective ends" which "rest on incentives," and "objective
ends" which "depend on motives valid for every rational being."[10] Kant
was interested in determining whether there was "something the existence of which in itself had absolute worth, something which, as an end
in itself, could be a ground of definite laws."[11] He found his answer by
turning to human beings or rational beings as that end which has absolute worth and value in and of itself. "Now I say, man and, in general,
every rational being exists as an end in himself and not merely as a
means arbitrarily used by this or that will."[12]

Kant proceeded to clarify this initial proposal by distinguishing between "things"—whose "existence does not depend on our will but on
nature" and which have only "relative worth as means"—and "persons"—
who are "rational beings. . . because their nature indicates that they are
ends in themselves."[13] Persons have an absolute worth as "objective ends"
or "beings whose existence in itself is an end."[14] On this basis Kant
could declare what he calls a "supreme practical principle and a categorical imperative for the human will" that is grounded in the presupposition that "rational nature exists as an end in itself."[15] That supreme
practical principle is the famous casting of the categorical imperative so
influential to Boston Personalism and King: "Act so that you treat humanity, whether in your own person or in that of another, always as an
end and never as a means only."[16]

Kant called this "principle of humanity" the "supreme limiting condition on freedom of the actions of each man."[17] He believed this because
it applied "universally" to "all rational beings generally and experience
does not suffice to determine anything about them," and because humanity should be "thought of as an objective end which should constitute the
supreme limiting condition of all subjective ends, whatever they may
be."[18] For Kant, this principle arises from "pure reason."[19] Thus every

[10]Ibid., 52.
[11]Ibid.
[12]Ibid.
[13]Ibid., 53.
[14]Ibid.
[15]Ibid.
[16]Ibid., 54.
[17]Ibid., 55.
[18]Ibid., 56.
[19]Ibid.

rational being is to be regarded as "giving universal law through all the maxims of its will, so that it may judge itself and its actions from this standpoint."[20] Kant went on to describe the "systematic union of different rational beings through common laws" as a "realm of ends" or what others have translated as a "Kingdom of Ends."[21] Rational beings belong to this "realm of ends as a member" by giving "universal laws in it [the realm of ends] while also being subject to these laws."[22] This realm of ends is particularly pertinent to an understanding of King's thought because of the way in which Kant distinguished between *price* and *dignity* within the realm of ends:

> In the realm of ends everything has either a *price* or a *dignity*. Whatever has a price can be replaced by something as its equivalent; on the other hand, whatever is *above all price, and therefore admits of no equivalent, has a dignity*. [my emphasis][23]

For Kant "morality and humanity, so far as it is capable of morality, alone have dignity."[24] Human beings esteem and respect that which lies beyond "market price" because of its "intrinsic worth" or "dignity."[25] Dignity, so defined, is to be recognized as the esteem and valuation that goes "infinitely beyond any price, with which it cannot in the least be brought into competition or comparison without, as it were, violating its holiness."[26] The basis for such an understanding of dignity lies in "participation" or "legislation" in the realm of ends; this is afforded every rational being in giving universal laws.[27] Rational beings participate in the legislation of laws because it is the destiny of human nature to participate, "free from all laws of nature and obedient only to those

---

[20]Ibid.

[21]Ibid., 58. "Kingdom of Ends" is found in H. J. Paton's translation and analysis of Immanuel Kant, *Groundwork of the Metaphysic of Morals* (New York: Harper Torchbooks, 1956) 35–36.

[22]Ibid., 59.

[23]Ibid., 60.

[24]Ibid.

[25]Ibid.

[26]Ibid., 60–61.

[27]Ibid., 61.

which he [the rational being] himself gives."[28] Kant named this rational freedom "autonomy." Autonomy, therefore, stands at the heart of Kant's ideal of dignity:

> The legislation which determines all worth must therefore have a dignity, i.e., unconditional and incomparable worth. For the esteem which a rational being must have for it, only the word "respect" is a suitable expression. Autonomy is thus the basis of the dignity of both human nature and every rational nature.[29]

Although King had studied Kant's epistemology extensively in the *Critique of Pure Reason*,[30] it appears that he also studied Kant's belief in the moral dignity of persons—the second formulation of the categorical imperative—as it was restated in Brightman's law of altruism: "Each person ought to respect all other persons as ends in themselves, and, as far as possible, to co-operate with others in the production and enjoyment of shared values."[31]

King heard more specifically of Kant's influence on Boston Personalism in DeWolf's class on personalism:

> [On Kant's Ethical Contribution to Personalism]
> 1. Kant's formal laws are acknowledged by many Personalists
> 2. *Every person is to be treated as an end and not as a mere means*
> 3. Kant taught that he had an interest in international relations.[32]

---

[28]Ibid.

[29]Ibid.

[30]King's study of Kant's writings was extensive. My archival research uncovered an exhaustive year, 1950, in which doctoral candidate Martin King struggled through a course on Kant. He did well, impressing his teacher with his analysis of synthetic and analytic judgments from the *Critique of Pure Reason*, and receiving an A– for the course. As one reads through King's notes on Kant, it becomes apparent that at Boston University a knowledge of this particular *Critique* was essential towards understanding the claims of Boston Personalism.

[31]Brightman, *Moral Laws*, 223.

[32]King, "Notes on Personalism.

King later employed the above mentioned formulation of the categorical imperative many times when critiquing segregation as a depersonalizing system that treats Negroes as things and not as persons:

> Segregation stands diametrically opposed to the principle of the sacredness of human personality. Immanuel Kant said in one formulation of the *Categorical Imperative* that "all men must be treated as *ends* and never as mere *means*." The tragedy of segregation is that it treats men as means rather than ends, and thereby reduces them to things rather than persons.[33]

King used various versions of this quotation countless times; it even appeared in 1967 in *Where Do We Go From Here: Chaos or Community?*[34] Yet King used more than this particular formulation of Kant's categorical imperative as he battled the system of segregation. King also appealed to Kant's third formulation of the categorical imperative—"Act according to the maxim which can at the same time makes itself a universal law"[35]—when he articulated standards of justice necessary for remedying the "racist legal system of the South":

> It is obvious, then, that what is needed is a reforming of the racist legal system of the South in such a way as to effectuate *substantive justice* within the procedural framework of the instrumentalities of law and order. By *substantive justice*, I mean that noble societal touchstone which involves reference to a criterion or set of values which is higher than or superior to statutory or procedural law. Such great philosophical thinkers as Aristotle, Hume, Kant, and Roscoe Pound have given us to know that this substantive justice is the ultimate standard of moral conduct and is consonant with the principle of giving every man his due. . . . Kant emphasized the democratic and egalitarian flavor of distributive justice, indicated that the final criterion of whether any action is in accord with such justice is the test of whether the standard drawn out of the particular action is acceptable as a universal principle for all mankind.[36]

[33]King, "Ethical Demands," 119.

[34]King, *Where Do We Go*, 97.

[35]Kant, *Foundations*, 63.

[36]Martin Luther King, Jr., "Address to Atlanta Press Club," 10 November 1965, Martin Luther King, Jr. Center Archives, Atlanta, GA, 13.

In King's reference to Kant lies an appeal to a "higher law" above the statutory, and therefore racist, laws of the South. King's concept of substantive justice could rely on Kant's understanding of moral laws because of their turn to a *universal standard* by which all particular laws and actions could be judged. I interpret this universal standard as King's way of describing Kant's universal laws. For King, however, the appeal to a universal standard could not be merely for the sake of demonstrating the primacy and autonomy of reason, as it was for Kant; King appealed to a universal standard also for the sake of granting substantive justice and citizenship rights to oppressed Negroes in the South.

King did not appropriate Kant uncritically, for he disagreed with Kant's view of freedom. Kant viewed freedom as "freedom of the will," a thing "presupposed as the property of the will of all rational beings."[37] King directly objected to this view of freedom, because it abstracted freedom from the entire person:

> A second reason why segregation is morally wrong is that it deprives man of that quality which makes him man, namely freedom. The very character of the life of man demands freedom. In speaking of freedom at this point I am not referring to the freedom of a thing called the will. The very phrase, "freedom of the will," *abstracts freedom from the person to make it an object; and an object almost by definition is not free. But freedom cannot be abstracted from the person, who is always subject as well as object and who himself still does the abstracting. So I am speaking of the freedom of man, the whole man, and not the freedom of a function called the will.* [my emphasis][38]

To speak of "freedom of the will" was to separate the whole person from a particular function of that person, valuing the *function* of that person rather than the person him or herself. Such abstraction, for King, would be depersonalizing because it would give value to an object, the quality of freedom, rather than value and dignity to the persons demanding their own freedom. Freedom therefore had to be freedom for the entire person. It is interesting that King would critique Kant's view of freedom by using a Kantian argument. King could criticize Kant so

---

[37]Kant, *Foundations*, 74–75.
[38]King, "America's Chief Moral Dilemma."

confidently because of his adherence to the principles of personality as elucidated by Boston Personalists and because of the concrete demands for an embodied understanding of such concepts as "freedom" and "justice" that the civil rights struggle imposed.

King and Hegel

King claimed to have been greatly influenced by the philosophy of G. F. W. Hegel, especially by three areas of Hegel's thought: his notion that "the truth is the whole," his dialectical methodology, and his philosophy of history.

King's class notes reveal more precisely both the manner in which he was taught Hegel's philosophy and the parts of King's philosophy which he claimed were "Hegelian." King's class notes from his course on the history of philosophy at the University of Pennsylvania in 1949–1950 show an intensive introduction to Hegel's thought as a whole.[39] To give a complete account of King's initial course on Hegel would go beyond the scope of this discussion. It is enough simply to mention that King's notes reveal exposure to Hegel's philosophy of logic, nature, and Mind. In this course King was introduced to two of the three Hegelian concepts influential in King's own philosophical construction: namely, the truth is the whole and dialectical methodology. There is no mention that he was introduced to Hegel's philosophy of history at this point.

King learned that Hegel followed Fichte and Schelling in their fundamental idealism:

> Hegel agrees with Fichte and Schelling that Ultimate Reality is Absolute Mind or Spirit which passes through stages of development in time, and becomes conscious of itself in human reason. Yet the Absolute is timeless, eternal, or all-embracing, and a self-completed whole.[40]

King's notes move quickly to a basic conception of the dialectic:

[39]King, "Class Notes on Hegel.
[40]Ibid., 27.

Hegel professes this process by means of a logical method which he calls the *dialectic*—how everything is connected in principle to everything else, and helps to constitute the whole. "*The truth is the whole.*"[41]

The notion of the "whole," as King learned it, described a "relationship of whole to parts" in an organic fashion:

> Any part of a whole is what it is because of its relation to the system as a whole, and to the other parts. Every part is determined by its relations to everything else. This is the *organic theory of Truth and Reality.*[42]

Everything, according to King's notes, must therefore be seen in accordance with this whole, rather than in terms of its separate, unrelated parts. This whole may be called the "Absolute," seen not as a creator apart from the world, but rather "the Absolute *is* the world."[43] Arising from this concept of the whole and the Absolute in Hegel's thought were the particular ways Hegel used the terms "concrete" and "abstract":

> If you look at a thing by itself apart from its relationships, you are looking at it *abstractly.* If, on the contrary, you consider it in its organic relationships, you view it *concretely.* Hegel distinguishes between an "abstract" and a "concrete universal." The "Absolute" of Schelling and Spinoza is an "abstract universal." It is mere identity. One can only say of it that it is. All specific difference would be limitation, and so have to be left out of it. This is why Hegel compares Spinoza's Absolute with the Lion's Den in Aesop's fable, and why he says of Schelling's Absolute that it's like "the midnight in which all cats are black." Hegel's own Absolute is wholly concrete. It is *all reality comprehended within a whole,* not some thing apart from other things.[44]

[41]Ibid.
[42]Ibid.
[43]Ibid., 28.
[44]Ibid., 27.

King's notes reveal what Ansbro has called the "Kierkegaard interpretation and criticism of Hegel"[45] prevalent among Boston Personalists in general. There is also a Marxist reduction of the complex subtlety of Hegel's concept of a dialectic into a simple triad—thesis, antithesis, and synthesis—shown in a brief sample taken from King's class notes: "Hegel's dialectic shows that any thesis implies its antithesis, and that the two are united in a higher synthesis."[46] This reduction of Hegel's dialectic to a triadic notion runs throughout King's notes and appears to serve as a useful pedagogical device for understanding Hegel:

> The Absolute Idea passes through a dialectic of many triads, each of which has its own thesis, antithesis, and synthesis. In the thesis a certain aspect of reality is revealed. In the antithesis a contrasting aspect appears. And the two are Aufgehobung [*sic*] in a higher synthesis. The synthesis, again, gives rise to a new triad, and that to another in time. There are triads within triads. Every member of every triad is the Absolute. According to Hegel, the dialectic is the actual order which the Absolute follows. The most general triad has Logic as thesis, Nature as antithesis, and Mind or Spirit as Synthesis.[47]

King learned of Hegel's specific influence on Boston Personalism in DeWolf's course on personalism. King's notes reveal the following:

1. In method Hegel has suggested an empirical logic of coherence.
2. A metaphysic which is dynamic through and through The Absolute is process.
3. His doctrine is one of idealism, the Absolute is Geist.
4. Coherence is the criterion of ethics.
5. Coherence is the criterion of aesthetic values.
6. The self is a unity in complexity.

---

[45]Ansbro, *King*, 127. Ansbro finds (p. 299) in Boston Personalism an acceptance of Kierkegaard's criticism of Hegel for being a "pantheist," as well as a mistaken view of Hegel's system as swallowing up the individual in the whole. King's notes reveal that he was taught that Hegel was a "rationalistic pantheistic idealist" ("Class Notes on Hegel," 28).

[46]King, "Class Notes on Hegel," 28.

[47]Ibid.

7. History is a quest for coherence.

His [Hegel's] pantheism is abhorrent to all Personalists moreover, the militarism that he has at times set forth is abhorrent to Personalists.[48]

At this stage we find that King was introduced to Hegel's notion of history and that Boston Personalists found many of Hegel's ideas useful in their own philosophical enterprise.

King received a more thorough reading of Hegel in Brightman's course on Hegel. Brightman himself was considerably influenced by Hegel's dialectic and "interpreted all experience in terms of the basic structure of the Hegelian dialectic."[49] Ansbro quotes Brightman's *Problem of God* to support this claim:

Everything which exists stands in contrast with something else. . . every thesis implies some sort of antithesis. . . every opposition leads to a higher level of life, and every struggle points to a higher meaning or synthesis.[50]

King studied three of Hegel's primary texts during the course: *Phenomenology of Mind, Philosophy of History,* and *Philosophy of Right.*[51] Peter Bertocci, who replaced Brightman after his death, recounted to Ansbro that King "almost took over the class" in his enthusiastic appraisal of Hegel's notion of the "dependence of the master on the slave for his consciousness of himself as master"[52] found in the *Phenomenology of Mind.*[53] Such a notion validated King's concept of "the value of community and the futility of any attempt by any individual or group to dominate another."[54]

[48]King, "Notes on Personalism."

[49]Ansbro, *King,* 127.

[50]Edgar S. Brightman, *The Problem of God* (New York: Abingdon, 1930) 135, quoted in Ansbro, *King,* 127.

[51]King (*Stride Toward Freedom,* 100) mentioned reading these books.

[52]Ansbro, *King,* 298 n. 63.

[53]G. W. F. Hegel, *Phenomenology of Mind* (trans. J. Baillie; New York: Macmillan, 1955) 236–37.

[54]Ansbro, *King,* 298.

From this Hegel course King also learned to affirm that "growth comes through struggle."[55] King found in Hegel a reassuring echo of his grandfather Williams's dictum that "progress never comes without challenge," and King found in the notion of a dialectic a satisfying philosophical and metaphysical description of historical conflict. For King this dialectic became a way of viewing the civil rights struggle in general and the nonviolence movement in particular. In *Stride Toward Freedom*, King proclaimed the way of nonviolence to be the "synthesis" of two opposing alternatives, "acquiescence and violence":

> Like the synthesis in Hegelian philosophy, the principle of nonviolent resistance seeks to reconcile the truths of two opposites—acquiescence and violence—while avoiding the extremes and immoralities of both.[56]

This casting of the nonviolent movement in Hegelian language also reveals King's awareness of the deep nuances of the notion of synthesis or *Aufhebung* as described in Hegel's *Philosophy of History*. Hegel saw *Aufhebung* as "annulment, a preservation, and also an elevation":[57]

> For Thought is that Universal—that Species which is immortal, which preserves identity with itself. The particular form of Spirit not merely passes away in the world by natural causes in Time, but is annulled in the automatic self-mirroring activity of consciousness. Because this annulling is an activity of Thought, *it is at the same time conservative and elevating in its operation.* [my emphasis][58]

As in other cases, King was able to take the concept of a Hegelian dialectic outside of the graduate classroom and make it applicable to his struggle for human dignity and civil rights. He applied the notion of thesis, antithesis, and synthesis in his evaluations of communism and capitalism. He cast the two as thesis and antithesis:

[55]King, *Stride Toward Freedom*, 101.
[56]Ibid., 213.
[57]Ansbro, *King*, 122.
[58]Hegel, *Philosophy of History*, 77.

The great weakness of Karl Marx is right here; that he did recognize that means and ends must cohere. Capitalism fails to recognize that life is social. Marxism fails to recognize that life is individual. Truth is found neither in the rugged individualism of capitalism nor in the impersonal collectivism of Communism. The *kingdom of God is found in a synthesis that combines the truths of these two opposites.* [my emphasis][59]

Philosophically, the expression "kingdom of God" for King is a powerful *synthesis* of the partial truths of the opposites of capitalism and communism. I believe that King means the following: the term "kingdom of God" denotes a higher and more coherent (in the personalist sense of all-inclusive) sense of truth than either capitalism or communism can offer. In *Strength to Love* King called the kingdom of God "neither the thesis of individual enterprise nor the antithesis of collective enterprise, but a *synthesis which reconciles the truth of both* (my emphasis)."[60]

King so enthusiastically embraced Hegel's concept of a dialectical progression that it became the standard way that meetings of the Southern Christian Leadership Conference were conducted:

"He [King] had a remarkable facility for sitting through long, contentious meetings, and then summarizing what everybody had said and synthesizing that" into a conclusion that appealed to all. That skill was not happenstance, but a repeated, practical application of the Hegelian method of thesis-antithesis-synthesis that King had been fascinated with and attached to ever since graduate school. Andrew Young understood the format. "He would want somebody to express as radical a view as possible and somebody to express as conservative a view as possible. We kind of did this sort of like a game and it almost always fell to my lot to express the conservative view. . . . He figured. . . *the wider variety of opinions you got, the better chance you had of extracting the truth* from that." [my emphasis][61]

[59]Martin Luther King, Jr., "Speech at the Frogmore Retreat," 14 November 966; Martin Luther King, Jr. Center Archives, Atlanta, GA.

[60]King, *Strength to Love*, 103.

[61]Garrow, *Bearing The Cross*, 464–65.

King had appropriated the dialectic (as he understood it) as a *way of processing thought, debate, and arriving at acceptable conclusions*. It was not merely an intellectual "game," as Andrew Young implied, but a method and way of thinking that King considered necessary and fruitful.

Hegel's philosophy of history contains the notions of "world-Historical Individuals" who have "insight into the requirements of the time—what was ripe for development,"[62] or the "*Zeitgeist*." I agree with Ansbro that King utilized this notion to interpret the actions of Rosa Parks, the woman who refused to give up her seat to a white passenger and whose arrest precipitated the Montgomery bus boycott.

> She was planted by her personal sense of dignity and self-respect. She was anchored to that seat by the accumulated indignities of days gone by and the boundless aspirations of generations yet unborn. She was a victim of both the forces of history and the forces of destiny. She had been tracked down by the *Zeitgeist*—the spirit of the time.[63]

Like Ansbro, moreover, I believe that King even applied the insight of being "in the grip of the Zeitgeist" to himself.[64] King believed that the *Zeitgeist* for freedom had captured not only him individually, but the Negro in general, as he stated in his Nobel reception speech:

> Something within the Negro has reminded him of his birthright of freedom, and something without has reminded him that it can be gained. Consciously and unconsciously, he has been caught up by the *Zeitgeist*, and he is moving with a sense of great urgency toward the promised land of racial justice.[65]

A careful study of King's texts reveals what King had said about himself, namely, that Hegel's thought held an important place in King's

---

[62]Hegel, *Philosophy of History*, 30.

[63]King, *Stride Toward Freedom*, 44.

[64]See Ansbro's section on *Zeitgeist* in *King*, 126.

[65]Martin Luther King, Jr., "Nobel Reception Speech" at Dinkler Plaza Hotel Atlanta, 27 January 1965; Martin Luther King, Jr. Center Archives, Atlanta, GA

philosophy. King did not accept everything about Hegel, however. King followed the Kierkegaardian-personalist tradition of condemning Hegel for "pantheism" and "absolute idealism": "His [Hegel's] absolute idealism was rationally unsound to me because it tended to swallow up the many in the one."[66]

King found inspiration in Hegel's determination to found a system of rational coherence." King's speeches and sermons articulated a point of view—that of Negroes—that America had not yet heard with such force and power. In this way the entire movement for human dignity and civil rights can be seen as adding to the "whole" or "Truth" of America. King spoke specifically of the nonviolent movement as being the emerging synthesis between acquiescence and violence.

King was able to apply with great facility selected elements of Hegel's dialectic, logic, and philosophy of history to the concrete social struggle of Negroes in the late 1950s and early 1960s because these resonated with his own interpretation of what was occurring historically. As a result of King's daily practical application of Hegel's idea, the reduced dialectic became more than an intellectual method and an accepted way of processing problems within the South Christian Leadership Conference. In this way, as with personalism, King was able to transcend a merely academic appreciation of ideas by directly applying the philosophical insights of *Zeitgeist* and of Hegel's dialectic to the struggle for human dignity.

Nonviolence

King's synthesis of personalism with nonviolence distinguishes his philosophical thought. His views on nonviolence have been exhaustively researched by numerous King scholars. Some of the best work on King's thought is in this area.[67] My task is not to duplicate their efforts, but to

---

[66]King, *Stride Toward Freedom*, 100–101.

[67]See Watley, *Roots of Resistance*; Adam Fairclough, "Martin Luther King, and the Quest for Nonviolent Social Change" in Garrow, *King*, 333–47; Shin eng Lee, "The Concept of Human Nature, Justice, and Nonviolence in the political Thought of Martin Luther King, Jr." (Ph.D. diss., New York University, 1979); Walter G. Mueldeter, "Martin Luther King, Jr.'s Ethics of Nonviolent Action," (paper presented at the King Center, Atlanta, 1985); Lois D. Wasserman, Martin Luther King, Jr.: The Molding of Nonviolence as a Philosophy and strategy, 1955–1963" (Ph.D. diss., Boston University, 1972); as well as Ansbro's discussion of "The Moral Obligation to Resist Collective Evil" in *King*, 111–63.

supplement them with my particular research in order to reveal the re-lationship between King's view of nonviolence and his understanding of human dignity. I shall demonstrate this relationship both by showing that King came to nonviolence as a strategy of synthesis that matured into a way of life and by relating concrete elements of King's nonviolent agenda to his view of human dignity through a chronological exegesis of King's texts.

Synthesis that Matured from Strategy to a Way of Life

Philosophically, King understood nonviolence as a Hegelian synthesis that could reconcile the two extreme options of oppressed persons—violence and acquiescence—into an effective means of protest for social change.[68] Nonviolence, in King's mind, balanced the violent resister's need to resist with the acquiescent person's need to resist in a nonaggressive fashion.[69] King saw immorality in both the nonresistance of the acquiescent and in the violence of the violent resister. Nonviolence embraced both, while at the same time "avoiding the extremes and immoralities of both."[70]

Part of the synthesis that comprised King's understanding of nonviolence also involved his appropriation of Mahatma Gandhi's profound views of nonviolence. David Garrow has traced King's evolution from a highly skeptical and critical attitude toward Gandhism and pacifism in general to his early talks with Glenn Smiley in Montgomery.[71] Garrow contends that King did not overtly demonstrate any strong interest in Gandhian principles of nonviolence until a long personal training period between Glenn Smiley and King:

> Smiley took an armful of books on nonviolence for their first meeting, and asked King about his familiarity with the doctrine. "I said to Dr. King," Smiley recalled, "'I'm assuming that you're very familiar and have been greatly influenced by Mahatma Gandhi.' And he was very thoughtful, and he said, 'As a matter of fact, no. I know who the man is. I have read some statements by him, and so on, but I will have to truthfully say'—and this is almost a direct

[68]King, *Stride Toward Freedom*, 213.
[69]Ibid.
[70]Ibid.
[71]Garrow, "Intellectual Development," 437–52.

quote. . .—'I will have to say that I know very little about the man.'" King stated that he nonetheless admired Gandhi, and Smiley described to King how the essence of nonviolence was a refusal to retaliate against evil, a refusal based on the realization that "the law of retaliation is the law of the multiplication of evil."[72]

Garrow's account goes on to say that this was the first of many long conversations that had a "profound effect on both King's thought and language" concerning Gandhian nonviolence.[73] Smiley reported to Garrow that King did not even use the word "nonviolence" at first, using instead the term "passive resistance."[74]

As I have examined the various texts from this early period in King's public life, I have been impressed with King's apparent attachment to the idea that the Montgomery bus boycott was a peaceful protest of "Christian people" using only the "weapon of protest."[75] This protest was not a violent one (King compares it to the violence of White Citizens' Councils), but one demonstrating the justice of the Negro's cause, its undeniable moral claim, and the practical application of Jesus' ethic of love from the Sermon on the Mount. The only tools with which these protesters would be armed were those of protest, justice, persuasion, and coercion.[76]

From the time of transition between using either of the terms "passive resistance" or "nonviolence" exclusively, I discovered only one text in which King uses both terms back to back.

We are not bitter. We are still preaching nonviolence. We are still using the weapon of love. We are still using the method of passive resistance.[77]

[72]Ibid., 444.

[73]Ibid., 443.

[74]Ibid.

[75]See Martin Luther King, Jr., "Holt Street Baptist Address," 5 December 1955, 1.

[76]Ibid., 1–2. It is interesting to note that the "tools of coercion" involve a reference to the "process of legislation" King felt necessary to make concrete changes in the segregated system.

[77]Martin Luther King, Jr., "Address to a Mass Meeting at Hope Street Baptist Church," Montgomery, AL, 22 March 1956; Martin Luther King, Jr. Center Archives, Atlanta, GA, 1.

It should be noted that Gandhi struggled with the best term for describing satyagraha or "holding to Truth." Gandhi, like King, moved through a stage of calling it "passive nonresistance," to "civil resistance," and eventually overthrew the term because of its emphasis on passivity, instead of the active protest that "nonviolent resistance" implied.[78]

As King read the works of Gandhi, his language became much more Gandhian. King appropriated many of Gandhi's fundamental ideas into his system of nonviolence. Of particular interest is the notion of noncooperation. Gandhi was convinced that persons oppressed by a system of government were morally obligated actively not to cooperate with that government:

> A citizen who barters with such a state shares in its corruption or lawlessness. . . . Rejection is as much an ideal as the acceptance of a thing. *It is as necessary to reject untruth as it is to accept truth. . . . Non-cooperation is a protest against an unwitting and unwilling participation in evil.*[79]

King's own phrase, "noncooperation with evil is as much a moral obligation as cooperation with good," has a similar ring.[80] King applied the concept to the Negro struggle for human dignity. For King, noncooperation with evil and following the principles of nonviolence enabled the practitioner to gain a deeper sense of dignity:

> This is not the drama of only one actor. More precisely, it is the chronicle of 50,000 Negroes who took to heart the principles of nonviolence, who learned to fight for their rights with the weapon of love, and who, in the process, acquired a new estimate of their own human worth.[81]

[78]See Mahatma Gandhi, *Indian Opinion*, 26 October 1907; *The Collected Works of Mahatma Gandhi* (21 vols.; Ahmdabad: Navajivan, 1961) 7. 304; idem, *Non-Violent Resistance*; idem, *Autobiography*.

[79]*The Essential Gandhi* (ed. Louis Fischer; New York: Random House, 1962) 166; quoted in Ansbro, *King*, 132.

[80]Martin Luther King, Jr., "Some Things We Must Do," sermon at Dexter Baptist Church, Montgomery, AL, 5 December 1957; Martin Luther King, Jr. Center Archives, Atlanta, GA, 19.

[81]King, *Stride Toward Freedom*, 9.

King sought to invigorate those who were passively acquiescent to the system of slavery. He called on them to "stand up" for their humanity:

> As I stated a few minutes ago, some people have lived with this thing [segregation] so long they have adjusted to it. They accept it. But that's also wrong. That's also evil. For the minute you accept an evil, you cooperate with it. Many of you accept segregation. You are a part of the perpetuation of segregation. Noncooperation with evil is as much a moral obligation as cooperation with good. So that isn't the way, just to acquiesce and resign and sit down and do nothing.[82]

For King, the only way to move from the evil of cooperative acquiescence with the evil system of segregation was to participate actively in nonviolent resistance. In his early public life King thought of nonviolent resistance as a method toward gaining greater freedom and dignity, as evidenced in the following:

> It [nonviolent resistance] is just as strong as the first method [violent resistance] because you do resist, but you do not sit down and resign yourself to the fate of oppression. You stand up and resist strongly, but without violence. I believe to the bottom of my heart that it is the greatest method open to the Negro as he struggles for freedom and justice in this nation. It is the greatest method open to oppressed people all over the world, whenever we use it. . . . It is one of the most powerful methods that has ever existed in this universe.[83]

King learned many other tenets of satyagraha from his study of Gandhi, of which the primary one was *ahimsa*, the principle of noninjury or renunciation of the will to kill or damage."[84] *Ahimsa* for Gandhi is a comprehensive principle" that consciously brings its practitioner to an awareness of the "deadly coil of himsa [the destruction of life]" in which human beings participate simply by living:

---

[82]King, "Some Things," 19.
[83]Ibid.
[84]Ansbro, *King*, 4.

Man cannot for a moment live without consciously or unconsciously committing outward himsa. The very fact of his living—eating, drinking, and moving about—necessarily involves some himsa, destruction of life, be it ever so minute.[85]

The best that a "votary [practitioner] of ahimsa" could do, in Gandhi's mind, was constantly to strive toward an inward attitude of *ahimsa* wherein "the spring of all actions is compassion."[86] The practitioner of *ahimsa* rejects internal violence of the spirit as well:

Not to hurt any living thing is no doubt a part of ahimsa. But it is its least expression. The principle of ahimsa is hurt by every evil thought, by undue haste, by lying, by hatred, by wishing ill to anybody.[87]

For Gandhi, *ahimsa* was the "positive and active state of love," or "Love-Force" that animated satyagraha.[88] Gandhi described this activity of love in satyagraha as "Soul-Force."[89] The practitioner of satyagraha, motivated by the active, noncooperating, and loving force of *ahimsa*, trusts that the opposition may be "converted by love."[90]

For Gandhi, one imbued with *ahimsa* opposed systems of tyrannical government, not individual persons.[91] Thus the spirit of *ahimsa* requires its practitioner to be "neither punitive nor vindictive nor based on malice or hatred."[92] Since *ahimsa* makes one aware of the "unity of all life,"[93] Gandhi insisted that one had to resist the evil system and not the persons representing that system, lest one harm oneself:

It is quite proper to resist and attack a system, but to resist and attack its author is tantamount to resisting and attacking oneself.

[85]Gandhi, *Autobiography*, 349.
[86]Ibid.
[87]Gandhi, *Non-Violent Resistance*, 41–42.
[88]Ibid., 6.
[89]Ibid.
[90]Gandhi, *Autobiography*, 347.
[91]Ibid., 276.
[92]Gandhi, *Non-Violent Resistance*, 161–62.
[93]Gandhi, *Autobiography*, 347.

For we are all tarred by the same brush, and are children of one and the same Creator, and as such the divine powers within us are infinite. To slight a single human being is to slight those divine powers, and thus to harm not only that being, but with him the whole world.[94]

Finally, Gandhi believed that one could not expect to make progress in *ahimsa*'s struggle against an evil system without suffering. Such suffering, from bodily harm or even death, was a "necessary condition for progress."[95] Gandhi also viewed suffering as part of the necessary "purification" that the satyagrahi, as well as the nation, needed in order to be free:

No country has ever risen without being purified through the fire of suffering. Mother suffers so that her child may live. The condition of wheat growing is that the seed grain should perish. Life comes out of death. Will India rise out of her slavery without fulfilling this eternal law of purification through suffering?[96]

King's speeches and sermons are filled with his own appropriation of Gandhi's thought about *ahimsa*. He was particularly interested in the notion of soul force being stronger than the brute and violent physical force that segregation could inflict on nonviolent resisters. In the following quotation, it is important to note how King reviews in his own particularly Christian way many of Gandhi's tenets concerning transforming the enemy with love, not harming the individual person, the necessity of suffering, and the power of soul force:

We must somehow stand up before our white brothers in this Southland, and see within them the image of God. No matter how bad they are, no matter what they do to us—no matter what they said about us, we must still believe that in the most recalcitrant segregationists there is the image of God. We keep on loving and we must believe that he can be transformed. . . . My friends, we must keep on believing that unearned suffering is redemptive. We

[94]Ibid., 276.
[95]Ansbro, *King*, 5.
[96]Gandhi, *Non-Violent Resistance*, 112.

must say to our white brothers all over the South who would try to
keep us down, we will match your capacity to inflict suffering with
our capacity to endure suffering. We will meet your physical force
with soul force.[97]

King's appropriation of Gandhi's thoughts concerning nonviolence is
significant to my argument because, as Negroes learned to practice these
methods, a new and deeper sense of dignity was gained. In one speech
King called the nonviolent protest of the Freedom Riders significant
because it created a "psychological forward thrust"[98] that had "fired the
imagination of the entire world."[99] The "prime impetus for this psychological change" had come from the "little people," the Negroes of Montgomery in their bus boycott.[100] King saw them as "nonviolent, serene
instruments of decisive action who demonstrated once and for all time,
the *Negro's ability to animate himself* and create a climate in which
justice would be rendered without benefit of skin coloration."[101] This
phrase demonstrates a transition in King's thinking from nonviolence as
a method to nonviolence as a way of life—a way that enabled downtrod-
den Negroes to animate themselves and gain a greater sense of dignity.

In a "Short Statement on Nonviolence" (1964) King develops the
phrase "the sword that heals" as a symbol of nonviolence. King uses
language that echoes Gandhi's words concerning nonviolence:

> Nonviolence is like a sword in that it strikes with power at hatred
> and evil, both inside a person and in society. It heals not by delib-
> erately injuring another, but by stimulating and challenging con-
> science and morality.[102]

Nonviolence heals in two ways for King. First, it "heals personally" by
asking individuals to confront themselves in the privacy of their own

[97]King, "Some Things," 19–20.

[98]Martin Luther King, Jr., "People in Action," 3 February 1962; Martin Luther
King, Jr. Center Archives, Atlanta, GA.

[99]Ibid, 2.

[100]Ibid.

[101]Ibid.

[102]Martin Luther King, Jr., "A Short Statement on Nonviolence," 1965; Martin Luther King, Jr. Center Archives, Atlanta, GA.

moral consciences.[103] This confrontation, in King's view, is redemptive because it leads to a changed life:

> Being nonviolent has dried up internal anxieties; renewed in them a sense of life purpose; changed their bitterness into forgiveness towards others and replaced vindictiveness with active good-will.[104]

King called this the "redemptive power" of the nonviolent sword. While King does not mention dignity specifically here, it is important to remember that nonviolence enabled a deeper sense of dignity, because it healed the person individually. From the above quotation I believe that King means that the redemption of those negative psychological traits such as anxiety, lack of purpose, bitterness, and vindictiveness involves their replacement by a lack of anxiety, purpose, forgiveness, and active good will as the necessary individual attributes of this new sense of dignity.

The second way that King saw nonviolence as a "sword that heals" was that it healed society. King noted that in the nonviolent movements in Mississippi, Birmingham, and Selma, society "saw nonviolent resistance stand with dignity against racial hatred."[105] Such dignified resistance captured the moral conscience of the nation, enabling society to progress from 1960 to 1965 in viewing "justice and opportunity for all Americans" as a "primary domestic matter."[106] For King, such a national concern "caused the emergence of a new, more sensitive dimension of social conscience."[107] Thus the dignifying nonviolent resistance of Negroes enabled the entire society to gain a more sensitive, more profoundly responsive moral conscience.

By 1965 King had developed a profound concern for the "disciplined cultivation of the power within our souls."[108] He appropriated Gandhi's thought about avoiding internal violence of spirit as a necessary way of life:

---

[103]Ibid., 2.

[104]Ibid.

[105]Ibid.

[106]Ibid.

[107]Ibid., 3.

[108]Martin Luther King, Jr., "Speech on Political Power," 1965; Martin Luther King, Jr. Center Archives, Atlanta, GA, 11.

The tactical non-violence which was sufficient in the past will be weighed in the balance and found wanting in the future. Men must begin to learn to love one another, not just restrain themselves from killing one another. The *non-violent attitude* will be every bit as important as the non-violent action.[109]

While King had mentioned as early as 1958 that "living through the actual experience of the protest, nonviolence became more than a method to which I gave intellectual assent; it became a commitment to a way of life,"[110] it is clear that by 1965 he had become a keen observer of even the most subtle forms of inner violence of spirit. King went on in the same speech to describe the ways in which a violent attitude is revealed and the need to change it:

Our speech must lose the harsh hostile tones which creep into our negotiations. Our eyes must soften their glances and be free of any residue of malice or resentment. This is not just a necessity for a non-violent movement, it is a necessity for the maintenance of human community.[111]

King spelled out the connection between dignity and nonviolence from the very start of the Montgomery bus boycott. In 1957 King wrote an article entitled "Nonviolence and Racial Justice" which stated that nonviolence enabled oppressed persons to wage their struggle "with dignity and discipline."[112] By avoiding "internal violence of the spirit," oppressed persons were able to "cut off the chain of hate" as they struggled for dignity.[113] Reflecting his increased awareness of Gandhi's thought on *himsa* and *ahimsa*, King called for the nonviolent resister to "project the ethics of love to the center of our lives."[114] I shall discuss King's views of love below. For now it is enough to note that the projection of the ethic of love into the center of one's life through nonviolent resistance

[109]Ibid.
[110]King, *Stride Toward Freedom*, 101.
[111]King, "Speech on Political Power," 11.
[112]See Washington, *Testament of Hope*, 9.
[113]Ibid., 8.
[114]Ibid.

enabled those struggling for human dignity to avoid bitterness within their own lives.[115]

In 1959 King spoke of the direct connection between nonviolent resistance and human dignity. In a speech before a high school audience he contrasted the degradation of being denied the right to vote with the dignifying power of nonviolent resistance:

> The denial of the vote not only denies the Negro of his constitutional rights—but what is even worse—it degrades him as a human being. And yet, even this degradation, which is only one of many humiliations of everyday life, is losing its ability to degrade. *For the Southern Negro is learning to transform his degradation into resistance. Nonviolent resistance. And by so doing he is not only achieving his dignity as a human being, he is advancing democracy in the South.* [my emphasis][116]

After the challenge of Stokely Carmichael's "Black Power" insurgency in 1965 and 1966 within the civil rights movement and the increasing disenchantment with nonviolence as an effective strategy for social change after 1966, King was forced to defend his adherence to nonviolence. King wrote that he was convinced that nonviolence offered the "only road to freedom for my people" for "practical, as well as moral reasons."[117] Furthermore, he spoke of nonviolence as having a mysterious "power" that could produce social change.[118] King critiqued marches that did not follow nonviolent discipline.

> Marching feet announce that the time has come for a given idea. When the idea is a sound one, the cause a just one, and the demonstration a righteous one, change will be forthcoming. But if any one of these conditions are not present, the power for change is missing also. A thousand people demonstrating for the right to use heroin would have little effect. By the same token, a group of ten

---

[115]Ibid.

[116]Martin Luther King, Jr., "Speech Before the Youth March for Integrated Schools," in Washington, *Testament of Hope*, 22.

[117]Martin Luther King, Jr., "Nonviolence: The Only Road to Freedom," *Ebony* (1966) 27–30; in Washington, *Testament of Hope*, 54.

[118]Washington, *Testament of Hope*, 59.

thousand marching in anger against a police station and cussing out
the chief of police will do very little to bring respect, dignity, and
unbiased law enforcement. Such a demonstration would only produce fear and bring about an addition of forces to the station and
more oppressive methods by the police.[119]

For King, nonviolence endowed marching feet with dignity because it
provided a high moral ground. Without nonviolence, marching simply
adds, in Gandhi's terms, to the forces of *himsa* and is ultimately self-
destructive.

King agreed with Gandhi that retaliatory violence only added to hatred. He would say repeatedly,

To meet hate with retaliatory hate would do nothing but intensify
the existence of evil in the universe. Hate begets hate; violence
begets violence; toughness begets a greater toughness. It is all a
descending spiral, and the end is destruction—for everybody.[120]

King maintained throughout his public career that ultimately nonviolence was the only choice between existence and destruction.[121] In doing
so he extended Gandhi's critique not only to the civil rights struggle, but
also to the entire world. King's view of the dignifying power of nonviolence moved him from a convenient wedding of nonviolence with the
ethics of Jesus taken from the Sermon on the Mount in his very earliest
public speeches to an increasingly comprehensive and all-embracing view
of nonviolence as a necessary way of life for everyone.

As King became more familiar with Gandhi's views on nonviolence,
his own views broadened significantly. King was particularly influenced
by Gandhi's concept of noncooperation, *ahimsa*, love, soul force, and the
redemptive power of unmerited suffering insofar as each of these concepts enabled the nonviolent resister to grow in dignity and self-respect.
King applied Gandhi's concepts in his own particular manner, that is, as
a Negro and Christian, to his developing philosophy of nonviolence.
King's view of nonviolence had a uniquely Christian tone, often appeal-

---

[119]Ibid.

[120]Martin Luther King, Jr., "The Current Crisis in Race Relations," 1958; in
Washington, *Testament of Hope*, 87.

[121]See Ansbro, *King*, 333 n. 136.

ing to such traditional Christian notions as the image of God when speaking of transforming the oppressor into a friend.

King synthesized Gandhian-influenced nonviolence with the claims of Boston Personalism within the framework of the teachings from his family and church community which had shaped his development from the start. Claims such as the "dignity of human personality" that King learned from Boston Personalists resonated with his family's strong tradition of somebodyness, and later with the claims for the sanctity of all life in Gandhi's formulations of *ahimsa*. The "inter-relatedness of all life" that King heard from DeWolf was echoed in Gandhi. The injunction from King's parents to "love whites as a Christian duty" found meaning in the struggle not to succumb to violence or acquiesce to racial injustice. Instead, utilizing what he had learned of Hegel's dialectic, King looked upon nonviolence as the necessary synthesis that would enable Negroes to resist injustice actively and without violence.

Nonviolence, in synthesis with the principled tenets of Boston Personalism, enabled King to present a comprehensive nonviolent agenda. This agenda called for the dignifying activity of resisting depersonalization through nonviolent resistance. It stated, in simple terms, that as the nonviolent practitioner learned to stand up to racial oppression nonviolently, to counter negative and destructive inner feelings and attitudes, and persuasively to transform the oppressor into a friend, he or she would also gain a heightened sense of self-respect and human dignity.

5

THEOLOGICAL FOUNDATIONS: KING'S VIEW OF HUMANITY AND LOVE

The concepts of the image of God and agape illuminate the theological foundations of King's thought concerning human dignity. Normally a theological investigation moves systematically through various traditionally recognized areas of analysis such as christology and ecclesiology. Due to the specific nature of this work, however, two aspects of theology as they relate to King's understanding of dignity are a more appropriate starting point: namely, theological anthropology seen in terms of King's doctrine of the image of God and theological ethics as observed in the primacy of agape within King's entire theological outlook.

Theological Anthropology

King's contribution to our theoretical understanding of human dignity cannot be fully understood without a careful look at his view of the human being. The previous two chapters have examined the philosophical bases of King's understanding of dignity with particular attention to the Boston Personalist understanding of the term "person." This chapter, however, explores the *theological* elements undergirding King's anthropology, specifically, his view of the image of God.

One of King's early research papers at Boston University, "How Modern Christians Should Think of Man," provides a suitable starting point.[1] King began the paper with the observation that his thinking was "going through a state of transition" between a "mild neo-orthodox view of man" and a "liberal view of man."[2] King attributed the "mild neo-orthodox" view to "certain experiences that I had in the South with the vicious race problem."[3] These experiences made it hard for King to believe "in the essential goodness of man."[4] King went on to affirm that his "liberal leaning," however, came from "another branch of the same root" by "noticing the gradual improvements in this same race problem I came to see some noble possibilities in human nature."[5] King attributed his liberal leaning to a "great imprint" left upon him by his training in "many liberal theologians," and "my ever present desire to be optimistic about human nature."[6]

Just beneath the surface of these statements lie revealing aspects of King's early understanding of human nature. First, King used the expression "neo-orthodox" to describe his own understanding of the views of human nature espoused by Reinhold Niebuhr in the first volume of *The Nature and Destiny of Man*. Ansbro, Zepp, and Smith have given excellent renderings of the important influence of Reinhold Niebuhr's theological anthropology on King's thought.[7] Without repeating their findings unnecessarily, I shall briefly review Niebuhr's critical claim that humanity is not "essentially reason" as the "modern mind" casts it.[8] Rather humans enjoy a sense of freedom and self-transcendence that lies be-

[1]King, "Modern Christians." The date of this work is unknown, as is the teacher (although I suspect it is DeWolf, based on the comment). For the work however, he received an A with the comment, "Very well done, you preserve balance throughout."

[2]Ibid., 1.

[3]Ibid.

[4]Ibid.

[5]Ibid.

[6]Ibid.

[7]Ansbro, *King*, chap. 3, esp. 87–90; Smith and Zepp, *Search for the Beloved Community*, 71–97. Both of these studies present thoughtfully researched information concerning the influence of Reinhold Niebuhr on King's thought.

[8]Niebuhr, *Nature and Destiny*, 123–24.

yond the narrow confines of idealism and naturalism as he defines them.[9] Niebuhr wants to claim that a properly conceived understanding of the human being is the Christian view of "man," which he sees as rooted in doctrines of the image of God and creature.[10] For Niebuhr, there are three important aspects to this Christian understanding of humanity.

First, within the doctrine of the image of God "the height of self-transcendence in man's spiritual status" is emphasized.[11] Second, the doctrine of the human as creature "insists on man's weakness, dependence, and finiteness, on his involvement in the necessities and contingencies of the natural world, without, however, regarding this finiteness as, of itself, a source of evil in man."[12] Third, Niebuhr's doctrine of sin "affirms that the evil in man is a consequence of his inevitable though not necessary unwillingness to acknowledge his dependence, to accept his finiteness and to admit his insecurity, as unwillingness which involves him in the vicious circle of accentuating the insecurity from which he seeks escape."[13]

King also used a Niebuhrian understanding of the term "liberal" in the sense that being "liberal" meant affirming the "essential goodness in man" while ignoring "man as sinner." L. Harold DeWolf's criticism of Niebuhr's generalization of the term "liberal" in his book *The Case for Theology in Liberal Perspective* (1959) had an influence on King.[14]

---

[9]Niebuhr sees "naturalism" as destroying the self because it fails to validate individuality by emphasizing consanguinity and other natural forces of social uniformity as the only basis of meaning" (*Nature and Destiny*, 69). He defines "idealism" as the identification of the self with reason, failing to recognize the "actual self" which is "a unity of thought and life in which thought remains in organic unity with all the organic processes of finite existence" (p. 75). Failing to recognize "to what degree finiteness remains a basic characteristic of human spirituality," the idealist view of self affirms "transcendence" of the mind, eventually equating "the highest reaches of the conscious mind with a divine or absolute mind, or at least with some socially or politically conceived universal mind" (p. 76).

[10]Ibid., 150–51.

[11]Ibid., 150.

[12]Ibid.

[13]Ibid. Niebuhr describes "Man as Sinner" more fully in chapters 7 and 8 (pp. 178–240).

[14]L. Harold DeWolf, *The Case for Theology in Liberal Perspective* (Philadelphia: Westminster, 1959).

King, moreover, was affirming what his teachers had taught concerning their own liberal tradition. At both Crozer College and Boston University, King's mentors, George Davis, Edgar Brightman, and L. Harold DeWolf, called themselves "liberal."[15] Within this moderate liberal tradition, King also embraced the social gospel of Walter Rauschenbusch, as he encountered it at Crozer.[16]

King solved the dilemma of this transitional period in his thought by attempting to "synthesize the best in liberal theology with the best in neo-orthodox theology."[17] Despite a disclaimer about his "limited" knowledge of neoorthodox theology, King criticized it for "one-sided generalizations."[18] King never elaborated on what exactly he meant by "one-sided generalizations." He immediately affirmed, however, neoorthodoxy's "emphasis on sin and the necessity for perpetual repentance in the life of man."[19] He did so by criticizing liberal theology's propensity to "too easily cast aside the term sin, failing to realize that many of our present ills result from the *sins* of men."[20] Here, again, he did not name specific liberal theologians or liberal theological texts to back his claim. It is important to notice in this criticism of both neoorthodoxy and liberal theology King's appropriation of the dialectical method. King said both "yes" and "no" to what he had been educated to view as two contending schools of thought. He moved forward with the assurance that *his* anthropology would be a *synthesis* of the best in both neoorthodox theology and liberal theology.

[15]See L. Harold DeWolf, *Present Trends in Christian Thought* (New York: Association Press, 1960) in which DeWolf delineates various forms of "liberal." He describes Martin Luther King, Jr. as a "moderate liberal" (p. 18) alongside Walter G. Muelder and Walter Rauschenbusch.

[16]Much excellent material has been written about the influence of Rauschenbusch on King (see Ansbro, *King*, and Zepp and Smith, *Search for the Beloved Community* in particular). It is unclear whether King understood Rauschenbusch to be affirming the goodness in human beings and ultimate perfectability or whether Rauschenbusch also embraced quite strongly the doctrine of "original sin." See Ronald G. White, Jr., *Liberty and Justice for All* (New York: Harper & Row, 1990) for other materials concerning African-American contributors to the social gospel movement.

[17]King, "Modern Christians," 1.

[18]Ibid.

[19]Ibid. See Niebuhr, *Nature and Destiny*, 219–27, 257.

[20]King, "Modern Christians," 1.

King's first claim about human beings was that "man is neither good nor bad by nature, but has potentiality for either."[21] King rejected as "one-sided generalizations" claims such as the "doctrine of original sin" and the "romantic idealization of man."[22] Such "one-sided generalization" included Barth's view that "man was once completely good, made in the image of God" and that "this complete goodness was lost in the Fall."[23] As King understood Barth, after the Fall "the once present image of God was totally effaced, leaving him [humanity] totally helpless in his desire for salvation."[24] King found such a claim "preposterous," although he conceded that Barth's view of humanity might just be "an inaccurate way of stating the fact that man sins on every level of spiritual and moral achievement."[25]

King saw overgeneralization in the opposite theological camp which he labeled "extreme liberal and so-called religious humanistic circles."[26] It is difficult to know exactly to whom King referred, although my research has indicated that J. McTaggart and Henry Weiman, two of the favorite "extreme liberal humanists" that DeWolf singled out, may have been the likely persons for this appellation.[27] Nevertheless, King accused this circle of "strong sentimentality about man" that is expressed in the

---

[21]Ibid.

[22]King apparently took this term from Niebuhr (*Nature and Destiny*, 81–92) as he critiqued romanticism for leading to a rampant religious "relativism" that degenerates into "nihilism" (pp. 86–87).

[23]King, "Modern Christians," 2.

[24]Ibid. King's understanding of Barth's view of human sinfulness appears to have been influenced by *Church Dogmatics*, vol. 3: *The Doctrine of Creation* (4 pts.; Edinburgh: T & T Clark, 1958) which has repeated stern injunctions about the corruption of man being "radical and total" (2. 28). Furthermore, Barth cannot affirm any essential valuation of human beings "in which man is not seen at strife with God and therefore sinful" (2. 28). King does not portray Barth's reasons for this emphasis very well, for Barth's emphasis is on Jesus as the Real Man of God, and humans are necessarily the covenant recipients of God's grace as revealed in Jesus. King also appears unaware of Barth's positive affirmation of the goodness of creation, including human goodness (1. 363–65).

[25]King, "Modern Christians," 2.

[26]Ibid.

[27]This becomes apparent in the attention paid to the works of Weiman and McTaggart in the syllabus of DeWolf's "Personalism" course; King even wrote a research paper comparing the views of Edgar Brightman and J. McTaggart for the class.

popular phrase, "supreme value and self-perfectibility of man."[28] King
called this understanding of religion "humane and its vision a lofty one."
At the same time, King noted that such "optimism" had been discredited
most profoundly by what he called the "brutal logic of events."[29] King
viewed the "extreme liberal" progressive view of human beings as completely inadequate:

> Instead of assured progress and wisdom and decency, man faces the
> ever-present possibility of swift relapse not merely into animalism,
> but into such calculated cruelty as no other animal can practice.[30]

Having criticized what he considers to be two "extreme" points of
view, King posited a view "closest to the authentic Christian interpretation of man."[31] King directed the reader to the "life and teachings of
Jesus" as the standard for "humble dependence upon God," as the source
of all good, and to Christ's appeal to a "hidden goodness in their [human
beings] nature."[32] King then came to his first synthesis, namely, that the
modern Christian should "believe that lives are changed when the potential good in man is believed in patiently, and when the potential bad in
man is sought to be overwhelmed."[33] I believe that this synthesis is the
first time King had presented a clearly argued *theological* basis for pursuing a course of social change that sought to convert the "enemy" by
specifically validating and affirming the potential goodness present in
even the most vicious of enemies and at the same time sought to over-
whelm the potentiality for evil. Such a claim, moreover, affirms human
dignity by uplifting the *equality of potentiality* in all persons for the
good as well as the bad, placing both oppressor and oppressed on the
same *moral* plane. Such a view theologically undergirds human equality.
   King's second point, that "man is a finite child of nature," affirmed
human beings' dependence on the "laws of nature."[34] King used a phrase

---

[28]King found this quotation in Charles Francis Potter, *Humanism, A New
Religion* (New York: Simon & Schuster, 1930) 14.

[29]King, "Modern Christians," 2.

[30]Ibid.

[31]Ibid.

[32]Ibid., 3.

[33]Ibid.

[34]Ibid.

reminiscent of Niebuhr by stating, "On every hand, human freedom is mixed with natural necessity."[35] King claimed that "man is a victim of nature" and a "victim of the blindness and cruelty of his neighbours."[36] King called the latter a "liberal emphasis" that he wished to affirm for the modern Christian because it took into account "those nonmoral sources of evil which often interfere with man and his salvation."[37] Such a "liberal emphasis" concerning humanity as a finite child of nature can also be seen in the writings on theological anthropology of King's mentor, L. Harold DeWolf.[38]

King's third point was that "man [is] a rational being."[39] King saw "rationality as one of the supreme resources in man."[40] For King the "mind of man distinguishes him from his animal ancestors."[41] Through the faculties of "memory" and "abstract thinking" human beings can interpret the world for themselves. This "rational element" serves as a "check" to "false thinking."[42] Human rationality "protects" us from "false revelation."[43]

King warned against the "pride of reason," a phrase that he consciously borrowed from Reinhold Niebuhr.[44] King saw reason as a "peril as well as a supreme gift" because of reason's ability to degenerate into "pride and self-sufficiency."[45] It is significant to note, however, that King followed this tribute to Niebuhr with a strong affirmation of the place of reason: "It is well to emphasize the fact that reason rightly used remains the prize gift of man."[46]

---

[35]Ibid.; see also Niebuhr, *Nature and Destiny*, 178–79, although Niebuhr's presentation of the "anxiety" that this "paradox of human freedom" creates is much more complete than King's presentation.

[36]King, "Modern Christians," 3.

[37]Ibid. King cited John C. Bennett, "The Christian Conception of Man," in David E. Roberts and Henry Pitney Van Dusen, eds., *Liberal Theology, An Appraisal: Essays in Honor of Eugene William Lyman* (New York: Scribners, 1942) 195.

[38]See DeWolf, *A Theology of the Living Church*, 156–60.

[39]King, "Modern Christians," 3.

[40]Ibid.

[41]Ibid.

[42]Ibid., 4.

[43]Ibid.

[44]Ibid.; see Niebuhr, *Nature and Destiny*, 195.

[45]King, "Modern Christians," 4.

[46]Ibid.

King went on to state his fourth point, "man is a free and responsible being."[47] King wanted to affirm the Kantian ideal of the human being as free *and* responsible: "The Kantian 'I ought, therefore I can' should stand out as a prelude in the modern Christian's thinking about man."[48] King defined what he meant by "free and responsible" by criticizing what he called "Calvinistic and contemporary Barthian thought."[49] In King's eyes, such thought affirmed human responsibility but was "lacking freedom."[50] For King such thinking led only into "needless paradoxes," for freedom and responsibility inhere in his own thought. King wanted to affirm the "liberal" tendency to "affirm that man is free and then to deny that his conscious purposes are predestined by God."[51] This casting of human freedom and responsibility appealed to King as a "more logical mode of thought" since it affirmed the power of human choice: "We must believe that man has the power of choosing his supreme end. He can choose the low road or the high road. He can be true or false to his nature."[52]

This tenet of King's theological anthropology, the power to choose our end, connected with the first point, namely, that there is a potentiality for both good and bad and that the good must be enhanced while the bad must be overcome. King viewed the choice to develop the good or to fail to do so as a *human* responsibility. It is not that King rejected God's salvific grace, as study of his sermons will amply demonstrate.[53] Rather, King wanted both to join the notion of human freedom and responsibility in moral choices and to honor the power of human beings to choose their end.

King's fifth point, "man as sinner," is directly appropriated from Reinhold Niebuhr.[54] King referred to this view as having its source in the "neo-orthodox point of view."[55] King wanted to hold on to the notion of human beings as sinners because "many of the problems in this world are

[47]Ibid.
[48]Ibid.
[49]Ibid.
[50]Ibid.
[51]Ibid.
[52]Ibid.
[53]At the end of his sermons, King repeatedly appealed to the congregation to "come home to Jesus," because God is a "seeking God" who is "searching" for us. See particularly King, "Lost Sheep."
[54]King, "Modern Christians," 4; see also Niebuhr, *Nature and Destiny*, 178-240.
[55]King, "Modern Christians," 4.

due to plain sin."[56] King decried as "perilous" the "tendency of some liberal theologians" to relegate sin to a "mere 'lag of nature' which will be progressively eliminated as man climbs the evolutionary ladder."[57] King wanted modern Christians to look at sin as more than "shortcomings" or "ignorance, finiteness, and hampering circumstances."[58] Rather, sin is a "mis-use" of human rationality "by envisaging and pursuing ends unworthy of pursuit."[59] Human beings, moreover, have misused one another as social beings by "making others bear the burden of our selfishness."[60] King agreed with Niebuhr's assessment that "men sin through intellectual and spiritual pride."[61] For King, the world is "full of examples of such sin," so that the modern Christian is compelled to view 'man as a guilty sinner who must ask forgiveness and be converted."[62]

This point suggests a synthesis of the previous "liberal" thesis concerning the power of human choice with what King probably considered its neoorthodox antithesis—human sinfulness. The two cohered for King not merely intellectually, but also because both honored his African-American rural background. This background combined a strong emphasis on human beings' choice to "come to Jesus" (most notably in revivals, although in many churches it takes place every Sunday) and the convicting preaching of his family concerning human sinfulness.[63]

King's sixth and final point about human beings was that "man [is] a being in need of continuous repentance."[64] King noted that repentance is an "essential part of the Christian life" that enables the believer to "be converted and brought into fellowship with God."[65] King stressed that the New Testament vision of repentance involves a "turning away from the

---

[56]Ibid., 5.

[57]Ibid.

[58]Ibid.

[59]Ibid.

[60]Ibid.; quoted from William Marshall Horton, "The Christian Understanding of Man," in *The Christian Understanding of Man* (ed. T. E. Jessop et al.; London: Allen & Unwin, 1938) 200.

[61]These were King's own words ("Modern Christians," 5); he then cited Niebuhr, *Nature and Destiny*, chap. 9.

[62]King, "Modern Christians," 5.

[63]Compare the connections James Cone makes along these lines in his excellent essay, "Theology," 215.

[64]King, "Modern Christians," 5.

[65]Ibid.

life of sin" by which a changed mind embraces a "new and better standard of life."[66] This process "may occur again and again."[67] Such "perpetual repentance" enables Christians (1) to "grow" spiritually, (2) to
"keep our consciences awake;" (3) it "preserves us from the sin of self-
righteousness," and (4) it "helps us to concentrate on our sins rather than
the sins of others."[68] King went so far as to say that repentance is an
"inestimable privilege."[69] Quoting William Newton Clark, a famous liberal Baptist preacher and theologian, King said that "perpetual repentance
is simply perpetual fellowship with Christ; performed once or a thousand
times it is a most precious act of moral unity with Christ the Saviour."[70]
In this final point we see the Baptist preacher in King shining through,
even supporting his claim by quoting a famous Baptist theologian.

It has been important to exegete this early essay of King's in some
detail in order to demonstrate that King built his theological anthropology on its systematic insights. "What is Man?" is a sermon that King
used in numerous variations; it shows the development of his anthropology.[71] In this sermon King began with an echo of his research paper.
King, identifying himself as a "realist," sought to "avoid the extremes of
a pessimistic naturalism and an optimistic humanism" by attempting to
"combine the truths of both."[72]

King affirmed a "strange dualism" which is "something of a dichotomy" with human beings.[73] Quoting Thomas Carlyle, King exclaimed

> There are depths in man that go down to the lowest hell, and heights
> that reach the highest heaven, for are not heaven and hell made out
> of him—ever lasting miracle and mystery that he is?[74]

[66]Ibid.

[67]Ibid.

[68]Ibid., 5–6.

[69]Ibid., 6.

[70]Ibid.; quoted from William Newton Clark, *An Outline of Christian Theolog.*
(New York: Scribners, 1898) 403.

[71]Martin Luther King, Jr., "What is Man?" in idem, *The Measure of a Man*
(Philadelphia: Fortress, 1988) 9–31. "What is Man?" is similar to "Who Are
We?" sermon preached at Ebenezer Baptist Church, 5 February 1966; Martin
Luther King, Jr. Center Archives, Atlanta, GA.

[72]Ibid., 10.

[73]Ibid.

[74]Ibid.

King noted that "man is a biological being with a physical body" and affirmed human "kinship with animate nature" because of our bodies.[75] This bodily kinship that human beings share with nature is *positive*:

> Since God made him that way there is nothing wrong with it. We read in the book of Genesis that everything God makes is good; therefore there is nothing wrong with having a body.[76]

King then asserted that Christianity's understanding of the sacredness of the body demands a concern for humanity's physical well-being:

> So the body in Christianity is sacred and significant. That means in any doctrine of man that we must be concerned with man's physical well-being.[77]

King condemned any religious doctrine of "man" that is "not concerned about the economic conditions that damn the soul, the social conditions that corrupt men, and the city governments that cripple them."[78] Such a doctrine "is a dry, dead, do-nothing religion in need of new blood" because it "overlooks the basic fact that man is a biological being with a physical body."[79] It is striking that this first point in King's sermon moves immediately from an abstract theological anthropology, systematically listing various categories of understanding human beings outside of their concrete social context, into a ringing theological critique. King turned what might be viewed as a simple observation that human beings are biological and have bodies into a *demand* that theo-

---

[75]Ibid., 12–13.

[76]Ibid., 13. King's positive valuation of the body is similar to that of L. Harold DeWolf. In *A Theology of the Living Church* (pp. 154–55) DeWolf writes, "The body, then, is not to be despised. It is not evil. . . . Nowhere in literature is there a more emphatic and exalted assertion of the rightful sanctity of human bodies than the passage in which Paul depicts them as 'members of Christ.'" The difference between King and DeWolf lies in the fact that DeWolf posits the sanctity of human bodies in Pauline and New Testament terms, while King cites the Hebraic Genesis account of creation's goodness.

[77]King, "The Measure of Man," 13–14.

[78]Ibid., 14.

[79]Ibid.

logical anthropology take note of any and all conditions that affect the body. This is so important for King because he desired his "doctrine of man to be realistic and thoroughly Christian."[80] As King undertook leadership in the civil rights struggle, he began to see that the physical conditions that bind human beings' bodies also affect their estimate of their own dignity. King changed the focus of his own initial theological anthropology by focusing *first* on the body.

King then made another startling connection. He described the human body as a chemical compound and listed all the chemical elements and materials that make up the body, claiming that in his time the "market value" of a body would be only $1.98![81] He then asked a series of rhetorical questions about whether the body's monetary value is a true measure of the human person.[82] He reached a climax with the ringing endorsement of the doctrine of *imago dei*, "man is a child of God."[83]

> There is something within man that cannot be reduced to chemical
> and biological terms, for man is more than a tiny vagary of whirl-
> ing electrons. He is more than a wisp of smoke from a limitless
> smoldering. Man is a child of God.[84]

At this point King conflated the image of God and rationality in human beings with the statement that "man is a being of spirit."[85] King identified the rational capacity that human beings possess as the quality that "distinguishes" us from "the lower animals."[86] Human beings are "God's marvelous creation" because of this tremendous mental capacity.[87] King marveled at the achievements of greatness and the transcendence of difficult situations that the human mind enables. All these things make up the "image of God":

> This is what the biblical writers mean when they say that man is
> made in the image of God. Man has a rational capacity; he has the

[80]Ibid.
[81]Ibid., 15.
[82]Ibid., 16.
[83]Ibid.
[84]Ibid.
[85]Ibid., 16–17.
[86]Ibid., 17.
[87]Ibid.

unique ability to have fellowship with God. Man is a being of spirit.[88]

King fleshed out another term from his early essay—"man is a sinner"—in terms of the doctrine of the image of God. King noted that while each human being was created a "free being made in the image of God," we have "misused this freedom."[89] As a result, "some of the image of God is gone."[90] The result of this loss is that each person is "a sinner in need of God's divine grace."[91]

King continued reaffirming the moral dichotomy within persons. Using the ethical language of moral philosophy King stated, "in a real sense the 'isness' of our present nature is out of harmony with the eternal 'oughtness' that forever confronts us. We know how to love, and yet we hate."[92]

King mentioned his agreement with Niebuhr's claim in *Moral Man and Immoral Society* regarding the increased power of collective sin in "our collective lives."[93] King used Niebuhr's insight to critique the racism and imperialism of America and Western civilization. He likened Western civilization to the prodigal son in Jesus' parable, who needs to return "home."

> Oh, I can hear a voice crying out today, saying to western civilization: "You strayed away to the far country of colonialism and imperialism. You have trampled one billion six hundred million of your colored brothers in Africa and Asia. But, O Western Civilization, if you will come to yourself, rise up, and come back home, I will take you in."[94]

It is intriguing that in this climax to "What is Man?" King conflated his previous ideas of freedom and responsibility, man as sinner, and man as a being in need of continual repentance into a specific critique of the

[88]Ibid., 18.
[89]Ibid., 18, 21.
[90]Ibid., 21.
[91]Ibid.
[92]Ibid., 22–23.
[93]Ibid., 23.
[94]Ibid., 29.

oppressive actions of Western civilization. Instead of a theological anthropology with an academic summary of the categories examined, King
ended with a prophetic challenge to the West. King called for Western
civilization to admit its sinful ways, repent, and take responsibility for
past wrongs.

King's theological anthropology is distinctive because these ideas are
not only spoken from a pulpit, but are also given life and substance in
the protests, marches, and demonstrations that transformed the ideas into
practices. King's ideas of human sinfulness, human responsibility to over-
whelm evil, and human potential for good became concrete through the
civil rights campaigns. I would add, moreover, that King inferred that
theological anthropology should be done in this manner, relating concrete sociopolitical struggles against oppression to an understanding of
what makes up the human being. Human beings, for King, are inexora-
bly tied to the forces of oppression and uplift. Such forces shape us,
confine us, and limit us. Yet our awareness of these forces can also
prompt us to take responsibility for their effects in the lives of the
victims of oppression. As part of his theological anthropology, King
challenged America to make a change for the better.

The Image of God as Freedom

King added the characteristic of "freedom" to his previous definition
of the image of God as "spirit" and "reason." Freedom, for King, was
something that is "innate" and "basic" to the human being:

> There seems to be a throbbing desire, an internal desire for free-
> dom within the soul of every man. And it's there. It might not
> break forth in the beginning, but eventually it breaks out. Men
> realize that freedom is something basic. To rob a man of his free-
> dom is to take from him the essential basis of his manhood. To
> take his freedom is to rob him of something of God's image.[95]

Freedom for King was the part of the Negro's *imago dei* that had been
"robbed" by the system of segregation. Yet there remained within the
soul of the Negro a "throbbing desire" for this freedom, and in King's
view that desire was breaking forth in the struggle for civil rights.

[95]Martin Luther King, Jr., "The Birth of a Nation," sermon, April 1957; Martin
Luther King, Jr. Center Archives, Atlanta, GA, 3–4.

King turned to Paul Tillich's definition of freedom to explain what he meant by the term. King defined freedom as the capacity to deliberate, to decide, and to take responsibility.[96] These are the exact terms that Tillich used to define freedom in his *Systematic Theology*.[97] King further defined freedom as operating "within the framework of destiny" and "destined structures."[98] There is great similarity between King's understanding and that of Tillich, who defines freedom and destiny as an "ontological polarity" wherein the "individual as the bearer of freedom" operates "within the larger structures to which the individual belongs namely 'destiny']."[99]

Through his claim that freedom is part of the image of God in all persons, King critiqued the system of segregation. Segregation "robs" Negroes of the part of their *imago dei* that is best called "freedom," because it has taken away the capacity to choose:

> The absence of freedom is the imposition of restraint on my deliberations as to what I shall do, where I shall live, or the kind of task I shall pursue. I am robbed of the basic quality of man-ness. When I cannot choose what I shall do or where I shall live or how I shall survive, it means in fact that someone or some system has already made these *a priori* decisions for me, and I am reduced to an animal.[100]

King immediately named the system of segregation as the system that has "wreaked havoc with the Negro" by altering Negro life to the point where "his [the Negro's] being cannot make the full circle of personhood because that which is basic to the character of life itself has been diminished."[101] King once again turned an aspect of his theological anthropology into a direct attack on the system of segregation, which he saw as virtually "diminishing" the image of God in Negroes. Since freedom is so inherently basic and fundamental to our understanding of what it

---

[96]King, "America's Chief Moral Dilemma."

[97]Paul Tillich, *Systematic Theology* (3 vols.; Chicago: University of Chicago Press, 1951) 1. 184.

[98]King, "Who Are We?" 7.

[99]Tillich, *Systematic Theology*, 1. 182.

[100]King, "America's Chief Moral Dilemma," 8.

[101]Ibid., 9.

means to be a human being created in the image of God, to rob people
of their freedom is deliberately to rob them of a vital part of their *imago
dei*. For the Negro, the robbed part can only exist as a "throbbing desire" that has broken forth into a ringing demand within the confines of
the nonviolence movement.

King insisted that the *imago dei* of Negroes had not been completely
eliminated by segregation's racism, only diminished in a way that is
immoral and sinful. King clarified this point in a late sermon, "Who Are
We?" by noting that freedom is the "highest expression of the image of
God."[102]

> Theologians have interpreted the image of God in many ways, and
> after studying all of them, I've come to the conclusion. The highest
> expression of the image of God in man is freedom. Man is man. . .
> because he's free.[103]

King's "Triangle of Personality"

As King sought to explain more fully the theological underpinning
of his understanding of the human person and human dignity, he described the human being as a "triangle" of personality. This image is
most clearly seen in his sermon "The Three Dimensions of A Complete
Life."[104] On one side of this triangle of life stands "the individual person, at the other angle stand other persons, and at the top stands the
Supreme Infinite Person, God."[105]

King began with the individual person. He was concerned that this
part of the triangle be fairly represented, for it enables the individual to
develop "his inner powers."[106] King did not condemn this development,
in fact he posited the existence of a "moral and rational self-interest."
Such self-love is a necessary prerequisite to love of others: "If one is
not concerned about himself he cannot be totally concerned about other
selves."[107]

---

[102]King, "Who are We?" 7.
[103]Ibid.
[104]King, "Three Dimensions," 35–56.
[105]Ibid., 37.
[106]Ibid.
[107]Ibid.

King desired that persons learn to "love your own self properly."[108] Such self-love enables each individual person to take the responsibility to "discover what he is made for," and after this discovery, to "set out to do it with all of the strength and power in his being."[109] Working in this way, each person comes to recognize that whatever job one has possesses "cosmic significance" because one is "serving humanity and doing the will of God."[110] In an impressive poetic flourish King proclaimed the dignity of all labor, a belief that was influenced by his father's work ethic.

> If it falls your lot to be a street sweeper, sweep streets as Raphael painted pictures, sweep streets as Michelangelo carved marble, sweep streets as Beethoven composed music, sweep streets as Shakespeare wrote poetry. Sweep streets so well that all the hosts of heaven and earth will have to pause and say, "Here lived a great street sweeper who swept his job well."[111]

This is King's "first dimension of life" and it is important to note that in this dimension King anchors his thought on the personal integrity of one's personal vocation, the dignity of all labor, and the responsibility of every person to discover that life's work. King also called this dimension the "length of life."[112]

King moved on to the "breadth of life," that second dimension wherein the individual rises "above the narrow confines of his individualistic concerns to the broader concerns of all humanity."[113] King described the "dangerous altruism" of the good Samaritan as a model for what it takes to be a "great man."[114] Greatness, in King's definition, is found in one who can "project the 'I' into the 'thou'"—a direct allusion to Martin Buber's famous book *I and Thou*.[115] King went on to remind his listeners that the world in which they lived was interdependent and that they were "all

[108]Ibid., 38.
[109]Ibid.
[110]Ibid., 41.
[111]Ibid.
[112]Ibid., 42.
[113]Ibid.
[114]Ibid., 43.
[115]King often mentioned Buber's "I and Thou" concept in sermons and speeches. See Martin Buber, *I and Thou* (New York: Scribners, 1958).

somehow caught in an inescapable network of mutuality."[116] Participatio
in the breadth of life broadens our human awareness of each other:

> I can never be what I ought to be until you are what you ought to
> be. This is the way our world is made. No individual or nation can
> stand out boasting of being independent. We are interdependent.[117]

King completed his triangle by directing individual persons who ar
also concerned with others "upward" to God.[118] This is the "height c
life" that rounds out the individual person.[119] King enjoined the listene
to "seek God and discover him and make him a power in your life."[1
King insisted that human beings must seek the "great things in thi
universe" which are "things we never see."[121] By seeking the invisibl
God who nevertheless is "still here," King criticized the materialist bas
of secular culture because it failed to provide the means for living
complete life.[122]

Standing well within the school of Boston Personalism, King pointe
to the developing invisible personality that is the *real* person:

> You look at me and think you see Martin Luther King. You don't
> see Martin Luther King: you see my body, but, you must under-
> stand, my body can't think, my body can't reason. You don't see the
> me that makes me me. You can never see my personality.[123]

By seeking the invisible and yet powerful God, the invisible huma
person is given a richer and more potent sense of life. The dimension c
God enables persons to "rise from the fatigue of despair to the buoyanc
of hope."[124] Furthermore, the dimension of God empowers persons

---

[116]King, "Three Dimensions," 48.
[117]Ibid., 48–49.
[118]Ibid., 54.
[119]Ibid., 56.
[120]Ibid., 54–55.
[121]Ibid., 51.
[122]Ibid., 54, 50–51.
[123]Ibid., 54.
[124]Ibid., 55.

'rise from the midnight of desperation to the daybreak of joy."[125] These are not merely poetic niceties for King, but represent his strong belief that God empowers individuals and enables them to transform negative situations into positive ones.

King summarized his triangle of personality in terms of *love*. The first dimension implies the injunction "Love yourself."[126] The second dimension fulfills the command to "love your neighbor as yourself."[127] Finally the third dimension of life points back to the "first and even greater commandment, 'Love the Lord thy God with all thy heart and all thy soul and all thy mind.'"[128] This suggests a vital link between King's theological anthropology and his doctrine of love. King saw the human personality in much the same way that Augustine described the human will as formed by the "object" of its "love."[129] King viewed each individual as capable of *willing the self to love*, first within its own self, then others, and finally God. This love is *constructive* in that it enables the human person to experience wholeness and completeness.

The Centrality of Agape

Some of the best scholarly material on King has focused on his understanding of love, particularly agape.[130] Smith and Zepp have given a full reading regarding the manner in which King's understanding of agape synthesizes elements of Paul Ramsey's *Basic Christian Ethics*, Anders Nygren's *Agape and Eros*, and Paul Tillich's *Love, Power, and Justice*.[131] Ansbro has carefully delineated how King's views of love as a power to achieve justice" combine the insights of Tillich with Gandhi's concept of *ahimsa*.[132] Ansbro has also looked at the influence of L.

---

[125]Ibid.

[126]Ibid.

[127]Ibid.

[128]Ibid., 55–56.

[129]Augustine *Civ. d.* 14. 7; ET: Augustine, *City of God* (trans. and ed. David Knowles; New York: Penguin, 1972) 536–37.

[130]See "The Redemptive Power of Agape," chapter 1 of Ansbro, *King*; Smith and Zepp, *Search for the Beloved Community*, 54–69. Smith and Zepp's analysis is particularly helpful in establishing the connection between Gandhi's ideas of *ahimsa*, King's understanding of nonviolence, and King's constructive moral form of agape.

[131]See Smith and Zepp, *Search for the Beloved Community*, 62–66.

[132]Ansbro, *King*, 7–8.

Harold DeWolf's understanding of agape on King.[133] I am in fundamen
tal agreement with these authors' conclusions concerning the syntheti
nature of King's view of agape. I shall focus, however, on that part o
King's doctrine of agape which reveals two concerns relevant to m
argument: the connection of agape to King's theological anthropolog
with regard to human dignity and the central place that agape held i
King's mind as the energizing force in the reformation of oppresse
human dignity.

King wanted to show that agape is the central energizing norm guid
ing the activity of nonviolence. Agape enables the nonviolent resister t
combine "tenderheartedness and toughmindedness" by avoiding the "com
placency and do-nothingness of the softminded and the violence an
bitterness of the hardhearted."[134] Such love enables the nonviolent re
sister to gain a greater sense of dignity because King saw it as "mankind
most potent weapon for personal and social transformation."[135] In King
view, love-empowered nonviolence enacted a transformation, creatin
"in the mind of the Negro a new image of himself."[136] Yet such lov
could not provide the catalyst for such personal transformation unless i
was appropriated into the "center of our lives" as a guiding and con
structive norm.

> At the center of our movement stood the philosophy of love. The
> attitude that the only way to ultimately change humanity and make
> for the society that we all long for is to keep love at the center of
> our lives.[137]

King's view of love should be seen, therefore, as a normative ideal tha
connects his high valuation of human beings as beings created in th
image of God and the reconstructive force necessary to heal oppresse
persons seeking to affirm their dignity. An exegetical analysis of King
1961 scholarly address, "Love, Law, and Civil Disobedience," reveal

[133]Ibid., 18–26.

[134]Martin Luther King, Jr., "A Tough Mind and a Tender Heart," a sermon i
idem, *Strength to Love*, 15.

[135]King, "Ethical Demands," 124.

[136]Ibid., 125.

[137]"The Power of Nonviolence," in Washington, *Testament*, 13.

he interrelation between King's views of the human person, nonvio-
ence, agape, and the laws of agape.

King began the address with a description of the precipitating factors
of a "crisis in race relations":[138] the "massive resistance" of southern
egislators and southern whites to the implications of the Supreme Court's
954 integration decision and the "determination of hundreds and thou-
ands and millions of Negro people to achieve freedom and dignity."[139]
This struggle for freedom and human dignity is rooted, according to King,
n the same longings for freedom and dignity seen in the "oppressed
people all over the world." Thus Negroes join an international "struggle"
or freedom that will not be aborted "short of full freedom."[140] King
herefore foresaw an inevitable struggle between those who cling to their
privileges" and those who fight for the dignity and freedom guaranteed
o all persons. The real question for King did not lie in the "struggle" as
uch, for King believed that it must continue until full freedom is won for
he oppressed, but in "how the struggle will be waged."[141]

King then looked at three possible responses to oppression that are
aken by oppressed persons: passivity and acquiescence, physical vio-
ence and hatred, or nonviolent resistance.[142] King chose to describe the
undamental principles of the nonviolent campaigns being waged by
tudents throughout the South as both the synthesis and the most appropriate response.

The first principle was that the "means must be as pure as the end."[143]
or King, the "ends and means must cohere." Thus King placed himself
nd the students against Machiavelli and Lenin who had stated unreserv-
dly that the end justifies the means. Not only must the means be pure,
ut the "end is preexistent in the means."[144] He concluded with the
trong statement that "immoral destructive means cannot bring about
noral and constructive ends."[145]

The principle of noninjury was the second principle of nonviolent
ampaigns. King appropriated Gandhi's concept of *ahimsa* by elaborating

---

[138]King, "Love," 44.
[139]Ibid.
[140]Ibid.
[141]Ibid.
[142]Ibid., 44–45.
[143]Ibid., 45.
[144]Ibid.
[145]Ibid.

on the ideal moral position of consistently refusing to "inflict injury upon another."[146] Thus the practitioner of nonviolence struggles to overcome two forms of violence: the *external physical violence* represented by retaliation and guns and *internal violence of the spirit*. Such a struggle enables the nonviolent to gain a more profound sense of inner discipline. This led King to the third principle, the centrality of the love ethic.

King distinguished three different levels of love: *eros*, *philia*, and *agape*. King described *eros* or "aesthetic love" as the Platonic longing for the realm of the divine.[147] *Eros* for King was the type of "romantic love" illustrated in the poetry of Edgar Allen Poe or Shakespeare. *Philia*, the "intimate affection between personal friends," is "reciprocal" and can also be called "friendship."[148] This corresponds to Aristotle's notion of love.[149] *Agape*, which King described as the "love of God operating in the human heart,"[150] is "higher" than *eros* or *philia*. It requires that its practitioners "rise" to the level of "understanding, creative good will to all."[151] Such love distinguishes between the evil deed and evil persons, for it insists upon "loving the person who does an evil deed while hating the deed that the person does."[152] As such, to use the term "love" while engaged in nonviolent resistance is to affirm Jesus' injunction from the Sermon on the Mount to "love your enemies."[153] King stated that this kind of love goes beyond "liking" the person, for King admitted to the fact that it is "difficult" to love someone who bombs your house or threatens your children.[154] Nevertheless, King affirmed the moral primacy of agape as an essential principle in nonviolent resistance. Such love engages the will of the nonviolent practitioner in understanding and creating good will between opposing parties.

The fourth principle of nonviolence was to defeat unjust systems, not persons. Agape energizes the nonviolent resister to attack the "unjust [social] system, rather than the individuals who are caught in that sys-

[146]Ibid., 46.

[147]Ibid.

[148]Ibid.

[149]See Aristotle, *Nichomachean Ethics* (trans. Martin Ostwald; Indianapolis Bobbs-Merril, 1962) 214–15, chap. 8.

[150]King, "Love," 46.

[151]Ibid.

[152]Ibid., 46–47.

[153]Ibid., 47.

[154]Ibid.

em."[155] King referred to individual racists as "misled" and "taught wrong," but did not personally attack them for being wrong. King was attentive to restoring the "moral balance within society" by ridding society of an unjust system. Three things are implied: first, that an unjust social system such as segregation must be eliminated as a moral obligation to a healthy society; second, that injustice creates a moral imbalance within society that remains until the unjust system is eliminated; and third, that agape is related to the defeat of social injustice by enabling persons to focus on defeating systems rather than persons.

The fifth principle was that suffering is a creative social force. King contrasted the ways in which violence and nonviolence view the efficacy of suffering as a powerful social force. Violence understands that one may achieve one's end by "inflicting suffering on another."[156] Nonviolence, by contrast, believes that suffering can become a powerful social force by the willing acceptance of "violence on yourself" or "self-suffering."[157] Such "self-suffering" gives the nonviolent resister the capacity to "suffer in a creative manner, feeling that unearned suffering is redemptive, and that suffering may serve to transform the social situation."[158] It is important to note that King never said directly that suffering was redemptive, but that it had the potential to redeem and transform, that it "can" or "may" be transformative of society. The unspoken implication is that it might not be redemptive at all.[159]

The sixth principle concerned the good potential of human nature. Quoting from Ovid, Augustine, Plato, and Carlyle, King described a strange dichotomy within human nature, the capacity for both good and evil.[160] King was impressed with the ability of Jesus or Gandhi to appeal

---

[155]Ibid.

[156]Ibid.

[157]Ibid.

[158]Ibid.

[159]In other texts King more explicitly tied the concept of suffering to agape. In *Stride Toward Freedom* (p. 105), King called agape the "willingness to sacrifice in the interest of mutuality." He further cemented agape's "sacrificial" nature by stating that the "cross is the eternal expression of the length to which God will go to restore broken community." It is significant that he followed this theological symbol with another: "The resurrection is a symbol of God's triumph over all the forces that seek to block community." The emphasis, clearly, is not on sacrifice in and of itself, but on sacrifice as that *attitude* which enables God's victory to be won.

[160]King, "Love," 47–48.

to the "element of human goodness," and, on the other hand, the ability of Hitler to appeal to the "element of evil within."[161] Nevertheless, King affirmed his fundamental conviction that "there is something within human nature that can respond to goodness."[162] He defined this "something" theologically in terms of the image of God which is never "totally gone" or "totally depraved."[163] Thus the nonviolent practitioner can go forth into conflict believing that "even the worst segregationist can become an integrationist."[164] Something in human nature "can be changed" for the better.[165] Such a belief was not stated by King naively, but points toward his underlying Christian belief in the conversion of all persons. King revealed here his adherence to the optimistic view of the related Christian doctrines of sin and redemption. In "Love, Law, and Civil Disobedience," King conflated all of his early research text on human beings into a short paragraph. He demonstrated, moreover, the confidence he had in agape's power to transform even the enemy into a friend.

The seventh principle asserted noncooperation as a moral obligation. "It is as much a moral obligation to refuse to cooperate with evil as it is to cooperate with good."[166] This moral centerpiece of nonviolent resistance enabled its practitioners to "stand up courageously on the idea of civil disobedience."[167] Such a moral declaration led King to answer carefully the objection that it is difficult to determine and judge the "difference between a just and unjust law."[168] King had a strong view of a moral law of the universe that judges whether a human law is just or unjust. In other places, such as the "Letter in the Birmingham Jail," King offered a deeper elaboration of this distinction, which he credits to Augustine's and Aquinas's distinction between "just law" and "unjust law."[169] A just law for King is a law that is in harmony with the law of

[161]Ibid.
[162]Ibid., 48.
[163]Ibid.
[164]Ibid.
[165]Ibid.
[166]Ibid.
[167]Ibid.
[168]Ibid., 48–49.
[169]See Martin Luther King, Jr., *Why We Can't Wait* (New York: Mentor, 1963) 76–95.

God, a "law that squares with that which is right. . . so that any law that uplifts human personality is a just law."[170] An unjust law is a law that does not square with the moral law of the universe," "does not square with the law of God," and "degrades the human personality."[171] In King's view, nonviolent protesters, by willingly enduring jailings, demonstrate that they are neither anarchists nor lawless, but that they have the "very highest respect for law."[172] Following the lead of Boston Personalist Edgar Sheffield Brightman, King described the term "moral law" as something woven into the fabric of the universe which is rational, orderly, and understandable to human beings. Such an understanding of law goes deeper than human laws or the laws arrived at through legislation and roots itself in the soil of the philosophical and theological traditions surrounding the term. Law, for King, is judged to be "just" or "unjust" by human "conscience."[173]

King's proposed goals were not phrased in the sharp, crisp language of legislation; rather, they broadly stated two overall aims. The first aim was a "positive peace," which is the fruit of justice between races. King stated that "true peace is not the absence of tension [which King calls 'negative peace'], but the presence of justice and brotherhood."[174] Within the term "positive peace" is the state of "true brotherhood, true integration, true person-to-person relationships."[175] King's second aim was "complete integration," not the "tokenism" of "just a few students and a few schools here and there and a few doors open here and there."[176] Integration, for King, was a highly valued term that meant access to all of American life. While he did not state it in this essay, elsewhere King elaborated on integration as access to housing, jobs, economic opportunities, professions, and education. King later described "integration" as true intergroup, interpersonal living" that is based upon "mutual sharing of power."[177]

[170]King, "Love," 48–49.
[171]Ibid., 49.
[172]Ibid.
[173]Ibid.
[174]Ibid., 51.
[175]Ibid.
[176]Ibid., 63.
[177]King, *Where Do We Go*, 62.

Love and Hope

In one of his later sermons, "The Meaning of Hope," King demonstrated how love operates with hope as an empowering force within the
lives of the oppressed. King first defined hope as that quality which is
"necessary for life."[178] The "hopeless individual is a dead individual,"
for in King's view hope has a transformative quality that keeps human
beings "alive" both spiritually and pyschologically.[179] Hope, therefore, is
"one of the basic structures for an adequate life."[180]

In the second place, hope must be viewed as "animated and undergirded
by faith and love."[181] King interpreted Paul as having put the three "right
together" (1 Cor 13:13) for this reason.[182] Thus, in King's mind, to "hope"
in something is to "love," and "if you really hope, you have faith in
something."[183] Hope is "generated and animated by love, and is
undergirded by faith."[184] Thus hope shares with love the belief that "all
reality hinges on moral foundations."[185] The inner essence of this "moral
foundation" is the "law of love in the universe" which is concomitantly
"the law of justice."[186] This "law of love and law of justice" is the "final
morality in the universe" that ultimately determines the fate of nations:[187]

> And there is a law of love in the universe. Try to break it if you
> will, it'll break you. History is replete with the bleached bones of
> nations and the crumbled wreckage of communities that failed to
> follow the law of love and the law of justice.[188]

In King's mind, hope enables one to have faith in the ultimate morality
of this "law of love and law of justice." Hope is a part of the moral
force through which love, justice, and faith operate together.

[178]Martin Luther King, Jr., "The Meaning of Hope," sermon, 10 December
1967; Martin Luther King, Jr. Center Archives, Atlanta, GA, 5.

[179]Ibid.

[180]Ibid., 6.

[181]Ibid.

[182]Ibid.

[183]Ibid.

[184]Ibid.

[185]Ibid.

[186]Ibid., 7.

[187]Ibid.

[188]Ibid., 6–7.

Finally, hope is the "refusal to give up" despite overwhelming odds.[189] King found the supreme example of this capacity of hope by turning to "our slave foreparents" who resisted giving up because they never had the "disease of 'giveupitis.'"[190] Through the power of love operating in hope the slaves had made "an agreement with an eternal power" that told them, "You ain't no nigger, you ain't no slave, but you're God's children."[191] This statement shows how love, hope, and the determined grip of the Negro on the doctrine of *imago dei* operated together in King's mind as necessary elements of Negro dignity. Negro dignity operated through a hope that was animated and generated by love and irrepressible faith.

From this representative text it is possible to make several important conclusions about King's understanding of love. As it is practiced within the parameters of nonviolence, love has the power to transform oppressed persons into dignified persons. Love, moreover, is a force that binds all persons together as brothers and sisters because it operates on the assumption that all are created in the image of God. The presupposition of a universal *imago dei* enables the nonviolent practitioner to believe even in the eventual transformation of a hardened enemy into a friend.

In King's thought, love may also be viewed as a norm or a guiding ethical principle for concrete proposals about social policy. King was not a legislator or a lawyer, but a preacher and social activist with a broad theological and ethical background that enabled him to explain how such theological notions of love, God, and moral law had any bearing on debates of social policy. He was deeply involved in the massive social policy debates surrounding the issue of civil rights of the late 1950s and the 1960s until his death in April 1968. He never swerved from insisting that love could be appropriately applied toward the struggle for human dignity.

Love, for King, is not an abstract and yet necessary "impossible ideal" that has little direct bearing on social policies and laws.[192] Rather, love is a social force that can utilize the committed self-suffering of nonviolent resisters toward the transformation of unjust laws within society.

[189]Ibid., 7.
[190]Ibid., 7–8.
[191]Ibid., 8.
[192]Reinhold Niebuhr, *An Interpretation of Christian Ethics* (New York: Scribners, 1935) 62–85.

Love is directly related to law because it serves as a powerful social force for confirming or denying the justice of human laws in accordance with the standard of a universal moral law. King further elaborated love as a motivating force, for love motivates action to eliminate not only unjust laws, but also unjust social systems. Love changes social attitudes toward oppressive and unjust laws because love reveals the brutality of injustice. As such, love is a convicting force that has the potential for pricking the conscience of a nation and even transforming oppressors into allies.

Love is revealed as a "positive peace" that is the active incarnation of justice. Justice, for King, is based on laws that uplift human personality, increase person-to-person relationships, and insist upon a mutual sharing of power between all parties. One might say that the social policy term "integration" and the theological and philosophical term "justice" are virtually interchangeable, so close was their relationship in his mind.

For King, love was not a matter of affectionate or sentimental feelings, but rather involved an actively engaged and directed will. This will moves toward understanding and creative good will for all persons. Such love is agape or God's love. King placed the categories of God, law, and love into the midst of the struggle for human dignity and a deeper sense of self-respect. King also injected these terms into social policy debate by presenting them as both necessary and morally appropriate to any just resolution of conflict between persons and communities.

King's understanding of the central role of agape in the struggle for dignity widens our knowledge of the place of love in both private and public spheres. King saw agape as having a role both in the stress and conflict engendered by public policy and legislative debates and in the personal transformation of the self. For King there was no sharp line of demarcation beyond which agape's power to transform and energize could not reach; agape could even influence the formation of legislation.

Love was the animating force that both generated and energized hope, that necessary quality of human dignity. Hope, for King, was an inclusive force that incorporated the energy of love and faith into the formation of dignified persons. Such persons, like the slave forebears, could resist giving up on life because their lives were animated by hope. In my interpretation of King, hope was a quality of a dignified life that incorporated a faith-driven adherence to the doctrine of *imago dei* within the animating power of agape.

In conclusion, King's view of dignity possessed a constructive view of the *imago dei* as fundamental to all persons. He held that an adequate theological anthropology must consider the whole person—bodily and material needs as well as the capacity to reason. King viewed agape as the energizing force that enabled the unification of all human beings into a community, the transformation of a robbed dignity into a new sense of self-respect, and a sturdy and resistant quality of hope.

6

KING'S LATER VIEW OF DIGNITY, 1962–1968

This chapter concerns the evolution of King's understanding of dignity from 1962 until his death in April 1968. An examination of some of the evolving motifs of dignity, especially the Emancipation Proclamation, demonstrates how King developed the symbolism of his understanding of dignity.

Emancipation Proclamation and Declaration of Independence

In an address in 1962 before the Civil War Centennial Commission in New York, King for the first time thoroughly developed the Emancipation Proclamation and the Declaration of Independence as representative symbols of dignity. King began by stating that humanity's search for dignity is that which makes human beings unique:

Mankind through the ages has been in a ceaseless struggle to give dignity and meaning to human life. It is a quest which separates it

from the animal, whose biological functions and anatomical functions resemble aspects of the human species.[1]

King then praised two historical documents of the United States, the
Emancipation Proclamation and the Declaration of Independence, as
having made an imperishable contribution to civilization.[2] King extolled
the Declaration of Independence for affirming the equality of every person in spite of the more common tradition of affirming the inequality of
persons:

> The Declaration of Independence proclaimed to a world organized
> politically and spiritually around the concept of the *inequality* of
> man, that the liberty and dignity of human personality were inher-
> ent in man as a living being that he, himself, could not create a
> society which could last if it alienated freedom from man.[3]

The personalist phrase, "the dignity of human personality," shines through
the statement, as does King's ideal of freedom as something fundamental
to all human beings. King affirmed the equality of persons by placing
the qualities of "liberty" and "dignity" in the forefront. He honored the
Declaration of Independence for championing these qualities.

King went on to call the Emancipation Proclamation the "offspring of
the Declaration of Independence" which countered a historical system
that denied liberty to all:[4]

> The Emancipation Proclamation was the offspring of the Declara-
> tion of Independence using the forces of law to uproot a social
> order which sought to separate liberty from a segment of humanity.
> The principle of equality on which the nation was founded had to
> be reaffirmed in the flames of a scorching war until rededication to
> liberty was once again recorded in the Emancipation Proclamation.[5]

[1]Martin Luther King, Jr., "Address to New York State Civil War Centennial
Commission," 12 September 1962; Martin Luther King, Jr. Center Archives,
Atlanta, GA, 1.
[2]Ibid.
[3]Ibid., 2.
[4]Ibid.
[5]Ibid.

King elaborated his critique of "contradictions" that have revolved around the "unresolved race question" throughout America's history. As demonstrated in his earlier texts, King often described American history as contradictory to its own highest ideals of freedom, dignity, and equality, and sometimes even defeating them.[6] In this address King calls the "unresolved race question" a "pathological infection in our social and political anatomy, which has sickened us throughout our history."[7] King utilized the powerful image of a social illness or disease to demonstrate vividly his concern for the social health of the nation.[8] He further elaborated several results of the "injury" inflicted upon the social health of the Negro, including a lack of economic equality, cultural deprivation, and limited opportunities.[9]

King contrasted two potent symbols, the Emancipation Proclamation and the "proclamation of inferiority"—a social reality of oppression experienced by all Negroes. King described the "proclamation of inferiority" by noting that all Negroes recognize that their "personality is corroded by a sense of inferiority, generated by this degraded status."[10] He proceeded to name the "proclamation of inferiority" the ideological "slave chains" of the contemporary world:

> The imposition of inferiority externally and internally are the slave chains of today. What the Emancipation Proclamation proscribed in a legal and formal sense has never been eliminated in human terms. By burning in the consciousness of white Americans a conviction that Negroes are by nature subnormal, much of the myth was absorbed by the Negro himself, stultifying his energy, his ambition, and self-respect. The Proclamation of Inferiority has contended with the Proclamation of Emancipation, negating its liberating force.[11]

King recognized that while the Emancipation Proclamation "liberated" Negroes from the legal and formal structure of slavery, the system imposing the ideology of inferiority had never been dismantled. King

---

[6]Ibid.
[7]Ibid., 4.
[8]Ibid., 5.
[9]Ibid.
[10]Ibid.
[11]Ibid.

emphasized his point with the claim that this "proclamation of inferiority" was a tremendously vicious form of enslavement because it "is invisible and its victim helps to fashion his own bonds."[12]

King nevertheless listed four positive "enduring results" of the Emancipation Proclamation. First, it "gave force to the executive power to change conditions in the national interest on a broad and far-reaching scale."[13] This was an important point for King, who almost weekly fired off telegrams to Presidents Kennedy and Johnson urging them to enact an executive order that would eliminate racism, open up voting opportunities, and enable equal access to jobs. Second, it "dealt a devastating blow to the system of slaveholding and an economy based upon it." In so doing, it "forced a change in which the area of maneuver enemies of the Constitution might deploy was limited."[14] This was also an important point for King, revealing his strong resolve that the Constitution was a document which could be appealed to as a basis for demanding equal rights, liberty, and dignity. Third, it "enabled the Negro to play a significant role in his own liberation with the ability to organize and to struggle, with less of the bestial retaliation his slave status had permitted to his masters."[15] This point is especially important since King later developed it in close relation to his idea of dignity. Fourth, it "resurrected and restated the principle of equality upon which the founding of the nation rested."[16]

King repeated the claim that the Emancipation Proclamation helped Negroes to liberate themselves:

> The Proclamation opened the door of self-liberation by the Negro upon which he immediately acted by deserting the plantations in the south and joining Union armies in the north.[17]

It is clear, then, that King wanted the listeners to realize his confidence and positive feelings about the Emancipation Proclamation, despite the pervasive under-cutting influence of the "proclamation of inferiority."

[12]Ibid., 6.
[13]Ibid., 7.
[14]Ibid.
[15]Ibid.
[16]Ibid.
[17]Ibid., 8.

King clarifies his intention by challenging those present to make the claims of freedom within the Emancipation Proclamation "real":

> There is but one way to commemorate the Emancipation Proclamation. That is to make its declaration of freedom real; to reach back to the origins of our nation when our message of equality electrified an unfree world, and reaffirm democracy by deeds as bold and daring as the issuance of the Emancipation Proclamation.[18]

King was appealing to a predominantly Caucasian audience's sense of the original equality on which the nation was founded. Such an appeal to the "origins" of the United States was ideal in content and persuasive in intent. King never appealed to a predominantly black audience with these same claims in this manner, but rather in a manner that encouraged blacks to fight for the rights guaranteed by the civil traditions of the United States.[19] King was appealing to the self-image of white Americans in order to challenge them to take responsibility for helping to make freedom and dignity real for all persons. Yet King did not ask for a handout of liberty or of dignity; he carefully explained the pervasive nature of racism's "proclamation of inferiority," and affirmed the process of self-liberation undertaken by the Negroes themselves.

It is significant that King developed the theme of self-liberation around the Emancipation Proclamation. In 1967 King molded the two into one powerful concept, "assertive selfhood," in *Where Do We Go From Here?*:

> Psychological freedom, a firm sense of self-esteem, is the most powerful weapon against the long night of physical slavery. No Lincolnian Emancipation Proclamation or Kennedyan or Johnsonian civil rights bill can totally bring this kind of freedom. The Negro will only be truly free when he reaches down to the inner depths

---

[18]Ibid., 10.

[19]For example, King referred to the Declaration of Independence as a "huge promissory note" when speaking to predominantly black audiences: "America signed a huge promissory note. . . . It didn't say, 'Some men,' it said, 'All men.' It didn't say 'All white men,' it said, 'All men' which includes black men" ("Address at Mason Temple Mass Meeting," Memphis, TN, 18 March 1968; Martin Luther King, Jr. Center Archives, Atlanta, GA, 8).

of his own being and signs with the pen and ink of assertive selfhood his own emancipation proclamation.[20]

King called this inner assertiveness "Olympian manhood"[21] because such self-liberation would enable Negroes to "throw off the manacles of self abnegation."[22] Thus through the imagery of the Emancipation Proclamation King developed the concept that Negroes could boldly move toward "self-affirmation" by inwardly striving to liberate themselves from psychological bonds.[23]

The manner in which King used the symbolism of the Emancipation Proclamation and the Declaration of Independence within the framework of "self-liberation" is particularly significant. Furthermore, it is significant that King used these historical documents to capture the essence of a pervasive psychological struggle for dignity within the Negro. King transformed well-known historical documents into living symbols of what Negroes were doing for themselves, that is, boldly asserting their selfhood and personhood despite the pervasive presence of the "proclamation of inferiority."

The "Battle" Based on Achievement

In an article entitled "True Dignity" King employed another evocative image of dignity, that of a "battle." While the article is undated, it is safe to assume that it was written somewhere between 1961 and 1963 because it mentions the Kennedy Administration and not that of Lyndon Johnson.[24]

King began the article with the statement that true dignity is "one of man's most precious goals" because it "involves a rare state of harmony" and "security of the inner person."[25] Such harmony and security of the inner person have been historically denied Negroes because of a "bewildering paradox" wherein two contradictory images of Negroes have been presented side by side: "His enemies have made savage use of caricature

[20]King, *Where Do We Go*, 45.

[21]Ibid.

[22]Ibid.

[23]Ibid., 46.

[24]Martin Luther King, Jr., "True Dignity," undated article; Martin Luther King, Jr. Center Archives, Atlanta, GA, 6.

[25]Ibid., 1.

epicting Negroes as *buffoons devoid of a scintilla of dignity*" (my em-
hasis).[26] This caricature of the Negro was bolstered by several familiar
images in literature and the media such as "Uncle Tom; the shuffling,
izy and mentally retarded individual, the ambitionless and cowardly
ype."[27]

At the same time "another and contradictory image" portrayed the
Negro as "possessing strength of character, the will to survive over ter-
ifying obstacles, and spiritual depth."[28] The most famous symbol of this
aricature is "John Henry. . . who symbolized the conviction of all
eople that man is mightier than a machine."[29] King found both images
nadequate and condemned them as products of an ideology of oppres-
ion.[30]

King then described the process of establishing inferiority in the Negro:

> The power holders were required to prove their victims were not
> only naturally inferior, but enjoyed and willingly accepted their
> deprived status. They were pictured as a special breed whose psy-
> chological structures could not absorb or retain the creative quali-
> ties of freedom. For them servitude was the desirable way of life;
> responsibility, growth, and self-respect were biologically and spiri-
> tually alien to the psyche of the Negro.[31]

he end result of this process of indoctrination was that the Negro "of-
en blamed his poverty and backwardness on himself rather than his
ppressor or his environment."[32] As King put it, "He [the Negro] was
rainwashed to honor his exploiter and dishonor himself."[33] This process
f the "ideological distortion of history" was bolstered further by the
iolence of "guns, chains, and the whip."[34] King affirmed that the "cre-
tive use of nonviolence" by Negroes had nevertheless disarmed those

[26]Ibid.
[27]Ibid.
[28]Ibid.
[29]Ibid.
[30]Ibid., 2.
[31]Ibid.
[32]Ibid.
[33]Ibid.
[34]Ibid., 1–2.

violent weapons and enabled a more accurate view of the history and contribution of Negroes in America.[35]

For King, dignity must be founded first on achievement. By achievement, King meant a rediscovery of "Negro attainments which would support a sense of pride."[36] He turned to a rereading of the history of the Negro in the United States to support his claim, mentioning the important role that blacks had in building the cotton economy of the South and honoring the "Negro carpenters" who "built the elegant mansions of the master."[37] King also mentioned the fact that the "care, safety and training of white southern children was a Negro task."[38] King honored such facts as part of a legacy of achievement in which Negroes could affirm themselves as some of the "nation's priceless and exceptional builders and creators."[39] King declared that the "modern Negro is thus a descendent of achievers no less decisive to the national growth than many of those honored as the country's leaders."[40]

King elaborated the legacy of achievement of Negroes in America.[41] He appears determined to prove that Negroes have always struggled to have an influence on the history of the United States through the contributions of "geniuses" such as George Washington Carver, "creative endeavor," and "folk art" such as "work songs, protest songs, and spirituals."[42]

Having established the contributions of Negro achievement, King described the need of Negroes for "valid self-appraisal."[43] This self-appraisal must arise despite the fact that the Negro, in King's view, is "doubly exploited; robbed of a fair share of his [the Negro's own] product, and deprived of much of his dignity."[44] It is important to emphasize the fact that King did not state that Negroes were robbed of all their dignity, just "much" of it. This view demonstrates once again that King

[35]Ibid., 2.
[36]Ibid.
[37]Ibid., 2–3.
[38]Ibid., 3.
[39]Ibid.
[40]Ibid., 4.
[41]Ibid., 5–6.
[42]Ibid., 7.
[43]Ibid.
[44]Ibid.

viewed dignity as something innate to every person, which nonetheless could be diminished by social injustice.

King then explained why the movement for freedom is important for dignity's growth. He described the movement as a "demand for recognition of their contributions of the past, their right to equality in the present, and their justifiable share of the future."[45] King portrayed dignity in this statement as being something found in the course of history—past, present, and future. Dignity is confirmed historically for King, not merely affirmed theologically without a concrete historical referent. King implied that dignity was based on actual and concrete rights—economic, social, and political—and not on empty promises.

King identified the "demand" of the movement as a "battle." The battle is first of all a combat against "the unAmericanism of the bigot, often with inadequate support from those who cherish our democratic traditions."[46] In this way the country would come to recognize Negro dignity, for King felt dignity would never be granted as a "gift," but must be gained through the fight: "They [white Americans] are slowly learning his [the Negro's] dignity belongs to him—they are merely obligated to recognize it."[47]

Negroes involved in the struggle were learning other things, in King's view. They were discovering that "dignity is not a matter of manners" and the tawdry imitation of white "patterns of behavior."[48] Rather, King declared dignity to be a "heritage."[49] This heritage is "innate" and can be cultivated and revealed "as a quality as much their own as their bodies and souls."[50] In this section of the speech King appears to attack directly those who would find their dignity outside of themselves, particularly those who define the "dignified life" as a life that imitates white patterns of behaviors, values, and standards.

King concluded his description of the battle for dignity by reminding the listener that the affirmation of one's heritage of dignity was "not a simple unfolding process."[51] It is, instead, a battle, since against this development are "arrayed centuries of subtle and crude propaganda de-

---

[45]Ibid., 8.
[46]Ibid.
[47]Ibid.
[48]Ibid., 7–8.
[49]Ibid., 9.
[50]Ibid.
[51]Ibid.

vices and institutions."[52] King listed discrimination, segregation, and patronizing attitudes as three of the most prominent opponents of dignity:

> Discrimination erodes dignity. Segregation smothers it. Patronizing attitudes belittle it. These are not all equal in effect. Discrimination is the worst disease inhibiting dignity's growth.[53]

King enumerates discriminatory actions such as "being forced into the most menial employment, to receive a second-class education, to live in slums."[54] The concrete debilitating effect of such acts are that they are "blows to dignity which cripple it and often crush its living force entirely."[55] Still, King wants to affirm that despite the existence of the "three evils," Negro dignity was not utterly destroyed:

> And yet, three hundred years of history prove that not even all of these three evils—not even the rape of Africa to initiate the process, was successful in destroying Negro dignity. It lived thru it all, and grew.[56]

An understanding of this statement is dependent upon our previous discussion of King's view of dignity as a quality innate to humanity and related to social status, citizenship, and civil rights. King pointed to an aspect of dignity that Negroes possessed simply because they were children of God, created in God's image. This aspect of dignity could be diminished but not destroyed, in King's eyes, because it is the possession of every person. It is necessary, however, to add that King clarified his statement by stressing the need for the battle for dignity as a quality related to social status and citizenship:

> The simple truth is that *dignity is created by man's constructive work and God's love and no power exists which can take either*

[52]Ibid.
[53]Ibid.
[54]Ibid.
[55]Ibid.
[56]Ibid.

from the Negro. His dignity will exist as long as he lives and fights for human rights. [my emphasis][57]

The addition reveals two important things. First, dignity is not only innate and related to the *imago dei*, but it is also the creative result of the combination of "constructive work" and God's love. We have seen already that King understood God's love (agape) as a binding and constructive force necessary in the creation of a greater sense of dignity. Second, King apparently felt that one should not silently acquiesce to racism's negating effects on the self, but rather that dignity for the Negro demanded the activity of struggle for human rights. The notion of the necessity of "struggle" has been discussed both in terms of its Hegelian valence (see chapter 3) and in relation to the understanding that King gained from his grandfather and father (see chapter 1). In this statement we find a mature King tying his understanding of "struggle" directly into his view of the battle for dignity that faces the Negro in racist America. In this sense, King also combined his own creative theological understanding of dignity with what he had learned from his family about the need for struggle.

King also referred here to "human rights." This is yet another significant phrase that became symbolic of King's mature view of dignity. I turn next to an analysis of what King meant by this term.

Human Rights: The "Dream" and King's World Perspective

King's discussion of "human rights" appears to have come at a time in his career when he wanted to clarify what he meant in his famous "I Have a Dream" speech of 23 August 1963. He did not mention "human rights" with great concreteness in his speeches before that time. The image of a dream was particularly offensive to many of the more radical elements of the black community, including Malcolm X.[58] I want to argue that King's understanding of the American "Dream" must be seen within the context of his vision of "human rights," so that both symbols articulated King's mature vision of human dignity. I shall first discuss King's vision of the American "Dream," then his view of "human rights,"

---

[57]Ibid.

[58]See Malcolm X's stinging criticism of the entire March on Washington in "Message to the Grass Roots" in *Malcolm X Speaks* (ed. George Breitman; New York: Grove, 1965) 1–17.

and finally the way in which he increasingly applied these insights to the global community.

King's understanding of the American "Dream" can best be understood as his unique contribution to what is now called "public theology."[59] For my argument, the "Dream" symbol has value as King's way of linking his trust in the American creed—taken from the Declaration of Independence's assertion about the equality of all "men"—to his constructive demand for greater dignity and rights for Negroes (and in fact, all people) living in the United States. An examination of the salient points of his speech, "The American Dream" (1961) reveals this tie rather clearly.

King began with the assertion that "America is essentially a dream, a dream as yet unfulfilled."[60] The "Dream" is of a land "where men of all races, of all nationalities, and of all creeds can live together as brothers."[61] King found the essence of the "Dream" in the egalitarian assertion of the Declaration of Independence, an assertion that he "lifts to cosmic proportions":

> The substance of the dream is expressed in those sublime words lifted to cosmic proportions: "We hold these truths to be self-evident, that all men are created equal, that they are endowed by their Creator with certain unalienable rights, that among these are life, liberty, and the pursuit of happiness." This is the dream.[62]

King found in this "dream" an "amazing universalism" that is ultimately inclusive of all persons.[63] King praised the Declaration of Independence for its direct language in asserting the "basic rights" of individuals not as linked to the "state," but as "God-given."[64] It is important to see the

[59]Max Stackhouse and Martin Marty have given much attention to this field of theological study as the interface of social ethics and theology; see Max Stackhouse, *Creeds, Society, and Human Rights* (Grand Rapids: Eerdmans, 1984) as well as Martin E. Marty, *Religion and Republic: The American Circumstance* (Boston: Beacon, 1987). Curiously, neither of these authors discuss King's contribution to the field, although Marty does mention King.

[60]King, "The American Dream," in Washington, *Testament of Hope*, 208.

[61]Ibid.

[62]Ibid.

[63]Ibid.

[64]Ibid.

connection in King's mind between "basic rights" and God-given rights. For King, basic human rights cannot be "conferred or derived" by the state, but are given legitimacy and authority because they are God-given.

Significantly, King's appeal to God-given rights forms a basis for using the Declaration of Independence as an authoritative document concerning dignity. Utilizing again the language of Boston Personalism, King tied the Declaration's call for equality into a recognition of the "dignity and worth of human personality":

> Very seldom if ever in the history of the world has a sociopolitical document expressed in such profoundly eloquent and unequivocal language the dignity and worth of human personality. *The American Dream reminds us that every man is heir to the legacy of worthiness.* [my emphasis][65]

A question arises at this point. Since King refers to the Judaeo-Christian heritage of the worthiness of every person (see chapter 5), did he implicitly conflate his understanding of the ethical demands of the doctrine of *imago dei* with what he proposes as the effect of the American Dream? That is to say, is there merely a similarity between the *imago dei* and the American Dream as ideals of human dignity, or does King unconsciously conflate the two?

Continued exegesis of this particular speech, which goes on to demand that the American Dream become a "reality," suggests an answer.[66] King listed four points whereby the "Dream" might become a reality. First, King stated that "all of us must develop a world perspective if we are to survive."[67] This point refers to King's often repeated injunction that "all of life is interrelated."[68] For King, the cultivation of this kind of interrelated "world perspective" would "realize the American dream."[69] Second, King called for the nation to "keep our moral and spiritual progress abreast with our scientific and technological advances."[70]

[65]Ibid.
[66]Ibid., 209.
[67]Ibid.
[68]King (ibid., 210) repeats this injunction later in this speech.
[69]Ibid.
[70]Ibid.

King utilized Weber's distinction between "civilization" and "culture" to make his point:

> Civilization refers to what we use; culture refers to what we are. . . . The greatest problem confronting us today is that we have allowed the means by which we live to outdistance the ends for which we live. We have allowed civilization to outrun our culture, and so we are in danger now of ending up with guided missiles in the hands of misguided men.[71]

King was determined to link the survival of the world with the realization of "our mission and dream of the world" by holding "the means by which we live abreast with the ends for which we live."[72]

Third, King called for the United States to "get rid of the notion once and for all that there are superior and inferior races."[73] He critiqued racism as both "resting on this fallacy" and as dehumanizing the Negro.[74] King's remedy was a challenge to Negroes to use actively all the "freedom we already possess" to achieve excellence.[75] He further challenged Negroes to remember that "inner determination can often break through the outer shackles of circumstance."[76] For King, all of these points were closely linked to his view of human dignity and his theological anthropology.

King's final point was that "we must continue to engage in creative protest in order to break down all of those barriers that make it impossible for the dream to be realized."[77] King rejoiced in the power of nonviolent resistance to "secure moral ends by moral means" and to achieve a more just society.[78] King warned against a philosophy of "black supremacy" as "substituting one tyranny for another."[79] King criticized black supremacy once again from the vantage point of what King believed to be God's understanding of human dignity:

[71]Ibid., 210–11.
[72]Ibid., 211.
[73]Ibid.
[74]Ibid.
[75]Ibid., 211–12.
[76]Ibid., 212.
[77]Ibid., 212–13.
[78]Ibid., 214.
[79]Ibid., 215.

Black supremacy is as dangerous as white supremacy, and God is not interested merely in the freedom of black men and brown men and yellow men. God is interested in the freedom of the whole human race and in the creation of a society where all men can live together as brothers, where every man will respect the dignity and worth of human personality.[80]

It is important to remember that King defined "freedom" as the "highest expression of the image of God" (see chapter 5). The emphasis on human freedom, the interrelatedness of all persons, and the dignity and worth of all persons seen in King's four points demonstrates that King's American "Dream" bears a strong resemblance to his basic theological anthropology, especially in relationship to his doctrine of *imago dei*. The two are, in a sense, parallel concepts, both united in their valuation of the human person as inherently worthy and possessing dignity.

The same concerns for dignity and the interrelatedness of all persons can be found in King's famous "I Have A Dream" speech. King reminded the crowd that the nonviolent struggle is the "high plane of dignity and discipline" that must not be allowed to "degenerate into physical violence."[81] King reminded the crowd further of the need for a "biracial army" marching together against racial injustice and appealed to his concepts of freedom and the interrelatedness of persons:

The marvelous new militancy which has engulfed the Negro community must not lead us to a distrust of all white people, for many of our white brothers, as evidenced by their presence here today, have come to realize that their destiny is tied up with our destiny and they have come to realize that their freedom is inextricably bound to our freedom. This offense we share mounted to storm the battlements of injustice must be carried forth by a biracial army. We cannot walk alone.[82]

King again referred to the American Dream as synonymous with the declaration of equality in the Declaration of Independence:

---

[80]Ibid.
[81]King, "I Have A Dream," in Washington, *Testament of Hope*, 218.
[82]Ibid.

> It is a dream deeply rooted in the American dream that one day this
> nation will rise up and live out the true meaning of its creed—we
> hold these truths to be self-evident, that all men are created equal.[83]

King elaborated other aspects of the "Dream" in an "Address befor
the National Press Club," particularly by explaining how economic "op
portunity" was an essential part of his vision:

> We are simply seeking to bring into full realization the American
> dream—a dream yet unfulfilled. A dream of equality of opportu-
> nity, of privilege and property widely distributed; a dream of a land
> where men no longer argue that the color of a man's skin deter-
> mines the content of his character; the dream of a land where every
> man will respect the dignity and worth of human personality.[84]

King developed more fully this notion of opportunity in his view c
human rights. King felt that there were two elements to human rights
"recognition" and "opportunity."[85] If these were "being granted equall
to all, there could be no people without dignity."[86] Dignity, so definec
rested on the recognition of one's achievements and worth as a person.[8]
King believed that such recognition was expanding in 1964. At the sam
time, King decried the apparent stagnation and recession in opportu
nity.[88]

King felt that opportunity could be gained by a continued "legal as
sault on the system of segregation" in proper balance with the "direc
action" of nonviolent protest.[89] King saw the two in complementar
relationship, each needing the other to "become more effective."[90] Kin
demonstrated his confidence that by the effecting of legal changes along

[83]Ibid., 219.

[84]Martin Luther King, Jr., "An Address Before The National Press Club,
Washington, DC, 19 July 1962; in Washington, *Testament of Hope*, 105.

[85]Martin Luther King, Jr., "World March Toward Human Rights," 28 Ma
1964; Martin Luther King, Jr. Center Archives, Atlanta, GA, 3.

[86]Ibid.

[87]Ibid.

[88]Ibid.

[89]Ibid., 3, 4.

[90]Ibid., 4.

side the pressure produced by nonviolent direct action, opportunities for
blacks could be increased. Furthermore, he had confidence that the "law
itself is a form of education" in which whites, as they were legally
compelled to include Negroes in the work force, could learn to respect
Negroes.[91]

In a later annual report to the Southern Christian Leadership Conference King expanded what he meant by "opportunities." In this report
King is especially concerned to demonstrate that the Negro "is not struggling for some vague abstract rights, but for concrete and prompt improvement in his way of life."[92] King demanded a higher "family income,"
higher paying jobs, and that the Negro "be absorbed into our economic
system" in a manner suitable to dignity.[93] He proceeded to state that the
struggle "at bottom, is a struggle for opportunities."[94] Such opportunities
are not "charity," or "languishing on welfare rolls," but the training and
"realistic aid" that will enable Negroes to seize the opportunity for economic equality as it is offered.[95] What King demanded by the term
"opportunity" was the realistic access and aid necessary for the Negro to
have economic dignity.

After King received the Nobel Prize in 1964 he appears increasingly
to have interpreted this honor as giving him a place to speak out on the
need for human rights and dignity throughout the world. King's concern
for global issues of oppression can be seen as early as the Montgomery
bus boycott (see chapter 1). From that time until the end of his life, he
saw the American Negro's struggle for dignity as part of a "worldwide
struggle" for dignity and human rights.

For King, one international concern of particular prominence was the
condemnation of the system of apartheid in South Africa as dehumanizing. In an address given in late 1965, King talked about the Pan-African
bonding that increased the dignity of all Negroes around the globe.[96]
King spoke of how the nonviolent struggle and attempt of the American

---

[91]Ibid., 5–6.

[92]Martin Luther King, Jr., "SCLC Annual Report," 2 December 1964; Martin
Luther King, Jr. Center Archives, Atlanta, GA, 15.

[93]Ibid., 15–16.

[94]Ibid., 16.

[95]Ibid.

[96]See Martin Luther King, Jr., "Address to the South Africa Benefit of the
American Committee on Africa," Hunter College, NY, 10 December 1965; Martin
Luther King, Jr. Center Archives, Atlanta, GA, 5.

Negro to "provide moral leadership" was affected profoundly by the "immense inspiration" of "the successful struggles of those Africans who have attained freedom in their own nations."[97] The capacity of black persons to "govern states, build democratic institutions, sit in world tribunals, and participate in global decision-making gives every Negro needed sense of dignity."[98] King called on this "powerful unity of Negro with Negro" and "white with Negro" to eliminate the "most potent and entrenched racism" of the world—apartheid.[99] Lastly, King condemned apartheid because it reversed the current positive historical trend of "advancing from pre-human to human" to one of "traveling backward in time from human to pre-human."[100] It is important to note how King spoke of dignity in terms of his analysis of the human being; he critiqued apartheid on the authority of the deontological principle of personalism that all persons must be respected in such a manner that affirms their entire personality.

The Last Years, 1966–1968: Somebodyness and the Dignity of Labor

As King's public influence began to encounter increasing criticism and outright rebellion from a separatist black militancy, he was compelled to respond to newer slogans and ideals such as "black power."[101] With the successful Selma campaign of 1965 and the passing of the Voting Rights Act, King's influence began to decline. In the James Meredith March of 1966, Stokely Carmichael first defied King with the slogans "Black Power" and "We Shall Overrun." The Chicago campaign of 1966 followed, with its inconclusive results. There was also a general decrease of congressional interest in passing legislation that would afford blacks an equal opportunity. Many liberal whites had been offended by the separatist tone of the new black militants and had left the movement. In such a turbulent and unsettled time it is fascinating to observe that King returned to two powerful symbols of dignity that he had learned

[97]Ibid.
[98]Ibid.
[99]Ibid., 6.
[100]Ibid.
[101]See Martin Luther King, Jr., "Black Power Defined," in Washington, *Testament of Hope*, 303–12, as it appeared in *New York Times Magazine*, 11 June 1967. For a fuller discussion of King's response to black power, see King, *Where Do We Go*, 23–66.

rom his family—somebodyness and "all labor has dignity." I want to lemonstrate how King enlarged these two terms so that they could speak with relevancy to the concerns of the late 1960s.

King had used the term somebodyness since the early days of his ublic life. Often he spoke of somebodyness in counterpoint with the ervasive sense of "nobodyness" afflicting the Negro:

> Nothing could be more tragic than to build a nation with a large segment of that nation feeling that they had no stake in this society; feeling that they have nothing to lose, and where thousands of people are jobless. Many live in rat-infested housing conditions, and they find themselves frustrated day in and day out, constantly fighting against a nagging sense of "nobodyness." For them it is often difficult to hear the pleas of nonviolence.[102]

King challenged his legislative audience to help those suffering the despair f "nobodyness" to realize their "sense of belonging, a sense of omebodyness,' and a feeling that they do count!"[103]

Later, in an interview on the Merv Griffin Show, King described ore completely the potential meaning of a sense of somebodyness. In nswering Griffin's question about what the civil rights movement had done for the Negro individually," King replied:

> Well, I think the greatest thing that it has done, is that it has *given the Negro a new sense of dignity, and a new sense of somebodyness.* And this is the greatest victory we have won. Turning away from the external changes that have come about, I think that the greatest thing that has taken place is the *internal change in the psyche of the Negro.* And the Negro has a *sense of pride* that he's desperately needed all along. And he is *able to stand up,* and *feel that he is a man.* [my emphasis][104]

---

[102]Martin Luther King, Jr., "Address to a Joint Convention of the Two Houses f the General Court of Massachusetts," 22 April 1965; Martin Luther King, Jr. enter Archives, Atlanta, GA, 11.

[103]Ibid.

[104]Martin Luther King, Jr., "Interview on Merv Griffin Show," 6 July 1967; lartin Luther King, Jr. Center Archives, Atlanta, GA, 6.

King went on to state that developing somebodyness is the "only way to solve the real problem and grapple with the problem of the future."[105] Through somebodyness the Negro "has straightened his back up," and it is "impossible to ride a man's back unless it's bent."[106]

King listed four qualities of this "new sense of dignity and new sense of somebodyness": an internal change in the psyche of the Negro, a sense of pride, an ability to stand up, and the feeling of being a "man." The sense of pride that we observed in King's early writing is retained here. Daddy King's term, "standing up," is incorporated into the sense of dignity and somebodyness and related to a stronger sense of being a "man."

The theological roots of King's understanding of "somebodyness" combine his conception of the *imago dei* with motifs concerning dignity from Boston Personalism and his family tradition. This becomes clear in an examination of a late sermon, "Lost Sheep," in which King used the parable of the lost sheep (Luke 15:1–10; Matt 18:12–14) to describe God as one who seeks every lost person. The second point of the sermon was that the parable of the lost sheep "tells us about the dignity and worth of all human personality."[107] King continued: "God is concerned about all of His children and He has stamped on all of his children a seal of preciousness. One lost child is significant to Him. Every individual is worthful."[108]

King's language, that of a Boston personalist regarding the worth and dignity of each and every individual person, is now quite familiar to us. He added another interesting image to his doctrine of *imago dei*, namely the "seal of preciousness." King elaborated further by articulating his understanding of somebodyness as originating in God's declaration of the worth and dignity of human beings:

> So if you're worried about your somebodyness, don't worry any longer because God fixed it a long time ago. He said, "I'm making all of my children in my image, and I will declare that every child of mine has dignity and every child of mine has worth."[109]

[105]Ibid.
[106]Ibid.
[107]King, "Lost Sheep," 6.
[108]Ibid.
[109]Ibid.

his quotation makes it clear that King placed his understanding of omebodyness within the parameters of his doctrine of *imago dei*, although he articulated this theological tenet in the language of Kantianinfluenced Boston Personalism.

We shall not have fully exhausted the resources within this sermon if e stop here, however, for King went on to claim that because God has iven worth to every individual by virtue of every person being God's child," then no matter what one's human status or educational level, ne has worth:

> Maybe you didn't get much education, maybe you didn't have the privilege to develop skills that made you articulate, but don't worry about it. The God that this parable talks about is a God who said, "The one who knows not the difference between 'you does' and 'you don't' is just as significant as the PhD in English.["]. . . The God this parable talks about tells me that the 'NoD' is just as significant as the PhD. The God that this parable talks about tells me that the man who's been to 'Nohouse' is as significant as the man who's been to Morehouse. So don't worry where you live and who you are, *you are somebody because you are God's child. He stamped dignity and worth on all of his children. And whenever we see this something happens in our souls that causes us to stand up because we know we are somebody.* [my emphasis][110]

In *Where Do We Go From Here?* King used his concept of someodyness as the answer to the dilemma of the "shattered dreams and asted hopes of the Negro's daily life."[111] Somebodyness is a "positive sponse" that overturns the instilled sense of "worthlessness" that King w as the legacy of slavery.[112] King then articulated a view of mebodyness that, through self-liberation, incorporated his previous mbols of dignified assertive selfhood and dignity:

> The Negro must assert for all to hear and see a majestic sense of worth. There is such a thing as a desegregated mind. We must no longer allow the outer chains of an oppressive society to shackle

[110]Ibid., 6–7.
[111]King, *Where Do We Go*, 122.
[112]Ibid.

our minds. With courage and fearlessness we must set out daringly to stabilize our egos. This alone will give us a confirmation of our roots and a validation of our worth.[113]

King affirmed the psychological necessity of self-liberation here. He spoke about an inner, mental state of worthlessness that only a "rugged sense" of somebodyness can overcome. This kind of somebodyness is the assertion of one's worth despite the racist culture's pervasive accusation and insinuation that one is worthless. Yet I would be remiss to allow the reader to believe that King was being simple-minded about the need for psychological self-liberation despite the unliberated nature of society. In *Where Do We Go From Here?* King demonstrated at length that a concern for dignity must be accompanied by the "elimination of poverty."[114] King desired that society guarantee "secure employment or a minimum income" in order to insure that dignity could come "within reach for all."[115] Thus it is necessary that this particular association of somebodyness with self-liberation not be misread as King's simplification of his demand that society be held accountable for the economic dignity of all persons. It is, rather, a strong articulation of the psychological factors (self-liberation) that necessarily combine with the economic factors.

King continued by stating that somebodyness "means the refusal to be ashamed of being black."[116] King chastised blacks for using "bleaching creams that promise to make us lighter," and "processing" hair in order to "make it appear straight."[117] King challenged the Negro to embrace instead "self-acceptance and self-appreciation" of dark skin and non-European hair.[118] King wanted black people to realize their own beauty without disparaging the beauty of whites, thus, "black people are very beautiful."[119] He turned to the musical image of a piano keyboard to describe an appreciation for the diversity of beauty: "Life's piano can only produce the melodies of brotherhood when it is recognized that the

[113]Ibid., 122–23.
[114]Ibid., 87.
[115]Ibid.
[116]Ibid., 123.
[117]Ibid.
[118]Ibid.
[119]Ibid.

lack keys are as basic, necessary, and beautiful as the white keys."[120]
King believed that if blacks gained self-acceptance and self-appreciation
of their beauty, then a process would begin whereby white Americans
could view integration as "an opportunity to participate in the beauty of
diversity."[121]

Finally, King defined somebodyness as *courage*:

> Courage, the determination not to be overwhelmed by any object,
> that power of the mind capable of sloughing off the thingification
> of the past, will be the Negro's most potent weapon in achieving
> self-respect.[122]

Such courage undergirds somebodyness with a "spirit" and a "drive"
inspired by "our slave forebears" who never gave up the hope to be
free.[123]

Until the end of his life, King continued to develop his understanding
of somebodyness as the necessary foundation of both psychological and
economic progress. In "An Address in Selma" in February 1968, King
once more enjoined the listeners to believe that they were "somebody"
and "God's children."[124] King associated the knowledge of one's status
with God as the basis for a better economic condition:

> If you are a child of God, you aren't supposed to live in a slum,
> where you don't have wall-to-wall carpet but wall to wall rats and
> roaches. *If you are a child of God, you aren't supposed to be at the*
> *bottom of the economic ladder.* We've got to believe in our hearts
> that we are somebody, and that we count, and that we aren't going
> to allow anybody to deprive us of our personhood and our freedom.
> [my emphasis][125]

---

[120]Ibid.
[121]Ibid.
[122]Ibid.
[123]Ibid.
[124]Martin Luther King, Jr., "An Address to a Mass Meeting in Selma," 18
February 1968; Martin Luther King, Jr. Center Archives, Atlanta, GA, 6.
[125]Ibid.

What did King mean here by "personhood and freedom"? He was no
drawing on his understanding of the person as inherently worthful, no
was he speaking about the person as rational. Rather, King appears t
have been speaking of the aspect of dignity that, in his understanding
can be "deprived" and diminished: the social aspect that reflects a grea
deal on economic security.

King was determined that the marchers present become aware that th
need to protest for better economic conditions is part of the struggle fo
human dignity. In King's view, dignity was not divorced from a person'
social and economic context, but influenced by it. By 1968 he was abl
to demonstrate through the symbol of somebodyness that protesting fo
greater economic opportunities was an essential aspect of the growth o
human dignity.

King's last campaign took place in Memphis during the spring o
1968 and came about because he decided to become involved in a strik
by black garbage workers. This strike provided King with an opportunit
to affirm another understanding of dignity that he had learned from hi
father—the dignity of all labor. Previously, King had affirmed the dig
nity of all labor. For instance, in a Louisville voter registration rally i
1967 King had stated that "all labor has dignity."[126] King elaborated th
claim:

> People talking about menial labor. The only thing that makes any
> job menial is the wage. . . . Now I contend that the man who
> sweeps the floor in the hospital is just as significant as the doctor.
> Because if that man doesn't sweep the floor, the germs will begin
> to circulate and could make the ill worse than before. And so that
> man deserves a livable income.[127]

In the Memphis campaign King inspired the striking garbage worker
to remember that they were "commanding that this city will respect th
dignity of labor."[128] King criticized those who could "overlook the sig

---

[126]Martin Luther King, Jr., "Which Ways Its Soul Shall Go," address to
voter registration rally, Louisville, KY, 2 August 1967; Martin Luther King, J
Center Archives, Atlanta, GA, 9.

[127]Ibid.

[128]Martin Luther King, Jr. "Address at Mason Temple Mass Meeting," Mer
phis, TN, 18 March 1968; Martin Luther King, Jr. Center Archives, Atlanta, GA
2.

nificance of those who are not in professional jobs, . . . or big jobs."[129] Instead King wanted the garbage workers to know that "whenever you are engaged in work that serves humanity, and is for the building of humanity, it has dignity, and it has worth."[130]

In phrases that recall the power of King's oratory, King built up to a climax (which the transcript recorder could not fully record) concerning the dignity of garbage workers:

> One day our society will come to see this. One day our society will come to respect the sanitation worker if it is to survive. For the person who picks up garbage, in the final analysis, is as significant as the physician. . . . If he doesn't do his job. . . (applause drowns out the rest of the phrase) All labor has worth.[131]

It is noteworthy that King used the maxim "all labor has worth" to make the case for a livable income as well as for greater social respect and dignity. It is fitting that King died in a struggle for the dignity of garbage workers because in this struggle the question of economics was so overtly combined with a demand for greater human respect. It is also fitting that King appears to have incorporated into this struggle the insights gained in his childhood regarding the inherent value and dignity of all forms of labor.

Conclusions

In this chapter I have discussed seven examples of historical documents, phrases, and symbolic metaphors. Between 1962 and 1968 King built these into motivic concepts[132] to describe his understanding of dignity. They are: (1) the Emancipation Proclamation and the Declaration of Independence, (2) self-liberation, (3) the Battle, (4) the Dream, (5) human rights, (6) somebodyness, and (7) "All Labor has Dignity."

In the first motif of dignity—the Emancipation Proclamation and the Declaration of Independence—King appealed to two authoritative documents in the history of the United States. In so doing, King established his understanding of dignity within the parameters of the nation's egali-

---

[129]Ibid.
[130]Ibid.
[131]Ibid.
[132]For a definition of "motivic concepts," see above p. xxiii.

tarian creed—"all men are created equal." King utilized the respect given to these documents by white Americans to undergird the moral and civil legitimacy of the struggle for dignity.

King derived the second motif of dignity, self-liberation, from the empowering effects of the first motif. Self-liberation involved the assertion of selfhood required to insure the proper self-respect necessary for a dignified person. King urged self-liberated Negroes to sign their own declaration of independence and make their own personal proclamation of emancipation from those structures within society that denied the Negro self-respect and dignity.

The third motif of dignity was the metaphor of the battle. Dignity was not simply granted by those holding power; it was fought for by those denied equality and human rights. As such, those involved in the nonviolent movement were also engaged, according to King, in a battle for their own dignity. Victory in this battle was insured, in King's mind, as long as nonviolent protesters continue to engage in *constructive work energized by God's love*. The battle motif incorporated elements of his grandfather's injunction to remember that progress can never be gained without a struggle, as well as King's own synthetic doctrine of agape. For King, the battle for dignity was a struggle to gain a firm and sure grip on the "heritage" of slave forbears who never "gave up" or "gave in" to the negating effects of slavery.

King's appropriation of the American Dream was the fifth motif of dignity. The dream for King was not just the theme of the famous and inspiring speech popular recently. It was also a concept of dignity that incorporates two norms: the *norm of inclusivity* guaranteed by the American Dream of equal opportunity for all and guided by the *theological norm of the imago dei* that undergirded King's inclusive vision of humanity. King elaborated the American Dream in a manner that made it parallel to his theological anthropology: that all persons are children of God, that all of life is interrelated, that freedom is an American right because it is a fundamental part of God's image within each of us, and that nonviolent protest is the most creative, morally appropriate, and powerful way of insuring human dignity for the oppressed.

In the fifth motif of dignity, human rights, King fleshed out certain concrete economic and social reforms necessary for the development of Negro dignity. Human rights, in King's mind, were founded on the recognition of one's innate worth, personhood, and heritage, on opportunities provided for the Negro to secure a livable income, a secure job, and decent housing, and thereby on secure economic dignity. The struggle for human rights was not limited to oppressed Negroes in the United States, for King, but had also motivated struggles in Asia, Latin America, and Africa.

King's doctrine of human rights was his way of clarifying the part of his understanding of dignity that was undeveloped earlier (see chapter 2). By appealing to human rights, King could criticize the United States and the West in general for robbing the oppressed of their dignity. Theologically, dignity cannot be utterly or absolutely "robbed," but it can be "robbed" through economic, legal, and political machinations. King's definition of dignity implies a social side that can be diminished, robbed, and denied by economic factors.

King's sixth motif of dignity, somebodyness, was the climax and synthesis of all the others, for it incorporated elements of the previous five. Those elements include the power of nonviolent resistance in the formation of dignity, the constructive power of love in dignity, and the reconstructive power of boldly and fearlessly asserting one's selfhood despite the persistent and pervasive presence of social pressure that instills a feeling of worthlessness.

Somebodyness, however, also involved the assertion of self-appreciation for the beauty of being black. While it might be possible to say that King simply appropriated the popular slogan of the day, "Black is Beautiful," such a statement is too simplistic. Rather, King incorporated ideas of black pride and black beauty directly into this powerful notion of somebodyness in order to affirm an aspect of dignity that he had not previously affirmed with such strength. Namely, King affirmed black pride in black bodies. Black bodies, traditionally denied value, are affirmed because they are part of the whole person. Black bodies are to be affirmed as a needed part of our God-given humanity, for King, just as the black keys are a necessary part of the piano keyboard. King overturned what Reinhold Niebuhr described as the "sin of pride,"[133] transforming "pride" into a vital element of human self-appreciation necessary in the formation of dignity. King's valuation of black beauty also demonstrates how he incorporated and modified the virtue of pride mentioned in his earlier view of dignity. King renamed pride as self-appreciation and self-acceptance. Furthermore, pride is achieved

---

[133]Reinhold Niebuhr held "the sin of pride" to be based on three "types": "pride of power, pride of knowledge, and pride of virtue" (*Nature and Destiny*, 188).

through the bold audacity of another virtue—courage. Courage for King involved the determination to slough off the "thingification" of the past and the determination not to be overwhelmed. Courage enables an appropriate pride in black beauty, as well as the strength to convince others of the diversity of beauty that is possible in a pluralistic society.

King's final motif of dignity was that all labor has dignity. This motif recalls his father's influential work ethic and the sermonic ethic of work in King's personal life. King was able to combine within this motif a criticism of those who denied respect to those whose work was not professional or "big paying" with a demand for a livable income for all persons.

The first five motifs appear particularly active in King's thought from 1961 through 1965. From 1965 until 1968, however, the last two motifs gained greater prominence. This is particularly interesting because the last two motifs, somebodyness and "all labor has dignity," are rooted in King's childhood. King used phrases originally heard from his father, mother, and grandmother to incorporate all of his previous concepts of dignity.

These seven motifs form a comprehensive symbolic understanding of Kings understanding of "dignity." King, of course, did not write a systematic exposition of dignity. I have provided a systematic framework within which King's symbolic motifs of dignity can be appreciated. It is now necessary to ask whether King's seven motifs provide us with an adequate resource for constructing a contemporary theory of dignity.

7

CONCLUSIONS AND CRITIQUE OF KING'S VIEW OF DIGNITY AS A RESOURCE FOR A THEORY OF DIGNITY

In this chapter I present a summary of King's view of dignity, analyzing its strengths and weaknesses. After presenting King's motivic symbols of dignity, I shall then revise King's understanding with the hope of retaining as many as possible of King's original intentions, but also with the hope of supplementing areas of his thought that are inadequate for our contemporary world. The normative criterion for determining the adequacy of King's thought for contemporary times will be that of *inclusiveness*, particularly gender inclusion. I shall employ the arguments of James Cone, Cornel West, Katie Cannon, and bell hooks that the norm of gender inclusion is one of the most important criteria for constructing a genuinely liberative understanding of dignity for African-Americans. I shall conclude with a suggestion for building a contemporary theory of dignity upon King's motivic symbol of somebodyness. Because somebodyness is the most inclusive and complex synthesis of all of

King's previous symbols of dignity, it is the most appropriate symbol for use in the creation of a new theory of dignity. Furthermore, somebodyness has the dynamic potential to be a meaningful step forward in our human understanding of dignity both in academic and pastoral contexts.

Summary

Martin Luther King, Jr.'s understanding of dignity was deeply rooted in the African-American community. He was profoundly influenced by both the protest tradition of the King fathers (Daddy King and Grandfather A. D. Williams) and the wisdom tradition of the King mothers (Grandmother Williams, Grandmother Delia Lindsay King, and Alberta Williams King). Particularly, King learned from the fathers that dignity consisted of "standing up like a man" to the system of racial injustice, that dignity consisted of being a minister who was a strong fighter and advocate for justice, and that all labor had intrinsic value and sanctity. From the mothers King came to understand that dignity meant that he was "somebody," beloved by God, and able to love even his enemies because of his Christian convictions.

Early in his public ministry (1955–1961) King was not able to articulate with great precision his understanding of dignity. He was, however, able to affirm that dignity was something that was both *inherent* to human persons, and *a thing to be fought for* through protest. At this time King viewed dignity as a quality of a *people*, belonging to nations as well as individuals. His emphasis was on the *growth and development* of dignity, seeing the public protest for greater citizenship rights as an important way both of becoming aware of one's inherent dignity and of developing a richer and deeper sense of dignity and self-respect.

King's early view of dignity was shaped by the virtues of hope and courage. Courage enabled protesters to march in spite of violent opposition. Hope, for King, was more than a theological virtue described in textbooks; it was based on empirically measured social progress. King was able to systematize his presentation of dignity into a historical typology (1962). Through this typology King described American history as having three discernible periods of race relations, each progressively more inclusive.

His view of dignity was informed by a Boston Personalist philosophical background that King incorporated into his view of nonviolence. King synthesized personalism's affirmation of the human person as the center of value with Hegel's view of historical conflict (dialectic) and with Kant's view of the inherent moral value of persons. To this synthesis King added a view of nonviolence that was particularly influenced by Gandhi's ideals of noncooperation, *ahimsa*, and love force. Nonviolence, for King, was both a strategy for social change and a philosophical basis for developing a new sense of dignity. Moreover, nonviolence provided a moral means to the moral end of greater rights and thereby instilled a profound sense of self-respect in its practitioners.

King's view of dignity was also undergirded by a theological anthropology that stressed the centrality of the doctrine that persons are made in the image of God. For King an adequate theological anthropology must necessarily affirm both human rationality and the needs of human bodies. He soundly criticized those theological anthropologies which cast the human being outside of the categories of concrete social and biological needs. Human beings, as created in God's image, are essentially beings of *freedom*, in King's view. Freedom was the highest expression of the *imago dei*. This freedom of the image of God can be diminished by social injustice, but can never be utterly removed. Through nonviolent protest, the diminished freedom of persons can be regained and restored. Ultimately, for King, the goal for human beings was to develop a "Triangle of Personality" wherein each individual person lives in loving relationship to self, neighbors, and God.

The theological ethic that energized King's view of dignity was expressed in his high view of agape. Agape, for King, served as the energizing force that binds persons together in a network of mutuality and self-respect. Agape permeates nonviolence and enables nonviolent protest to transform "nobodies" into "somebodies." Agape creates hope, a virtue King held to be the theologically essential quality of life: hope enables the oppressed never to give up and hope empowers them to continue resisting self-degradation while looking forward to a better future.

I have systematized King's later view of dignity (1962–1968) into seven evolving motivic symbols (see p. xxiii). The seven motifs found their eventual apotheosis and complex synthesis in the symbol of somebodyness, because within somebodyness the values, programs, and intention of all the previous symbols are incorporated.

Strengths and Weaknesses

One of the greatest strengths of King's view of dignity is its ability to combine theological, philosophical, and ethical categories into a program meaningful for concrete social change. His view was conceived out of elements of African-American church spirituality and protest as King experienced these as a child in Atlanta. Into these elements King incorporated the philosophical facets of his academic training, as well as theological and ethical tenets, in order to address directly the social injustices experienced by Negroes within the system of segregation. Thus King's view of nonviolence not only enabled Negroes to have a new sense of dignity and self-respect, but it also provided access to non-segregated public facilities, helped to goad Congress into passing progressive civil rights legislation, and began opening economic doors of opportunity to a larger segment of the black population. By doing so, King's understanding of dignity firmly tied progress in terms of individual self-respect to progress in terms of inclusive social legislation. Furthermore, his work demonstrates that a view of dignity may transcend the context of the academy to become meaningful directly to the masses of the oppressed and to become influential in the formative debate of social policymakers and legislators.

King's view of dignity may also be appreciated for its ability to combine into a coherent whole the insights of different academic fields of discipline. Its unique strength lies in its ability to draw from widely disparate sources of inspiration—from philosophers such as Augustine, Aquinas, and Plato, to literary figures such as William Cullen Bryant and George Bernard Shaw. King incorporated each source using the ideas to provide a framework for a more inclusive view of human dignity. While it may be well argued that King followed the convention of borrowing from great preachers, or that King's persuasive rhetoric is common within the African-American oral tradition,[1] such an argument fails to account for the rich variety of philosophical, theological, and ethical traditions that King was able to synthesize. Specifically, King was able to pull together the German school of idealism—in particular Kant and Hegel—the American school of Boston Personalism, the Christian realism of Reinhold Niebuhr, and the Christian social gospel of Walter Rauschenbusch with the protest and oral traditions of the black church.

King's view of dignity should also be valued for its contribution of naming the concrete ties between economic conditions and human dignity. King developed a system of dignity that stated in statistics current

---

[1] The presentation of King as rhetor is persuasively argued by Keith D. Miller in two articles: "Martin Luther King, Jr. Borrows a Revolution: Argument, Audience and Implications of a Secondhand Universe," in Garrow, *King*, 643–60; and idem, "Composing Martin Luther King, Jr.," in *Proceedings of the Modern Language Association* 105 (1990) 70.

o his time the specific status of Negroes in the American economy. King described dignity not only in terms of the American civic traditions of the Emancipation Proclamation and the Declaration of Independence, but also in terms of economic opportunities and appreciation for past contributions to the American market economy. By doing so, King enabled Negroes to claim as honorable what had been for many the shameful past of slavery. Moreover, it forced European Americans to concede the positive economic contribution of Negroes in slavery, a past that many whites used in negative ways against Negroes. Such a revalorizing of the historical economic contribution of Negroes (but importantly not of slavery itself) enabled a new sense of the worth and dignity of Negro labor from slavery until the present time.

Fundamentally, the greatest strength of King's view of dignity may be described as its dynamism. This dynamism arises because dignity is both an *inherent quality* and a *process*. Dignity as an inherent quality is insured: it is given because humans are created in God's image, and while it may diminished or increased by social factors, it can never be completely lost. Dignity as a process is a quality attained and achieved through nonviolent protest and energized by the force of agape. Thus Negroes, who were experiencing the pangs of diminished inherent dignity, could nevertheless, through nonviolent protest, fight for increased dignity. They could, in other words, gain dignity with dignity. At the same time, nonviolent demonstration against social injustice empowered the process of gaining or developing a new sense of dignity.

King and the Boston Personalists with whom he studied built upon the Kantian tradition of viewing persons as ends in themselves. Furthermore, King's view of dignity presupposed the primacy of human reason in defining the parameters of personhood, or as Kant put it, that persons are rational beings.

Is such a view of dignity, which looks at persons only as rational beings, enough? In this age of ecological consciousness, many voices have called for a widening of the terms of dignity. Carol Christ speaks of the "earth, my sister," and writes about her "sense of connection to this earth."[2] Indeed, many feminist theologians have challenged the Christian tradition to widen its concern for persons to a concern for all forms

---

[2]Carol Christ, *Laughter of Aphrodite* (San Francisco: Harper & Row, 1987) 15. Christ borrows the term, "this earth is my sister," from Susan Griffin, *Woman and Nature: The Roaring Inside Her* (New York: Harper & Row, 1978).

of life. Rosemary Radford Ruether links her concerns for an ecological consciousness to the Christian doctrines of creation and redemption.[3]

Liberal white male theologians have joined feminists in calling for a new ethic of life. Particularly appropriate to this discussion is John Cobb. Jr., who presents a revised version of Kant's doctrine of dignity: "The recognition that every animal is an end in itself and not merely a means to human ends."[4] Cobb calls such a tenet an ethic beyond anthropocentrism. He elaborates by saying that such an ethic would recognize "in every animal, including humans, both end and means."[5] He stresses that such an ethic would introduce the notion that animals and other forms of nonhuman life have value themselves and are not given a value by human estimation.[6] Cobb also states that "concern for human beings especially for the oppressed, and concern for animals are closely related."[7] Without saying so explicitly, Cobb is calling for those who claim concern for the oppressed of this world to recognize the value of animals and all other forms of nonhuman life. For Cobb, concern for oppressed persons should reinforce a concern for all life. Cobb states that this new ethic would greatly expand Kant's doctrine of the kingdom of ends.[8]

What then are we to do with King's adherence to an ethic that limits itself to human personhood and dignity? Such a view of dignity is far too narrow for our contemporary period of global and ecological concern. Yet King himself seemed to be aware of the inexorable movement toward a global consciousness. In the last chapter of *Where Do We Go From Here?* King presented a vision of a "World House."[9] As King understood this "World House," all people belong to a "world-wide neighborhood," a global community. Such a community has been brought together by the "scientific and technological revolutions," as well as the "world-wide freedom revolution."[10]

[3]Rosemary Radford Ruether, *Womanguides* (Boston: Beacon, 1985) 37–59 195–214.

[4]John B. Cobb, Jr. and Charles Birch, *The Liberation of Life* (Cambridge: Cambridge University Press, 1981) 151.

[5]Ibid.

[6]Ibid.

[7]Ibid.

[8]Ibid.

[9]See King, *Where Do We Go*, chap. 6.

[10]Ibid., 169.

> The universe is so structured that things go awry if men are not diligent in their cultivation of the other-regarding dimension. "I" cannot reach fulfillment without "thou." The self cannot be self without other selves. Self-concern without other-concern is like a tributary that has no outward flow to the ocean.[11]

The ethical norms of the "World House," according to King, would be other-preservation and other-concern, replacing self-preservation and self-concern.[12] King once again affirmed his commitment to interdependence, asserting that the "World House" is the consciousness that all life is interrelated.[13] I would argue that King's ethical norms of other-preservation, other-concern, and the interdependency of all life, although they were articulated in the language of human concern, leave room for incorporating a concern for animals, water, and the earth itself. King's ethical norms may be supplemented by the identification of specific ecological concerns provided by authors such as Christ, Cobb, and Ruether. King probably would have not been opposed to such additions to his thought, since part of his view of the "World House" included revulsion at the destruction by napalm bombs of rice paddies, villages, and valleys in Vietnam.[14] While King did not specifically name his revulsion as "ecological," this reaction does conform to contemporary concern for the preservation of ecosystems. It should be noted that consciousness of ecology, like that of feminism, was in its nascent stage in the 1960s. Nevertheless, King's view of a "World House" provides a congenial framework for ecological consciousness and could be supplemented by the works of Christ, Cobb, and others in order to become more appropriate to our contemporary recognition of the importance of ecological consciousness.

At the same time, much of contemporary ecological discussion could gain moral depth from King's view of the dignity and value of persons, and of oppressed persons in particular. It is disturbing that so much academic attention is given to the nonhuman world when human beings are still allowed to exist in undignified living conditions. Strong theological censure of human injustice as well as concern for the nonhuman world is needed. Without such censure one suspects that ecological

[11]Ibid., 180.
[12]Ibid.
[13]Ibid., 181.
[14]Ibid., 182.

concern could become an abstract exercise of those detached from and unconcerned about genuine human oppression. Expressing moral concern for the nonhuman world without an explicit call for human dignity leads to an inadequate view of dignity. Embracing King's understanding of human dignity could be a helpful supplement to the scholarship of ecological consciousness by including the suffering of human beings with the suffering of the world.

One fundamental weakness of King's view of dignity was his lack of awareness of the presupposition of male dominance within his thought. King lived at a time when the assumptions of women's proper role as confined to the private sphere and women's lack of public power were normative. While much of King's thought about human dignity utilized gender inclusive terms such as "assertive personhood,"[15] King often spoke as well about the need for an "Olympian manhood."[16] Does such a phrase reveal that King had a predominant interest in uplifting the dignity of men, or is it merely an example of King's following the male-exclusive linguistic conventions of his time? While it is impossible to read King's mind on this issue, it is possible to examine his view of women's social role and place with the goal of reconstructing his understanding of the dignity of both men and women. Thus a contemporary construction of dignity that is based on King's thought must discern the purview of King's own norm of inclusion. Did King include women in his view of dignity, or did he have a separate view of women's dignity? If so, then is it possible to supplement the male-exclusive and male-dominant valences of King's description of "manhood" with a gender inclusive norm?

Gender Inclusion: A New Norm as described by West, Cone, Cannon, and hooks

I turn to the works of four African-Americans, two men and two women, who have demonstrated the necessity of developing a more gender inclusive norm within the black community. Such a turn is not inconsistent with King's own thought, since he spent the majority of his life concerned about the dignity of the black community. The thought of West, Cone, Cannon, and hooks provides a needed supplement to King's contribution toward a theory of dignity. Furthermore, as an African-American Christian male who wishes to stand in solidarity with those members of the

[15]Ibid., 43.
[16]Ibid.

community who are striving to develop a more inclusive understanding of human beings, I see my work as an addition to the conversation already in progress within the African-American community.

My personal motivation to regard the ending of male domination as primary to the liberation of the entire community has been profoundly shaped by black womanist and feminist critiques of sexism. As I have been confronted with my own sexism, I have learned to take responsibility for it and to begin changing not only my outward behavior, but also my inner attitudes. Such self-transformation has not been easy, nor is it yet complete. Rather, by learning to listen to the radical voices of black women, I have been spurred to take steps toward the creative reconstruction of my own masculinity as part of the work necessary for a contemporary understanding of dignity. In this reconstructive effort I am dependent on the analysis of black womanists and feminists, for indeed no male can critique his own masculinity without incorporating the powerful analysis of sexism that is offered by womanism and feminism. By incorporating the gender inclusive norm presented by West, Cone, Cannon, and hooks, the sexist blind spots of King's view of dignity, otherwise left unexplored, may be revealed.

Cornel West's *Prophetic Fragments* contains an essay that honors black women's critique of sexism, thus revealing his commitment to a gender inclusive norm. His essay, "The Prophetic Tradition in Afro-America," includes womanism as part of West's understanding of Afro-America's "prophetic tradition."[17] West sees this prophetic tradition as distinguished by "Pascalian leaps of faith in the capacity of human beings to transform their circumstances, engage in relentless criticism and self-criticism, and project vision, analyses, and practices of social freedom."[18]

West praises black women for giving the "first national articulation of black prophetic practices in the USA."[19] He follows this with another accolade, that the first "nationwide protest organization among Afro-Americans was created by black women."[20] Showing that the National Federation of Afro-American Women (1895) predated the NAACP (1909) and the National Urban League (1900), West proceeds to describe the antilynching activism of Ida Wells-Barnett. He also honors lesser known figures such as Anna J. Cooper for her "neglected book *A Voice From*

---

[17]West, *Prophetic Fragments*, 38–39.
[18]Ibid., 38.
[19]Ibid., 45.
[20]Ibid.

the South (1892)," which he calls a "sophisticated case" for linking together racism and sexism.[21]

West proceeds to elaborate on the career of Ida Wells-Barnett, as well as on the work of black women who took part in the Communist Party U.S.A. during the 1930s, the women who participated in the freedom struggles of the 1960s, and the writers of the 1970s and 1980s.[22] West names many black women, from Bonita Williams, Eloise and Andley Moore, Fannie Lou Hamer to Gayl Jones, Alice Walker, and Audre Lorde. Unfortunately, West does not systematically treat any of the critical ideas about sexism or incorporate any of these women's viewpoints into a constructive analysis of sexism. He does mention, however, that the "common denominator" among all of them is their "protracted struggle against the effects of race, class, and gender oppression in the USA and those of class and gender in Afro-America."[23] While I am thankful that West recognizes the multidimensional reality of oppression, it is clear that his intention is to present womanism within his own framework of a philosophical and political analysis of black prophetism. Nevertheless, by naming the specific historical contribution of black women, he honors and uplifts the dignity of their prophetic struggle within the African-American community.

James Cone is more forthcoming and systematic in his analysis of sexism, calling for a more gender inclusive norm. In *For My People* Cone devotes an entire chapter to "Black Theology, Black Churches, and Black Women."[24] Cone, unlike West, begins by addressing some disturbing questions to black men about our lack of concern or interest in the topic of black male sexism. He asks:

> Why is it that many black men cannot see the analogy between racism and sexism, especially in view of the fact that so many black women in the church and in society have expressed clearly their experience of oppression? What is it that blinds black men to

[21]Ibid., 46. Womanist theologian Karen Baker-Fletcher has taken up the challenge of giving a thorough reading and analysis of Cooper's religious thought in her Ph.D. dissertation, "A Theological Anthropology of Voice: The Life and Thought of Anna Julia Cooper as a Resource for a Womanist Theology" (Ph.D. diss., Harvard University, 1991).

[22]West, *Prophetic Fragments*, 46–47.

[23]Ibid., 47.

[24]James H. Cone, *For My People* (Maryknoll, NY: Orbis, 1984) 122–39.

the truth regarding the suffering of their sisters? What is it that makes black church men insensitive to the pain of women minis-ters, and why do we laugh when they tell the story of their suffer-ing that we have inflicted on them?[25]

Such questions must be at the root of any analysis of sexism addressed to black males. They are direct and specific. Cone challenges and de-mands self-critique.

Cone, like West, then turns to a historical grounding of black women's aspirations and achievements with regard to freedom and the black com-munity. He states that black feminism "developed in the context of the abolitionist movement and the rise of white feminism in the second half of the nineteenth century."[26] He then uplifts Frederick Douglass as not only a "great abolitionist", but also as one who was an "outspoken ad-vocate of women's rights."[27] Cone infers that black men can emulate models of antisexist behavior such as Frederick Douglass.

Cone praises the advocacy of women's rights championed by Sojourner Truth, Mary Church Terrell, and Ida B. Wells-Barnett. He describes these women as "victims of double jeopardy," who could "not choose between the issues of sexism and racism" because they were "victims of both."[28] He then proceeds to critique the sexism that black women, such as Jarena Lee, faced *within* black churches.[29] Taking on the sexism within the A. M. E. church, Cone, an A. M. E. theologian, grapples with his own denominational history.

Cone critiques the sexism of black males as it developed in the 1960s and 1970s. He criticizes the fashion in which major figures such as Ella Baker, Anna Hedgeman, Fannie Lou Hamer, Ruby Doris Robinson, and Diane Nash Bevel were belittled.[30] Cone charges that the "invisibility of black women in the freedom movement and the hostility of black men toward women's equality helped drive black women to form their own feminist organizations."[31]

---

[25]Ibid., 123.
[26]Ibid.
[27]Ibid.
[28]Ibid., 122–25.
[29]Ibid., 126.
[30]Ibid., 127–28.
[31]Ibid., 128.

Cone's charge is not empty; it is fleshed out by his detailed descri-
tion of the types of "hostility" toward women's equality that typified t
sixties and seventies. He names the following: an "inordinate emphas
on violence and masculine assertiveness," a "stress on black womer
passivity and weakness," a "glorification of the pimp and the black male
sexual exploits" (he lists the titles of several movies and Broadway play
and the thematizing of "rape as a political act" by Eldridge Cleaver.
Furthermore, Cone articulates a concern that must be addressed by
contemporary analysis of sexism and motivates a gender inclusive vie
of dignity. This concern lies in the fact that for many black males,

> freedom meant the assertion of their manhood, which they identi-
> fied as violence against the white man with guns, rape of the white
> woman, and unlimited physical and mental brutality against the
> black woman.[33]

This is the first sweeping indictment of black male sexism written by
black male theologian. Cone's chapter does not end with this indictmer
however, for he proceeds to demonstrate the validity and necessity
black women doing their own theology for themselves.[34]

Cone concludes with a systematic and constructive statement of blac
men's responsibilities as churchmen and Christians. This statement a
firms his commitment to a regulative gender inclusive norm.[35] Fir
black males need to see "women's liberation as a viable issue."[36] F
Cone this means that black men must "recognize it and help others
the church to treat it seriously."[37] Cone emphasizes the point by sayin
"It is not a joke."[38] Cone challenges ministers to help make whatev
inner attitude changes are necessary in order to recognize women's o
pression as analogous to the oppression of blacks by whites.[39] Secon
Cone urges black men to "learn how to listen to women tell their stori

[32]Ibid.
[33]Ibid.
[34]Ibid., 135.
[35]Ibid., 136–37.
[36]Ibid., 137.
[37]Ibid.
[38]Ibid.
[39]Ibid.

pain and struggle."[40] Cone counsels black men to recognize that "the
[of listening is not easy, especially for oppressors whose very position
power inhibits them from hearing and understanding anything that
ntradicts their values."[41] Third, Cone counsels black men to "read as
uch as possible about the history of sexism and women's struggles" in
der to have a greater comprehension of sexism's complexity.[42]

The fourth responsibility Cone enumerates is for black men to "insist
 affirmative action for black women in churches and in the commu-
ty."[43] This is Cone's practical suggestion for the implementation of
als that would include women in "positions of responsibility in churches
d community organizations."[44] As blacks had a "plan of action," so
ould the "principle of affimative action" be logically applied to the
sue of women's positions, in Cone's view.[45]

Finally, Cone challenges black men to "support black women in their
tempts to discover role models."[46] As black men join black women in
ading role models from the past and present, "they can share experi-
ces with each other and thereby be encouraged to keep fighting for
cognition and justice in the churches."[47]

Cone's recent volume, *Martin & Malcolm & America*, provides a
itically appreciative and comparative analysis of King and Malcolm X.
e devotes an entire section of a chapter to a frankly critical portrayal
King's sexism.[48] Cone's intention is similar to mine, that is, to retrieve
itically those aspects of King's thought (and those of Malcolm X as
ell) helpful for our contemporary setting. He criticizes King's short-
mings honestly but without sensationalism.

Katie G. Cannon's *Black Womanist Ethics* affirms the necessity for a
nder inclusive norm that honors and names black women's experience
 a distinctive experience of oppression.[49] Cannon contributes a strong

---

[40]Ibid.
[41]Ibid.
[42]Ibid.
[43]Ibid., 138.
[44]Ibid.
[45]Ibid.
[46]Ibid.
[47]Ibid.
[48]James H. Cone, *Martin & Malcolm & America* (Maryknoll, NY: Orbis,
91) 272–80, in chap. 10, "Nothing But Men."
[49]Katie G. Cannon, *Black Womanist Ethics* (Atlanta: Scholars Press, 1988) 2,
4.

claim about the oppositional dignity of black women who are compelled to "create and cultivate values and virtues in their own terms so that they can prevail against the odds with moral integrity."[50]

Criticizing traditional white male ethical reflection as based on the presupposition of "freedom" and a "wide range of choices," Cannon insists that such a standard is "false" to the "less gracious boundaries" in which most black people, and black women in particular, must "live, work, and have their being."[51] Cannon describes black women's experience as a distinctive "tridimensional experience" of oppression that incorporates race, class, and gender.[52] Cannon's description of the dignity of black women cannot therefore be founded on the Kantian presupposition of freedom and the autonomy of the will.

Cannon's black womanist ethics are based on the Christian presupposition that all persons have a god-given dignity. Cannon incorporates into her ethical reflection the theology and ethics of Martin Luther King Jr. and Howard Thurman as important "moral resources" for the "struggle which still lies ahead."[53] She finds agreement between King's affirmation of human dignity and that of Zora Neale Hurston because both define dignity as "a birthright, a non-negotiable need."[54] Cannon praises Thurman and King for their "strong affirmation of the dignity of all Black people grounded in God" as the same "starting point" of Hurston's own concerns.[55]

Cannon brings the concern for human dignity of Thurman and King together with that of black women. Moreover, she demonstrates that her theological ethics are motivated by an underlying desire to uplift the dignity of all persons, and of African-American women and men in particular. Cannon thereby provides an ideal partner for problematizing King's vision of dignity, since both Cannon and King articulate the norm of inclusion in dignity's construction.

bell hooks[56] provides us with a final challenge regarding the necessity for a regulative norm of gender inclusion. Unlike many Caucasian feminists, African-American womanists and feminists like hooks are con-

---

[50]Ibid., 2.
[51]Ibid., 144.
[52]Ibid., 2–3.
[53]Ibid.
[54]Ibid.
[55]Ibid.
[56]The uncapitalized name is bell hooks's trademark.

erned in their analysis with including and directly addressing black men. hooks's work emphasizes the need for men to learn to listen to the "liberated voice" of black women.[57] hooks acknowledges that "the reconstruction and transformation of male behavior, of masculinity, is a necessary and essential part of the feminist revolution."[58] This transformation can only take place as men learn to hear and dialogue with the liberated voice" of women.

What is this "liberated voice" for hooks? She describes it by first analyzing "silence." hooks notes that in a "patriarchal society silence has been for women a gesture of submission and complicity, especially silence about men."[59] In a moving paragraph she describes her childhood in a patriarchical "southern black, working-class household" where she feared any form of "speech" around her father.[60] Such a household had two social spaces," one in which women and children could laugh freely, talk, and even speak loudly because the man was not present, and the other in which they retreated into silence in the presence of the father: We feared speech. We feared the words of a woman who could hold her own with a man."[61]

hooks goes on to explain that "the very act of speech wherein a woman talks to a man, carries embedded in that gesture a challenge, a threat to male domination."[62] In a former stage of feminism, she sees silence being "marked as a signifier, a marker of exploitation, oppression, dehumanization," while the act of speaking becomes the way in which women "come to power, telling our stories, sharing history, engaging in feminist discussion."[63] She wants to move to yet another stage in which there is a *confrontation* provoked by women's speech: "the confrontation between women and men, the sharing of this new and radical speech: women speaking to men in a liberated voice."[64]

This liberated voice is "confrontational, fundamentally rebellious and defiant" of male domination.[65] Such speech identifies the participants as

[57]bell hooks, *Talking Back* (Boston: South End Press, 1989) 130.
[58]Ibid., 127.
[59]Ibid., 128.
[60]Ibid.
[61]Ibid.
[62]Ibid.
[63]Ibid., 129.
[64]Ibid.
[65]Ibid.

"in a revolutionary feminist struggle" in which women speak to themselves and to men without fear.[66] Furthermore, such a liberated voice is spoken within the intimate confines of male-female "primary love relationships," the context in which many women find themselves.[67]

hooks extends the possibility that the sharing of this liberated voice may transform and radicalize men.[68] Since it is a voice that is "informed by a politic that resists domination" and is "humanizing and liberatory," men can be transformed and changed.[69] hooks seeks a "place of solidarity" where women "can speak to and/or about men in a feminist voice."[70] Such a "place of solidarity" would be a place "where our words can be heard, where we can speak the truth that heals, that transforms—that makes feminist revolution."[71] For hooks, such a space could include men, not all men, but men who are actively engaged in the process of transformation and radicalization. It is the liberated voice of black women's speech that will transform not only black women, but also those black men who dare to be "comrades" in the feminist revolution.[72] Moreover, while such black men can learn to *share* radical speech, the responsibility of males is to learn to *hear* and *listen* to the liberated voice as women speak defiantly, rebelliously, and critically of male domination.

hooks is clear that the responsibility of males engaged in feminist struggle is that of transforming other men. She calls on men to engage in "exposing, confronting, opposing, and transforming the sexism of male peers."[73] Males should demonstrate a "willingness to assume equal responsibility in feminist struggle" by "performing whatever tasks are necessary."[74] There is an important distinction, in my view, between women speaking in a liberated voice and this voice of male responsibility. I interpret hooks as suggesting that men have the responsibility of speaking to one another in what I would call a *radicalized voice*: male voices that have been transformed and given "critical consciousness"[75] by lis-

---

[66]Ibid.
[67]Ibid., 130.
[68]Ibid.
[69]Ibid., 133.
[70]Ibid.
[71]Ibid.
[72]bell hooks, *Feminist Theory: from margin to center* (Boston: South End Press, 1984) 80.
[73]Ibid., 81.
[74]Ibid.
[75]hooks uses this term in *Talking Back*, 130.

tening and learning to hear the *liberated voice* of women. This "critical consciousness" enables men and women to approach the "place of solidarity" that both desire.

The radicalized voice of men engaged in feminist revolution is a necessary reaction to the liberated voice of women. It is not something that men create for themselves outside of a confrontational dialogue with women. hooks disdains "men's liberation groups" which make facile comparisons between the oppression women experience and the "pain" and "hurt" that sexism produces in men.[76] For hooks, the radicalized voice of men engaged in feminist struggle is a voice learning to be "honest—aggressive in their human pursuits. . . boldly passionate, sexual and sensual."[77] The radicalized voice of men, in concert with the liberated voice of women is an important part of a gender inclusive norm and of a contemporary theory of dignity.

King and the Women Close to Him

Was King able to practice the humanizing theological ethic of dignity that he espoused toward women as well as men? The voices of the women closest to him help us to answer this question.

King's wife, Coretta Scott King, told Alice Walker that King was the kind of "strong man" who allowed her to be a woman:

> It was such a good feeling that Martin gave me, since the first time I met him. He was such a strong man that I felt like a woman. I could *be* a woman, and let him be a man. Yet he too was affected by the system, as a black man; but in spite of everything he always came through as a man, a person of dignity.[78]

She goes on in the same interview to mention that she missed sharing things with her husband. Her book, *My Life with Martin Luther King, Jr.*, is filled with many glowing accounts of the love, the family, and the movement that they shared together. To be sure, however, she characterized her husband's attitude toward a woman's "role" as "ambivalent":

---

[76]hooks, *Feminist Theory*, 78–79.

[77]Ibid., 79.

[78]Coretta Scott King's words as recorded by Alice Walker, "Coretta King; Revisited," in idem, *In Search of Our Mother's Gardens* (San Diego: Harcourt Brace Jovanovich, 1983) 152.

> On the one hand, he believed that women are just as intelligent and
> capable as men and that they should hold positions of authority and
> influence. But when it came to his own situation, he thought in
> terms of his wife being a homemaker and a mother for his children.
> He was very definite that he would expect whoever he married to
> be home waiting for him.[79]

Coretta King's characterization of King's attitude toward women makes
it quite clear that King adhered to the traditional understanding of a
woman's role as homemaker and mother to children. It is possible to
suggest from her comments that King believed that the dignity of women,
or at least of his wife, was most properly understood as confined to the
private sphere in the domestic roles of homemaker and mother. Furthermore, there is no textual evidence in the King archives that support
Coretta King's statement that King was ambivalent about the role of
women. He never openly supported women holding equal positions of
power and authority in the public sphere with men.

Coretta King's description of her husband's attitude toward women is
far more gentle than that which other King biographers have uncovered.
Garrow claims that Coretta "openly complained about her husband's
insistence that she take care of the home and family and not become
involved in movement activities."[80] Garrow quotes Andrew Young as
saying that "Martin didn't want her to get too active."[81] Garrow goes on
to recount Bernard Lee's testimony about his interpretation of King's
views on sex roles in the marriage: "Martin was absolutely a male chauvinist. He believed that the wife should stay home and take care of the
babies while he'd be out there in the streets."[82] What can be safely said
about the discrepancy between Garrow's research and Coretta's memories
is that there probably was some conflict generated between Martin and
Coretta over *her role* as his wife in the movement. King's view of
women's place was so "traditional" that Bernard Lee could accuse him
of being a "male chauvinist."

The most damaging and controversial revelations about King's life
have not been about how King treated the women closest to him, but

---

[79]Coretta King, *My Life with Martin Luther King, Jr.* (New York: Holt, Rinehart
& Winston, 1969) 60.
[80]Garrow, *Bearing the Cross*, 375.
[81]Ibid.
[82]Ibid., 375–76.

about his alleged sexual affairs with many unnamed women. Such controversy goes to the heart of understanding a possible gap between King's professed views of human dignity and his own personal respect for the dignity of women. Recent biographers of King's life have described King as "a Casonova. . . but with quiet dignity" and as having a "compulsive sexual athleticism."[83] King did not honor women as equals who possessed equal authority, at least in his personal practices with women. His professed beliefs about the sanctity of sexuality and marriage were undermined by the allegations that he himself was sexually promiscuous.

It is interesting to note, however, that King was painfully honest about these shortcomings. While Ralph Abernathy does not report that King had any remorse concerning his sexual promiscuity, Branch reports that King could never rest easy with these extramarital activities. Branch records that King insisted on calling his sexual activities a "sin" and that King strained relationships with his otherwise admiring group of male comrades by having "endless cycles from hedonism to self-recrimination and back."[84] Branch reflects that for the male circle attending King, all of these sexual activities were a "natural condition of manhood, or of great preachers obsessed by love, or of success," and that they eagerly *imitated* him.[85]

It is certain, then, that King's sexual behavior was enacted within a male-dominated context that supported promiscuity, although King himself was never at ease with the apparent conflict between the depersonalization caused by sexual promiscuity and his own teachings concerning the necessity of respecting persons. King never completely made the connection between his practice of sexual promiscuity, which implied that another person's body was a thing to be used, and his dignifying theological anthropology. King's theological anthropology rested on the presupposition that all persons, men and women, are created by God and are children of God. Such an anthropology implies an ethic of respect in personal as well as public relationships, an ethic that respects each person as a child of God and not as a thing to be used. Thus King's alleged sexual promiscuity was in conflict with his public denunciation of the depersonalization of racism.

King did not affirm women's equality in actual, concrete practice. Instead, King practiced a dynamic of power in which women were sub-

---

[83]Ibid., 375.
[84]Branch, *Parting the Waters*, 860.
[85]Ibid.

servient to men and viewed as sexual objects for men's sexual pleasure; women were not worthy of the kind of "I–Thou" exchange that he publicly demanded of whites toward blacks.

It should be noted that King's life and ministry occurred entirely before the eruption of feminist consciousness in the early seventies. King's attitude toward women was no different from that of the majority of men in his time. His conformity in this area surprises us now because he was advanced in his thinking in other areas. For instance, King was able to connect with the revolutionary struggles of Asia, Africa, and Latin America at a time when few others recognized that connection. King was also able to employ a multidimensional form of analysis that named racism, militarism, classism, and colonialism as the most urgent forms of oppression for the West to redress and correct.

Positively stated, there is no firm recording of King's philosophical, theological, and public view of women that would substantiate any claim that he had developed a sexist view of women's role. Instead it is better to say that King's practice toward women demonstrated his practical acceptance of women's inequality and his lack of critical reflection on the subject. Because King was assassinated in 1968, we can only speculate on how the feminist revolution would have affected his thinking about the oppression of women or his behavior toward women.

King's Thought as a Resource for a Contemporary Theory of Dignity

As a Christian African-American male who longs for solidarity with womanist colleagues and such males as West and Cone who have begun a transformation, I argue that one can utilize selectively much of King's thought for the construction of a liberating theory of dignity. In particular, I turn to King's most comprehensive symbol of dignity, somebodyness, as possessing the most gender inclusive potential.

For the purpose of clarification, any constructive theory of human dignity in our contemporary world written by an African-American Christian male is simultaneously *privileged* by gender and *limited* by race. While King's vision of somebodyness is philosophically grounded in the universalist deontological and moral claims of Kant, I am cognizant of the limitations of my maleness, my African-American perspective, and my experience of racism, as well as of the privilege of holding Christian beliefs and a middle-class background and education. Thus, the following constructive work limits itself: it is concerned with the dignity of African-American males and it is in solidarity with the struggle for the dignity of African-American women. My wish to stand in solidarity with

African-American womanists is a position that I have reached because of my exposure to womanists like Katie Cannon and Karen Baker-Fletcher, as well as feminists like Sharon Welch, Mary Daly, and Margaret Miles, who have challenged me to examine the sexist practices and beliefs that I have held. Their challenge has led me to reinterpret those of my former understandings of Christianity that did not challenge assumptions of male dominance. My construction of dignity will be judged and criticized by black men and women who question whether *any* male can or should be thinking about dignity with the issue of sexism in the forefront. Such a construction of dignity could be ignored or ridiculed because it speaks with a male voice to challenge the dominance of black males.

As a Baptist pastor, however, I have a particular calling to address the effects of sexism, classism, and racism both in academic and pastoral contexts. The following outline of a constructive theory of human dignity, therefore, speaks in the particular understanding of Christianity that most Baptists hold in common.

Cognizance of my privileged and limited perspective enables the following analysis of King's understanding of somebodyness to be supplemented by a norm of self-criticism that is open to other voices besides itself, particularly the voices of black womanists. To employ a musical image, I envision myself to be striking a chord similar to that of those men and women who desire the equality of all persons. Like a chord, which shares with other chords many overtones both audible and beyond the scope of human hearing, my theological and ethical beliefs resonate with those of other men and women. At the same time, it is necessary that the other "chords"—black male theologians and black womanist theologians and ethicists—with which I hope to resonate, make their own *distinct* and *unique* tonality. I do not wish to sound like them, nor they like me.[86] I hope that there is a resonance. If something within my proposed theory of dignity strikes a dissonance rather than a resonance, then hearing the correcting voices of those other "chords," as well as the norm of self-criticism, should guard against facile claims that this theory is liberating if it is not.

Somebodyness is an appropriately oppositional symbol rooted in African-American history, generative of the important values of self-affir-

---

[86]By this image of "resonance" I do not wish to exclude those white feminists, male and female, who are interested in taking the issues of race, class, and gender seriously.

mation and self-appreciation, and pertinent to understandings of the human body and economics. The nonviolence of somebodyness may address the pressing needs of African-American urban males in particular.

Somebodyness: African-American Roots

King's development of the concept of somebodyness grew out of the African-American community's understanding of black dignity as rooted in the common ancestry that all persons share as "children of God." I demonstrated in chapter one how King first heard that he was "somebody" from his mother after a situation in which he was questioning that status. The term "somebody" is "oppositional," a word Cornel West uses to define "the maintenance of self-respect in the face of pervasive denigration."[87] Oppositionality contains elements of a "combative spirituality" within "prophetic Black Christian practices" such as "supernatural and subversive joy" and "an oppositional perserverance and patience."[88] Thus, when King's mother reminded him that he was "somebody," she was being *oppositional*, helping him to maintain his self-respect in the face of pervasive denigration. This "pervasive denigration" is a refined way of speaking of the daily racist encounters that any African-American, not just Martin Luther King, Jr., may confront even now.

One may question whether somebodyness is a communally recognized term. I would answer with a story from my own family history. My grandmother, Annie B. Parham, who was born and raised in the segregated southern town of Thomaston, Georgia, at the turn of this century, named her daughter "Superia." Such a name, when spoken in a southern accent, means "superior"! One day, when her daughter Superia, my mother, had just been accepted into Case Western Reserve University as a math major, her peers in the classroom (both white and black) began teasing her about her unusual name. She came home asking her mother loudly, "Why did you give me that *name*?" Grandmother Annie's face lit up, and with pride in her voice she answered, "Oh darling, I named you 'Superia,' so that everybody would have to call you that! I wanted you to know that *you are somebody!*" Although I cannot estimate how many other African-American families have similar stories, it is significant to note that my grandmother named her child something oppositional—calling a black child "superior" at a time when all the laws, customs,

---

[87]West, *Prophesy Deliverance!*, 70.
[88]West, *Prophetic Fragments*, 43.

and mores of the United States, North and South, dictated otherwise. Moreover, when asked to explain the name, my grandmother turned to the expression, "you are somebody" as an oppositional source of encouragement in much the same way that King's mother used the expression.

The exact roots of the expression, "you are somebody," are buried forever in the mists of African-American slave history. One cannot cite a particular author, but only acknowledge both the community that produced the expression and the context of pervasive racism out of which it emerged. What is fascinating, however, is that the notion of being "somebody" apparently merged quickly in black church culture with the Christian doctrine of the *imago dei*. Benjamin Mays chronicles a sermon by Reverend Joseph Corr, an A. M. E. preacher in 1834, which Mays interprets as abolishing "in the mind of the Negro the feeling of inferiority—to make him feel that he is 'somebody'—that he is made in the image of God."[89] Although a full reading of this sermon goes beyond the scope of my work here, the following questions indicate the fervent nature of the sermon:

> Then let me ask the important question, Why! O Why! should not the coloured American citizen be equal, in all the qualities of heart, and the powers of the mind, with his white brother? Has nature made him inferior? Has his Creator designed him to be less, in any respect? Has he [God] at any time, or on any occasion declared it? . . . Ask the standard of truth; let Heaven's own inspiration be heard, and God himself will speak! "All souls are mine," is his express declaration, "for my ways are equal," saith the Lord.[90]

Mays's volume quotes other sources from the late eighteenth century into the early twentieth century. Mays sums up his conclusions with the following exposition of the doctrine of *imago dei*:

> There is no divine right of race. The rights of humanity are divine and they cannot be divested by reason of race. We are all God's creatures. God created the Negro in His own image. He has made

[89]Benjamin E. Mays, *The Negro's God* (Kingsport, TN: Atheneum, 1968) 44–45.

[90]Ibid., 45.

> no superior races and no inferior races. The Negro is God's most
> perfect handiwork. The human family is united in God.[91]

I would correct Mays's exclusive usage of the male pronoun for God
and for Negroes. The idea, however, remains: God created all persons
equally. The phrase about being somebody owes its theological origin to
a confidence that all people, including Negro people, are created in God's
image. Its roots, the roots to which King appealed, go back into the
depths of black history. It was employed by King's mother, like my
grandmother, as an oppositional expression of encouragement.
Somebodyness is not something taken for granted, but involves a struggle,
a battle. Somebodyness arises in the oppositional struggle that African-
Americans wage daily against the pervasive denigration of racism. To
attain a sense of somebodyness, there is a battle, as King put it, to attain
the awareness that one is a somebody. Thus, while one is a somebody
because one is a child of God, created in the image of God, the *sense*
of somebodyness involves an oppositional struggle; as King described it,
a battle for the awareness and self-affirmation that indeed one is a somebody. It is important to uplift this martial metaphor in any realistic
appraisal of the dignity of African-Americans, for it recognizes that dignity
for African-Americans is something worth struggle. Although dignity is
based on the Christian theological assumption that all persons are created by God and share in the image of God, unless it is fought for, its
application for blacks is not recognized or honored in the socioeconomic
sphere of American society.

Somebodyness, as I reconstruct it, takes seriously the claims of Katie
Cannon that blacks in general and black women in particular do not
make moral decisions in an ideal social sphere of freedom. Somebodyness
struggles for the freedom to make choices. It carves out spaces for
decisions to be made despite a social dynamic that negates social choice
and social power for black women and men.

Somebodyness and Values

The values of self-affirmation and self-appreciation form the ethical
foundation of King's concept of somebodyness. King's critique of skin
bleaching and hair straightening—beautification techniques that negate
blackness—is of great importance to my reconstruction. King felt that

---

[91]Ibid., 250.

one could not achieve a sense of somebodyness without affirming one's own beauty. Today womanist theologians such as Karen Baker-Fletcher and Chandra Taylor Smith are writing on the importance of black women affirming their particular African beauty.[92] We do not, however, have any writings concerning African-American males affirming their own beauty. Is this because black men do not wish to view themselves as "beautiful?" Is it because the whole concept of "beauty" is synonymous with women in most men's minds?

The affirmation of African-American male beauty is an important and necessary step in our recovery of dignity and in our gaining a deeper sense of somebodyness. Black men must learn to rejoice in the rich chocolate-colored skin that God has created for us. Such beauty should be understood beyond traditional definitions of male beauty which appreciate the virtues of "strength" or "power." African-American males should strive to value themselves despite what the rest of the world values about us. The entertainment world values the black male for his "talent," the sports world for his "ability." Yet these are not self-affirming values, but heteronomous values, coming from outside black male selves and being imposed from the outside. The call for self-affirming values involves a call for affirming *autonomous values*—values whereby black men affirm themselves despite the social pressure to succumb to the heteronomous market values of a racist society. We need to affirm the beauty of our voices, the way we speak to each other, the way we sound when we sing together, the way we encourage one another, and the way we bond together for support.

African-American male beauty involves an appreciation of the muscular "John Henry" grandfathers and great-grandfathers who worked the land and fed their families. Although they were slaves and sharecroppers, these men carried themselves with a poise and a sense of personal dignity that contemporary African-American males could benefit from emulating.

The black male body has been a source of fascination, terror, and sexual fantasy for the white Western world. As black men, we must begin to define for ourselves what our bodies mean to us. To elaborate an ethic of African-American male beauty goes beyond the confines of

---

[92]See Chandra Taylor Smith, "Black Women and Body-Spirit Dualism: Illuminating the Need for an Authentic Wholistic Black Woman's Theology and Ministry" (M.Div. Thesis, Harvard Divinity School, 1988); and Karen Baker-Fletcher, "Roundtable Discussion: If God is God She is Not Nice," *Journal of Feminist Studies in Religion* 5 (1989) 115–17.

this chapter. Nevertheless, black ethicists are called upon to develop an ethic that is concerned with the sense of self-appreciation and celebration possible for black males. The values of self-appreciation and self-affirmation can form the foundation of a new dignity for black males

King used the image of a piano keyboard to show the importance of black keys and white keys together. The keyboard was one of his favorite symbols for affirming the inclusion of blacks as human beings along with whites. I would widen King's keyboard imagery to recognize that as the black and white keys produce the sounds, the variety of tones comes from a balance of the treble (women) and the bass (men) Somebodyness, when seen as a piano, involves the appreciation not only of the keys, but of high and low pitches—pitches that make the music when played together.

Within King's understanding of somebodyness, the values of self-appreciation and self-affirmation need to be combined with his appreciation of diversity. By combining values that emphasize self-appreciation, self-affirmation, and autonomy with King's relational view of diversity rich possibilities for a dialogue with other persons open up. King was interested in African-Americans gaining a greater sense of somebodyness, but that sense of somebodyness should not be attained in isolation. To be a somebody is to be somebody in relation to other somebodies. This is what keeps somebodyness from collapsing into mere self-concern and psychologism. Somebodyness presents the appreciation of diversity as a moral imperative. Such diversity is energized by a real sharing of power and the inclusion of differences along racial, gender, and class differences. Somebodyness embraces and celebrates that kind of diversity.

Somebodyness and Economics: The Body

For King, somebodyness became increasingly tied to the necessity for an adequate living wage. I cannot speak of an adequate theory of dignity for African-American males without speaking of an affirmation of the dignity of work. To earn one's keep and to work for one's wage is fundamental right of all persons. This right has increasingly been taken away from black men, so that now, a generation after King's death, we find that black males are less employed than they were then. In order to insure the dignity of black males, it is imperative to have fair economic opportunities for black males. To gain a sense of somebodyness, black men need jobs, decent housing, and reasonable hopes for advancement

Black men have traditionally earned their wage through hard physical labor. Whether farming or lifting heavy objects in a factory, African

American males have utilized their bodies to gain at least a limited sense of economic freedom. To be somebody ultimately means to be "some" "body" and includes awareness of one's body. For King the body was part of God's good creation, something to be valued and appreciated. King desired that blacks would come to a place of self-affirmation and self-appreciation of our bodies. King's hopes can still be useful today. Black male bodies have been presented as "super-athletes" such as Bo Jackson and Hershel Walker, both multitalented athletes who excel in several sports. The black male body has been valued for its *utility* and *function*. Now, African-American males need to reexamine what our bodies mean to us. The question of how to value the black male body needs to be developed carefully in a further work. It is obvious, however, that the answers will involve much more than a discussion of African-American history and will necessarily include American history and values. African-Americans are Americans who are influenced, shaped, and molded by American values. Perhaps it is impossible to speak of blacks appreciating ourselves and valuing our bodies until America has learned to do the same for itself.

King's symbol of somebodyness presupposed a practiced grounding in his understanding of nonviolence. For King, nonviolence provided the morally rigorous and disciplined life-style that enabled its practitioners to gain a heightened sense of dignity and self-respect. As nonviolent protesters learned to resist the urge to respond to the violent opposition they often faced, they gained a deeper sense of conquering the fear of bodily harm. From this emerged an inner sense of strength and a powerful sense of courage. The oppressed, those who formerly thought of themselves as "nobodies," learned to say, "I am somebody."

Our world is exploding with gang violence. The nonviolent core of somebodyness could provide an alternative to young African-American males who are particularly vulnerable to succumbing to the violent "street ethic" whose ethos is "only the strong survive, so shoot first." The lack of respect for life, for caring, and yet the longing for community and intimacy becomes chillingly apparent as these are lauded in the songs of such rappers as Ice T or Easy E.[93]

Rappers such as Ice T, Easy E, and Public Enemy are representative of the impassioned artistic call for human dignity coming from urban

---

[93]See Ice T, *The Iceberg: Freedom of Speech But Watch What You Say* (Jive Records, 1989); and Easy E, *Easy Does It* (Jive Records, 1989).

poor males in particular. While the language of rap is often filled with rage at injustice, it is also laced with a jarring demand for respect, a call for recognition of the interdependence of all human beings, witty sarcasm, humor, and a longing for intimacy.[94] In rap songs, the longing for intimacy and love are often conflated with violent sado-masochistic acts.[95] Moreover, one of the most obvious aspects of the street ethic rap songs reveal is the "soldier" norm that involves following orders, dying for a cause, and sacrificing one's self for the "good" of the gang. It is considered an "honor" to die in so-called gang-banging—a war between rival gangs.

The street ethic is promoted with every drug deal that goes sour and turns into a fire fight. It is promulgated every time another young black child is shot, caught in the middle of two warring gangs. It is reinforced by fear of retaliation by other gang members. It cannot be broken by a theory of dignity as such. Yet it is my hope that such a theory of dignity could enable those working with young men off the streets to encourage them to begin a new life.[96] Nonviolence works best in groups, in a supportive community. Those accustomed to gangs are also used to the power that the many have when operating together toward one purpose.

Nonviolence enabled young Negroes in the fifties and sixties to gain a sense of somebodyness. Potentially, a specific application of nonviolence in the nineties may provide young African-American males with an alternative way of being a "man," of being somebody outside of the self-destructive lifestyle of street gangs. This can become possible by the promulgation of King's teachings on nonviolence and dignity, with the express purpose of translating his thought into forms that are relevant to our contemporary situation. For example, one could have a "Nonviolence Workshop" or "Dignity Workshop" much along the same lines as King, Abernathy, and Smiley did in the civil rights movement

[94]See the social critique embedded in the rap artistry of Public Enemy, *Fear of a Black Planet* (Jive Records RCA, 1990). Unfortunately it goes beyond the scope of this volume to provide quotations of these rap songs. In future work however, such lyrics can provide a fertile ground for the critical construction of a dignifying ethic to counter the negating effects of the street ethic.

[95]Ice T, *The Iceberg: Freedom of Speech but Watch what You Say* (Jive Records 1989).

[96]This theory in reality targets the recreation facility directors and the pastors and youth directors of urban churches who have direct access to these young people.

In those workshops the teacher prepared the students for the potentially violent actions of crowds and hostile police during a demonstration. Such a workshop now would also prepare young black males to learn how to face the police nonviolently (always a dangerous encounter for African-American males) or how to handle a conflict on the street non-violently. As the workshops of the sixties were fun and entertaining, so a "Dignity Workshop" would need to find ways that these potentially deadly encounters could be transformed into instances that demonstrate a profound commitment to nonviolent dignity.

Dignity is based on a sense of having and owning one's heritage, but the African-American heritage is erased by media stereotypes in our contemporary world. "Dignity Workshops" would have to find a way to present black history to young African American males in King's affirming manner. Many of these young men have not read black history, were not taught black history before they dropped out of school, and believe that blacks have no history worth recounting. Finally, these "Dignity Workshops" would enable young black males to gain a sense of connection to the generations of other African-American males who have achieved something and whose lives are not in vain. Establishing this connection in their minds would insure that the responsibility to *live* for honor and dignity is better than the call to *die* in order to fulfill the demands of a street ethic. Such a view of somebodyness could effectively utilize the sense of group honor and group discipline already present in these young men, guiding it to nonviolent transformation.

Harvard Dissertations in Religion

Previous Titles in the Series